GLOBAL ECONOMIC STUDIES SERIES

INFLATION: CAUSES AND EFFECTS

Global Economic Studies Series

The U.K.'s Rocky Road to Stability
Nicoletta Batini and Edward Nelson (Editor)
2009. ISBN: 978-1-60692-869-1

The Financial Crisis and the European Union
Klaus G. Efenhoff (Editor)
2009. ISBN: 978-1-60741-987-7

Inflation: Causes and Effects
Leon V. Schwartz (Editor)
2009. ISBN: 978-1-60741-823-8

GLOBAL ECONOMIC STUDIES SERIES

INFLATION: CAUSES AND EFFECTS

LEON V. SCHWARTZ
EDITOR

Nova Science Publishers, Inc.
New York

For permission to use material from this book please contact us:
Telephone 631-231-7269; Fax 631-231-8175
Web Site: http://www.novapublishers.com

LIBRARY OF CONGRESS CATALOGING-IN-PUBLICATION DATA
Available upon request.

ISBN 978-1-60741-823-8

Published by Nova Science Publishers, Inc. ✣ New York

CONTENTS

PREFACE

In economics, inflation is a rise in the general level of prices of goods and services in an economy over a period of time. The term inflation once referred to increases in the money supply (monetary inflation); however, economic debates about the relationship between money supply and price levels have led to its primary use today in describing price inflation. Inflation can also be described as a decline in the real value of money—a loss of purchasing power in the medium of exchange which is also the monetary unit of account. When the general price level rises, each unit of currency buys fewer goods and services. A chief measure of general price-level inflation is the general inflation rate, which is the percentage change in a general price index, normally the Consumer Price Index, over time. Inflation can have adverse effects on an economy. For example, uncertainty about future inflation may discourage investment and savings. High inflation may lead to shortages of goods if consumers begin hoarding out of concern that prices will increase in the future. Economists generally agree that high rates of inflation and hyperinflation are caused by an excessive growth of the money supply. This new important book gathers the latest research from around the globe on this issue.

While this study tries to consider HRM in the public sector as a whole, the focus is mainly on HRM at the central ministries (civil service organizations) in DCs in general and in sub-Sahara Africa (SSA) in particular. This is because it is usually among civil service organizations in SSA that the administrative crisis is most serious, where privatisation measures are least likely in the future, and where, to date, most attention both by national governments and donor agencies has been devoted to improving service delivery.

Chapter 1 has four sections, the first one being this introduction. Section 2 reviews the literature on HRM in the civil service in general and in the DCs in particular. Section 3 discusses the practices and challenges of HRM in sub-Saharan African (SSA) nations while section 4 carries the concluding remarks.

Chapter 2 investigates accuracy and rationality of Japanese consumer price index (CPI) forecasts from April 2004 through August 2008. It finds that the majority of zero-month forecasts are inferior to the naïve "last observation" forecast, which is the simple copy of the latest realization of CPI (at the time forecast was made). Moreover, almost all forecasts are irrational in the sense that their forecast errors could be reduced using the latest realization of CPI. These results present a striking contrast to the past literature.

Chapter 3 uses frontier nonparametric VARs techniques to investigate whether the Fisher Effect holds in the U.S. The Fisher Effect is examined taking into account structural breaks and nonlinearities between nominal interest rates and inflation, which are trend-stationary in the two samples examined. The nonparametric time-detrended test for the Fisher Effect is formed from the cumulative orthogonal dynamic multiplier ratios of inflation to nominal interest rates. If the Fisher Effect holds, this ratio statistically approaches one as the horizon goes to infinity. The nonparametric techniques developed in this paper conclude that the Fisher Effect holds for both samples examined.

Chapter 4 employs implicit gross domestic product (GDP) deflator and consumer price index (CPI) for forecasting inflation in Canada and USA. Inflation in these countries is modeled using non-Gaussian signal plus noise models that incorporate non-normality and conditional heteroskedasticity that may be present in the series. Inflation forecast from unrestricted non-Gaussian signal plus noise models and their restricted versions are compared with the inflation forecasts obtained from the Gaussian signal plus noise models for all the series.

The non-Gaussian signal plus noise models are estimated using filtering algorithm due to Sorenson and Alspach (1971). The results show that non-normality cannot be rejected in all the series even when the conditional heteroskedasticity is excluded from the models. When compared to the Gaussian signal plus noise models, the non-Gaussian models employed are able to take into account the outliers and level shifts in the inflation series.

The results from the present empirical exercise show statistically significant evidence of predictability of inflation in Canada and the USA series. The results obtained from non-Gaussian signal plus noise models show that there does not appears much disparity among the mean inflation forecasts for Canada using GDP Deflator and CPI series. However, substantial disparity does exist among the results for USA inflation forecasts obtained using CPI and GDP deflator.

Chapter 5 presents evidence on a non linear "inflation-relative prices" relationship in three Latin American countries with very high inflation experiences: Argentina, Brazil and Peru. Our results show a non concave relation during the episodes of higher price instability, and particularly at hyperinflation. This non concavity is mainly explained by the component of unexpected inflation, which suggests that the volatility associated to episodes of extreme inflation can be particularly relevant to understand the non neutrality of inflation

In Chapter 6, we investigate what is the best measure of labor market pressure for predicting wage inflation in Japan. Principal components analysis is used to select a subset of independent variables from 11 labor market variables. The first component is interpreted as the active opening rate and the second component is interpreted as total hours worked. We estimate a standard Phillips curve for wage inflation that incorporates the active opening rate and total hours worked as regressors. We find that (hourly) real wage growth is positively related to the active opening rate and negatively related to total hours worked. The second component (representing total hours worked) may help explain why wage inflation has not risen substantially despite Japan experiencing high active opening rates in the mid-2000s, when both total hours worked and active opening rates increased. Although higher active opening rates put upward pressure on real wage growth, this upward pressure is offset by longer working hours, which tend to reduce (hourly) real wage growth.

There has been an ongoing debate on the causes of inflation in developing countries. The debate focuses on the degree of fluctuations in the exchange rate in the face of internal and external shocks in order to curb inflation. As exchange rate policies are mostly geared toward containing inflation in developing countries, it is necessary to evaluate the effects of exchange rate fluctuations on price inflation. Demand and supply channels determine these effects.

To summarize Chapter 7, currency depreciation increases net exports and increases the cost of production. Similarly, currency appreciation decreases net exports and the cost of production. The combined effects of demand and supply channels determine the net results of exchange rate fluctuations on price.

In the context of a new Keynesian macroeconomic model, Chapter 8 studies the optimal monetary policy in an open economy setting. This policy depends on the preferences of the central bank, but also on the inflation persistence. Indeed, the inflation rate is the higher and the monetary policy should be all the more contractionary as the inflation inertia is high after positive fiscal, demand or foreign inflationary shocks. Then, in the event of a negative supply shock, the monetary policy is all the more expansionary as the monetary authority aims at sustaining the economic activity and as the inflation persistence is low. Finally, the monetary policy is only more expansionary if the inflation persistence increases after a positive shock on the foreign interest rate.

In Chapter 9, we extend a spatial autoregressive AR (SAR-AR) model, which is proposed by Elhorst (2001), to SAR-AR(p) model and construct the efficient strategy of Markov chain Monte Carlo (MCMC) methods to estimate the parameters of the model. Our approach is illustrated with both simulated and real data sets. By the simulated data set, we present that Griddy-Gibbs sampler is more efficient than Metropolis-Hastings (M-H) algorithm in sampling the spatial correlation parameter. In the example by real data set, we examine electric demand in Japan. From the empirical results, SAR-AR(1) model is selected and we find that electric demand in Japan has a strong time correlation with the first order lagged dependent variable. Through the model comparison, we find that the spatial interaction plays an important role in Japan.

Chapter 10 presents a new advantage of output contracts vs. inflation contracts not yet considered in previous literature [Beestma and Jensen (1999) and Røisland (2001)]. The analysis develops in the common agency framework used by Dixit and Jensen (2003), whichmodels the political pressures that national governments (principals) in a monetary union exert on the common central bank (agent) through inflation contracts. In this context, we show that the deflation bias obtained in this last article can be avoided if one government designs an output-related contract and its counterpart does the same or, instead, offers an inflation contract.

In: Inflation: Causes and Effects
Editor: Leon V. Schwartz, pp. 1-25
ISBN: 978-1-60741-823-8

Chapter 1

PRACTICES, CHALLENGES AND PROSPECTS OF HRM IN SUB-SAHARAN AFRICA (SSA)

Mussie Tessema[1,a], Mengsteab Tesfayohannes[2,b], Hamid Yeganeh[1,c] and Baekkyoo Joo (Brian)[1,d]

[1]Winona State University, MN, USA
[2]NeXt Research Center ,Wilfrid Laurier University, Waterloo, Canada

Introduction

In every country, people are the lifeblood of the public service. This underscores the need to value people highly and to develop and manage human resources with great care (UN, 2005: vii). Ingraham, Selden, and Moynihan (2000: 56) explain that "Members of the public service are...government's most important resource. Failure to understand and value that resource will inevitably be linked to lack of capacity and performance." Similarly, Tjiptoherijanto (2007) is of the view that improving the way human resources are managed is central to improving the quality of services offered by governments. Thus, public organizations need to effectively manage their human resources if they are to realize their objectives (Boxall, 2003; Klinger & Nalbandian, 1998; Paauwe, 2004).

Given the reality of manpower shortages in Developing Countries (DCs), effective Human Resource Management (HRM) especially in the civil service has become of great importance. For, this is the only way that DCs can hope to have an adequate and continuous supply of qualified, committed, and motivated work force (CAFRAD, 2000; Kim, 2007). In their review of the most successful development projects and programs from a variety of DCs, the ECA (1989) and the World Bank (1997) found out that a common feature in these projects was the high priority placed on human resource development and utilization. Successful organizations attribute their past successes partly to the way they deal with their people. Hence, effective HRM now more than ever before is a crucial ingredient in the development

[a] E-mail address: mtessema@winona.edu
[b] E-mail address: haryohruth@rogers.com
[c] E-mail address: HYeganeh@winona.edu
[d] E-mail address: BJoo@winona.edu

process of DCs. However, HRM has come under strong criticism in many DCs with their effectiveness thrown in considerable doubt (e.g., Budhwar & Debrah, 2004; Hilderbrand & Grindle, 1997; Jaeger et al., 1995; Kiggundu, 1989; Praha, 2004; Tessema & Ngoma, 2009).

Many studies conducted in many DCs indicate that HRM has not been effective and is a major limiting factor in the development programs. The main reasons for the failure of development projects and programs as well as of government routine operations in these countries are shortages of competent public servants and an inability to effectively utilize the expertise of the existing public servants (Brewer & Choi, 2007; Dirk, 2008; Kiggundu, 1989; Hilderbrand & Grindle, 1997; Munene et al., 2000; Tjiptoherijanto, 2007). These problems are compounded by the fact that DCs are increasingly unable to retain the trained personnel employed in the civil service. They also are unable to effectively utilize the expertise of those who do not leave the civil service. Beyond that, moonlighting and corrupt rent-seeking practices have become a way of life for public servants in many DCs (Bennell, 1994; Das, 1998).

While this study tries to consider HRM in the public sector as a whole, the focus is mainly on HRM at the central ministries (civil service organizations) in DCs in general and in sub-Sahara Africa (SSA) in particular. This is because it is usually among civil service organizations in SSA that the administrative crisis is most serious, where privatisation measures are least likely in the future, and where, to date, most attention both by national governments and donor agencies has been devoted to improving service delivery.

This chapter has four sections, the first one being this introduction. Section 2 reviews the literature on HRM in the civil service in general and in the DCs in particular. Section 3 discusses the practices and challenges of HRM in sub-Saharan African (SSA) nations while section 4 carries the concluding remarks.

Literature Review

The word *civil service* was first used in British administration in India and was popularised by Sir Charles Trevelyan (Sills, 1968: 495). It is difficult to provide a universally accepted definition of this term because its meaning and scope of coverage vary from country to country. Nevertheless, the following definitions have been suggested by scholars. The term *civil service* refers to the branches of public service excluding the legislative, judicial, and military sectors and in which positions are typically filled on the basis of competitive examinations and a professional career public service exists, with protections against political influence and patronage (Berman et al., 2001: 356). A *civil service* is the body of government officials who are employed in civil occupations that are neither political nor judicial; in many countries, it refers to employees selected and promoted on the basis of a merit and seniority system, which may include examinations (Encyclopaedia Britannica, 2008). From the above definitions, the following important points can be identified:

- The precise categories of personnel officially included in a civil service vary somewhat from one country to another, within a single country over a period of time and from one region of the continent to another. However, custom and law everywhere exclude elected officials and members of the armed forces.

- Despite the vagueness in accepted definitions and variations in its usage, a civil service does identify the expanding corps of trained manpower that must be maintained by every modern polity to carry out governmental functions.
- The role of the civil service must be defined in the political system generally. The universal expectation is that the civil service should be neutral. However, practices vary a great deal from country to country although responsiveness by the administrative staff to the directives of political leaders is an objective commonly sought, even among political regimes that differ greatly in other respects.
- Civil service systems are composed of political appointees and career civil services. Although the system as a whole is staffed primarily on the basis of merit, top-level administrators are appointed on the basis of patronage.
- In the context of most DCs, civil service as an institution came into being due to the outcome of their colonial experience. The process of establishment of colonial governments in these countries was marked by the replacement of the pre-colonial traditional administrative systems with modern administrative structures and institutions of the mother countries notably the British, French and Dutch. Hence, it can be said that the establishment of the civil services of most of the DCs and particularly that of African countries was a product of their colonial rule.

In the words of Pfeffer (1994: 33), "having good HRM is likely to generate much loyalty, commitment, or willingness to expend extra effort for the organization's objectives". Stone (1998: 4) also writes that "HRM is either part of the problem or part of the solution in gaining the productive contribution of people". The above quotes suggest that if organizations are to realize their objectives, they need to effectively manage their human resources.

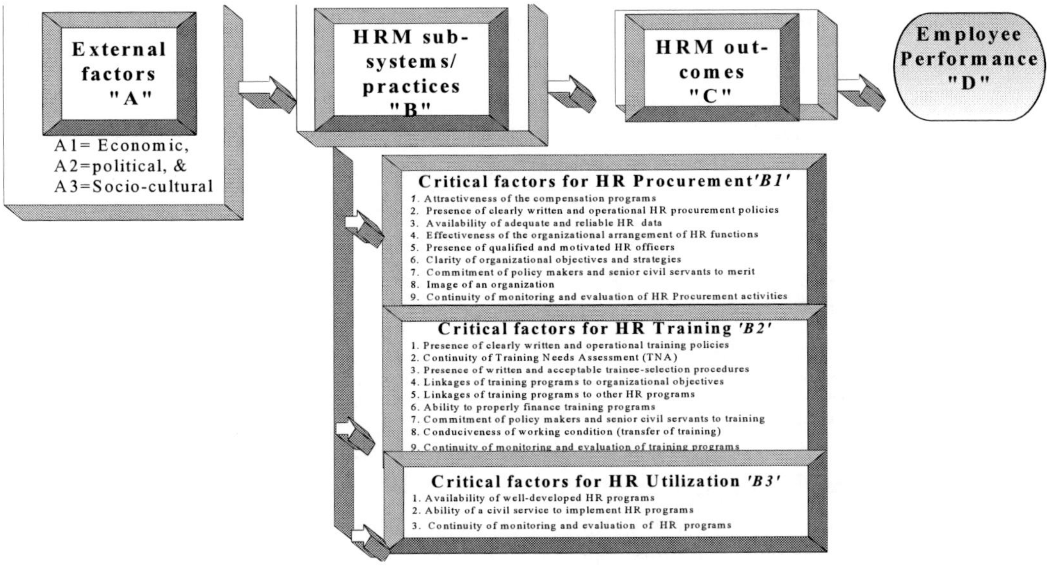

Figure 1. Conceptual framework for assessing HR practices, challenges and prospects in a civil service.

The main objective of this chapter is to assess HRM practices, challenges and prospects in the civil service in SSA. To this end, we developed the conceptual framework presented in Figure 1[1]. The conceptual framework was based on the following assumptions:

- External or environmental factors (economic, political, and socio-cultural) affect the three HRM sub-systems (HR procurement, training and utilization), which in turn affect HRM outcomes (e.g., HR competence, motivation, role clarity and retention), which subsequently affect employee and organizational performance.
- The HRM system has several functions. In this study, they are grouped under three categories or sub-systems, namely HR procurement, training and, utilization. The logic is that organizations first tend to procure human resources, then train and utilize them to realize their objectives. Overall HRM effectiveness depends to a great extent on the effectiveness of the above three sub-systems of HRM.
- The three HRM-sub systems are, in turn, affected by some factors, which we have called 'critical factors'. They are a sort of 'checklist'. In the words of Hiltrop (1996), the checklist chosen should depend on the problems being researched and the kinds of predictability sought. Hiltrop further notes that variables in a checklist can be interrelated and their exact number and labels are somewhat arbitrary. It should also be noted that as with any checklist, our checklist might be incomplete and in some cases, has overlapping factors. Nevertheless, it is useful for diagnosing and understanding HRM practices, challenges and prospects in SSA.
- In assessing HRM practices, challenges and prospects in SSA, 21 critical factors of the three HRM sub-systems were identified as shown below:

  - ***HR procurement/staffing:*** The main objective of HR procurement is to procure or hire the right quality (kind) and quantity (number) of human resources required to realize the desired objectives (e.g., Dessler, 2007; Berman et al., 2001). From an extensive literature review, the following critical factors, which affect HR procurement, are identified: [a] attractiveness of the compensation programs, [b] presence of clearly written and operational HR procurement policies, [c] availability of adequate and reliable personnel data, [d] effectiveness of the organizational arrangement of HR functions, [e] presence of qualified and motivated HR officers, [f] clarity of organizational objectives and strategies, [g] commitment of policy makers and senior civil servants to merit principles, [h] image of an organization, and [i] continuity of monitoring and evaluation of HR procurement activities.
  - ***HR training/development***: The main objective of HR training is to upgrade or improve the skills, knowledge and behaviour of human resources in order to be able to enhance their fit to the job and organization (Thomas and Theresa, 1995: 7; Berman et al., 2001: 234). From an extensive literature review, the following critical factors affecting HR training, have been identified: [a] presence of clearly written and operational training policies, [b] continuity of training needs assessment, [c] presence of written and acceptable trainee-selection procedures, [d] linkages of training programs to organizational objectives, [e] linkages of training programs to other HR

[1] As Hiltrop (1996) points out, having a framework through which to discuss HRM practices helps avoid the problem of randomly discussing policies and procedures.

programs, [f] capacity of the government to finance training programs, [g] commitment of the policy makers and senior civil servants to training, [h] conduciveness of the working condition (transfer of training), and [i] continuity of monitoring and evaluation of training programs.

- ***HR utilization:*** HR procurement and training are necessary but not sufficient conditions for an effective management of civil servants. This suggests that HR utilization is an important aspect of HRM. No discussion of HRM would be complete without considering the role of HR utilization (e.g., Ahmad & Schroeder, 2003; CAFRAD, 2000; Hilderbrand & Grindle, 1997; Wescott & Jones, 2007; Tessema et al, 2005; UN, 2005). The following three factors are crucial ingredients to effective HR utilization: [a] availability of well developed (clear) HR programs, [b] ability of a civil service to successfully implement HR programs, and [c] continuity of monitoring and evaluation of HR programs.

Practices and Challenges of HRM in the Civil Service in Sub-Sahara Africa

Sub-Sahara Africa refers to the 45 African countries, excluding the Arab countries of North Africa that are often identified with the Middle East (World Bank, 1997). In a number of studies, many scholars and researchers have treated SSA collectively, as part of the world with more or less similar HRM-related practices and challenges (e.g., Das, 1998; Tessema & Soeters, 2006a; Beugre & Offodile, 2001). It has also been noted that, although sub-Saharan African countries differ among themselves, they share many commonalities. We are well aware of the fact that each country has its own unique environmental context. Nevertheless, discussing HR practices in the civil service of the countries in SSA can provide us with good insights into the general situation of HRM among these countries. The main objectives of this chapter are, therefore, to highlight the way and context within which civil servants have been managed (procured, trained and utilized) in the SSA countries.

According to Beyene (1994), the situation in SSA in the last four decades could well be explained according to four characteristics, one for each decade: [a] the 1960s is described as the decade of euphoria; [b] the 1970s, the decade of strain, stress and decline; [c] the 1980s, the decades of socio-economic crisis, and [d] the 1990s as the decade of transition from a state-dominated economic order to a market-based economic system. The World Bank (1994: 121) also observes that since independence, most sub-Saharan African countries' policies toward the civil service have had three common features, each undermining institutional capacity: first, they expanded the size[2] of the public sector faster than the economy grew; second, they favoured employment growth over income growth in the public sector, driving down the real wages of public sector employees; and third, they favoured pay increases in the lower ranks, reducing pay differences between skilled and unskilled employees. As a

[2] In fact, African civil services have the least manpower per capita (i.e., for the population they serve) in the world. They also spend the least on their civil services (30% of GNP compared to 40-50% for OECD and Asian tigers). The ratio of civil servant per population is 1: 16 for OECD countries but 1: 150, 1: 155, 1: 120 and 1: 190 for Zambia, Ghana, Uganda and Ethiopia respectively (UN, 1992). If we take the Eritrean case, it is roughly 1: 117 (Tessema & Soeters, 2006b). As a result, Ozgediz (1983: 3) underlines African countries, on the average, have fewer public employees per capita than Asian and Latin American countries.

consequence, civil services are larger than these countries need, more costly than they can afford, and less effective and productive than they should be. Thus, African governments have been confronted with formidable challenges in the management (procurement, training, and utilization) of their civil servants.

With the foregoing issues in mind, we now discuss HR practices (HR procurement, training and utilization) and challenges in SSA.

Procurement of Civil Servants in Sub-Sahara Africa

HR procurement practices with respect to SSA are discussed below by taking into account the nine (9) critical factors for HR procurement (Figure 1).

Attractiveness of the Compensation Programs

Most SSA countries have been unable to put in place compensation programs that are competitive on the market. A number of studies of the civil service in SSA have warned that un-competitively low salaries threaten to undermine the SSA governments' ability to attract, motivate and retain competent civil servants (e.g., Hilderbrand & Grindle, 1997; Clemens & Pettersson, 2007; Das, 1998; ILO, 1998; World Bank, 1997).[3] The gap between wages in the civil service and private sector has widened, and it has become more and more difficult for the civil service to recruit and keep qualified civil servants. This problem is still creating difficulties in inviting and selecting the best applicants. The main factor that has inhibited SSA governments from developing attractive and competitive compensation are the serious economic challenges that they have faced in the last three decades. Recently, efforts have been made to improve compensation management (improve salary level and wage decompression- mainly on project basis that is not adjusted regularly); however, the situation still is not very attractive (see also ILO, 1998; Prah, 2004; Marfouk, 2008).

Presence of Clearly Written and Operational HR Procurement Policies

It has been observed that in many SSA countries, the civil service has been politicized (CAFRAD, 2000; Das, 1998; ECA, 2005; Heady, 1996). Das (1998: 19) argues, for example, that "politicization has resulted in the total erosion of traditional civil service values such as political neutrality, probity, rectitude, and objectivity". This situation, therefore, has been aggravating the practice of not properly following HR procurement policies and procedures. To reverse this trend, Tessema & Soeters (2006b) suggest that efforts should be made to change the patronizing attitude that has been prevalent in many African countries and to prevent the nepotism that is common in the management of civil service. For instance, in a study of managers' motivation in Africa, Beugre (1998, quoted in Beugre & Offodile, 2001: 537) writes that African managers are required to satisfy the social needs of their relatives. Behind every African worker, there is a family requesting attention, time and, mostly, money.

[3] Most World Bank reports emphasize the point that SSA countries do not have adequate capabilities to effectively attract and retain qualified civil servants (World Bank, 1994, 1997).

Obligation to relatives often leads to nepotism and/or favouritism. For example, helping one's relative for a job is considered normal. Furthermore, the World Bank (1994) observes that recruitment to the civil service is mostly based on considerations other than merit. As a consequence, some systems are 'civil service' in name only and function as 'spoils systems.' In other words, the government's personnel system may be nominally merit but practically political (Heady, 1996). Even though there are procurement guidelines they are not properly followed.

Effectiveness of the Organizational Arrangement of HR Functions

The organizational arrangement of HR functions of a civil service in most SSA countries is *somewhat centralized*[4] in that principal responsibilities are frequently placed in the hands of an independent agency (central personnel agency or civil service commission) or the office of the president/prime minister (Heady, 1996; Bennell, 1994; Turner & Hulme, 1997; Das, 1998; UN, 2005). According to Bennell (1994: 8), the principal characteristics of such kind of organizational arrangement are authoritarian, hierarchical, centralized rules and procedures based on rigid bureaucratic notions of legal authority and rationality. The centralized system of administration has eliminated most of the discretionary managerial authority over personnel decisions at the level of line positions. The World Bank (1994: 45) states that

> "matters relating to posts to be created, vacancies to be filled, promotions and incentives as also the expenditure to be incurred, are all centrally determined. All individual personnel decisions such as, transfers, postings, incentives, and punishments are made only by central authorities. Central control has effectively taken away decisional authority from line managers in the civil service".

In most of SSA, personnel departments in operating ministries/organizations play a relatively passive role, administering these (mostly outdated) rules rather than actively developing and pursuing policies for improving the civil service management (e.g., Komache, 2002; Ovadje &Ankomah, 2004).

One of the major obstacles to the effective HR functions in general and recruitment and selection in particular in most SSA countries is the excessive concentration of decision-making and authority within central government (Beugre & Offodile, 2001).[5] As a consequence, the protracted bureaucratic and all too often unfair nature of the recruitment process discourages large numbers of talented people from applying for jobs in the public sector. Although competitive entrance examinations are employed, these are frequently poorly designed since they fail to test for relevant job skills and knowledge required for effective job performance (see also Beugre & Offodile, 2001; Blunt & Jones, 1997; Ovadje &Ankomah, 2004).

HR practices in the civil service of most SSA have been seriously plagued by the regulatory type of public administration inherited from the colonial days (Dirk, 2008; Bennell,

[4] The organizational arrangement of HR functions in SSA countries is, generally, somewhat centralized (for details, see World Bank, 1994; Bennell, 1994).

[5] Many scholars believe that many of the personnel rules and procedures date back to the colonial period and as such intend to ensure control and stability rather than encourage high quality individual performance and promote necessary change (see also Heady, 1996; Bennell, 1994; Turner and Hulme, 1997; Mudhoo, 1995).

1994; Mudhoo, 1995). In many SSA, the civil service commission jealously guarded its control over HR policies and practices. Individual ministries have had little control over recruitment. Many SSA have continued till now to apply the systems which prevailed during the colonial days (e.g., Turner & Hulme, 1997; World Bank, 1994; Heady, 1996). The key word is still very much bureaucracy - red tape and an inflexible or mechanistic approach - despite the fact that the response is no longer appropriate in a fast changing world (see also Hilderbrand & Grindle; 1997; Tessema & Soeters, 2006a)[6].

On the basis of the foregoing discussion, one can conclude that, on the one hand, most countries in SSA prefer centralized organizational arrangement of HR functions (such as recruitment and selection), on the other hand, the central personnel agencies are not well staffed, structured, and funded, whereas the HR Information Systems (HRISs) are weak (see also Grindle, 1997; Bennell, 1994; Ghebregiorgis & Karsten, 2007).

Adequacy and Reliability of Personnel Data

Despite the importance of efficient HRIS, in most SSA countries, personnel records are maintained manually, are updated infrequently,[7] and are too cumbersome for the aggregate analysis needed for formulating policies, determining staffing and training requirements, or monitoring policy implementation (see also ECA, 1989; Bennell, 1994). Personnel data available in most SSA civil services are relatively limited both in terms of quality and quantity, which in turn suggests that personnel data have to be used with utmost care.[8] For instance, Polgreen (2006) notes that the Cameron government found 45,000 "ghost workers" on its payroll, a phantom workforce costing the country almost $10 million. ECA (1989) notes that questionnaires that merely ask each organization to state its net additional requirements of personnel over a five or more year period have ended up being little more than 'wish-lists'. Not surprisingly, the temptation for most organizations has been to over-inflate their HR estimates in the almost certain knowledge that only a small proportion of these requirements will ever be realized. Thus, like the budgetary process itself, HR planning in many SSA countries has become highly politicized. ECA (1989) and Mudhoo (1995) argue that HR planners in many African countries have also been excessively preoccupied with deriving HR estimates for additional personnel rather than analysing the utilization of personnel who have already been employed. However, with the introduction of civil service reform, most countries in SSA have begun to provide due attention to the HRISs,[9] which in turn are expected to play a crucial role in supplying policy makers with the required data (ECA, 1989; Tessema & Soeters, 2006a).

---

[6] It is important to bear in mind that our focus here is not to advocate decentralized arrangement of HR functions. However, it is to suggest that excessive centralization could be counter-productive.

[7] For instance, in 1993, when the personnel data of the civil service in the Central African Republic was updated, the following anomalies were noted: 3,876 had no dates of birth; 4,962 had no retirement dates; 5,325 had no establishment dates; 3,050 officials were on the payroll and not on the departmental records, while 2,277 officials were on the records and not on the payroll (for details, see Rambourg et al. 1995: 31-33).

[8] The head of an African civil service once said, we do not know how many we are, we don't know how many we need, but we are told to cut by 15 percent (Bennell, 1994).

[9] The ILO (1998: 18) remarks that it is indispensable to have a regular update and censuses in order to identify ghost workers, determine staffing needs, improve staff functions, verify payrolls, and facilitate statutory retirement. In doing so, there is a need of strengthening the capacity of the personnel office both centrally and organizationally.

Availability of Qualified and Motivated HR Officers

There has been a lack of skills and motivation on the part of the HR officers, which, in turn, has adversely affected the performance of HR functions (Branine, 2004; Ghebregiorgis & Karsten, 2007; ILO, 1998). Bennell (1994: 8) also notes that HRM tends to be the responsibility of relatively low status, poorly educated and trained staff in public sector organizations. Most personnel offices at organization level go little beyond record-keeping and drafting personnel procedures. Most advanced techniques for studying HR issues (manpower planning, job evaluation, position classification, performance assessment, counselling, staff development and various statistical methods) are rarely employed (CAFRAD, 2000; Kim & Hong, 2006; UN, 2005). It has long been known that African countries have inadequate supplies of skilled and experienced specialists. "In recent years, perhaps the most critical shortages are in the areas of management and administration" (Kiggundu, 1989: 63). As a consequence, personnel offices in many SSA countries remain staffed with civil servants who are in less demand elsewhere and who stress passive administrative tasks over more controversial management concerns that require robust policy research and analysis. HRM has all too often remained narrowly preoccupied with the administration of usually complex, legally defined and enforced sets of uniform rules and procedures governing all HR functions (Bennell, 1994: 8). Thus, unlike in the private corporate sector, there is no well-developed professional cadre of HR managers with clear responsibilities for all aspects of HRM. This is certainly the case in most SSA.

Many scholars suggest that what is missing is a team of actors specialized in the field of HRM to spearhead and bring some new concepts and ideas to fruition. Furthermore, until and unless the supervising officers of departments are themselves convinced of the necessity for achieving excellence and promoting it throughout their respective areas of operation, not much progress can be expected (see also Branine, 2004; Mudhoo, 1995; Kim & Hong, 2006).

Clarity of Organizational Objectives and Strategies

Many civil service organizations in SSA do not have clear objectives and strategies (e.g., Beugre & Offodile, 2001; Das, 1998; Kiggundu, 1989; Austin, 1990). Das (1998) notes that many governments in SSA do not set clear objectives or monitorable measurements of achievement. This, in his view, makes HRM so opaque that no accountability can be enforced (1998: 21-23). Quite often, the African organization's means and goals are not clearly articulated and the organization lacks a clear sense of purpose and direction (Kiggundu, 1989: 9). Politicians in most of SSA are not well-prepared to spell out their organizational objectives in a sufficiently precise manner (e.g., Kiggundu, 1989; Das, 1998).

Many African countries have three to five years development plans that identify national goals, priorities, targets, resources, and strategies, and that are similar to mission statements or officials goals for individual organizations. These plans are often broken down by sector, ministry, or government agency or corporation. However, most of the time, they do not properly specify how many employees with what types of skills would be needed to realize the stated objectives (see also Bennell, 1994; Kiggundu, 1989; ECA, 1989). Despite its importance, HRM is not always perceived as being integrated into strategic planning and policy development. Kiggundu (1989: 71) also states that "reading the national development plans, and watching public servants at work in these organizations, it is not always clear how the two complement each other". In particular, development goals and objectives at the national and sectoral levels have been poorly defined, and there has frequently not been political commitment to translate planned objectives into practice (see also UN, 2005; Kiggundu, 1989). Mainly due to the above situation, many SSA countries not only have HR functions, which have been poorly managed but also there has been a marked absence of any strategic HRM directly linked to and supportive of the overall goals and objectives of each organization (UN, 2005).

Commitment of Policy Makers and Senior Civil Servants to Merit Principles

Commitment of the policy makers and civil service managers to merit principles is a sine qua non for successful recruitment and selection of civil servants. However, such kind of commitment does not usually prevail in many SSA governments, which has resulted in the politicization[10] of the civil service.

Image of an Organization

The prevailing situation in the civil service in most SSA countries has adversely affected the image of these countries. As many scholars have argued, civil service organizations in most SSA countries are not prestigious places which can attract and retain qualified and experienced personnel (Ghebregiorgis & Karsten, 2007; Clemens & Pettersson, 2007). This may imply that many competent and qualified individuals are not willing to join these organizations.

Continuity of Monitoring and Evaluation of HR Procurement Activities

Many studies indicate that there are no proper monitoring and evaluation mechanisms for HR activities in general and that of the HR procurement in particular (Grindle, 1997). Once civil servants are procured and placed, there is almost no follow-up as to whether they are in the right positions or they are the right persons for the positions (e.g., Wekita, 2002). For instance, it is common to find overstaffing of civil servants in some departments while others are understaffed. This is the case because of lack of proper monitoring and evaluation of HRM. Recently, many countries in SSA began conducting *functional reviews* to pinpoint the main constraints to efficient and effective staffing. Accordingly, they have identified staff who need to be retrenched, re-deployed or retrained (Kim & Hong, 2006; Das, 1998). However, despite their importance, most countries have not been conducting functional reviews regularly.

---

[10] All efforts made to be guided by the meritocracy principles fall short of expectation (see also Waiguchu, 1999; Heady, 1996).

To summarize:

- civil servants who are well qualified, motivated and productive is a goal common to SSA; yet, this simply stated goal is usually not achieved. This is mainly due to a number of reasons; inter alia economic constraints, politicization of civil service, and indigenous social arrangements, which, in turn, encourages nepotism and favouritism;
- the above factors have a cumulative impact upon the image of the civil service in SSA. As a result, many governments in SSA are finding it increasingly difficult to attract and retain the professionals that they need in the civil service;
- although some improvements have been made in many SSA countries mainly due to the introduction of HRM reforms, still a lot needs to be done.

Training of Civil Servants in Sub-Saharan Africa

Over the past four decades, governments in SSA have been attempting to improve the skills and knowledge of their civil servants by providing both local and overseas training programs. However, despite all the efforts made so far, civil service training has had limited impact on the capacity of the civil service organizations in most SSA countries (Cohen & Wheeler, 1997; ILO, 1998; Kerrigan & Luke 1987; Hilderbrand & Grindle, 1997; Clemens & Pettersson, 2007). In spite of the increased training activities they are still unable to make significant visible contribution to the shortage of skilled manpower problems in the sense that still many civil service organizations have been experiencing acute shortages of high-level technical and managerial skills in many areas (Aredo, 2002; Tessema & Ngoma, 2009). The most disturbing thing is that the ability of civil service organizations to retain and effectively utilize their well-trained civil servants has been adversely affected. For instance, Haddow (quoted in Cohen & Wheeler, 1997: 125) notes that

> "the government must train four officers to retain one for a long period of time... [this] serious retention problem... is reaching alarming proportions...[it] must be addressed squarely...[efforts must be made] to change and improve the management and utilization of trained professionals in Government so as to create an environment in which graduates will enjoy a challenging and rewarding professional career in the Civil Service".

Marfouk's study (2008: 6) shows that

> "10 out of the 53 African countries have lost more than 35 per cent of the their tertiary educated labor force and countries such as Cape Verde (68 percent), Gambia (63 percent), Seychelles (56 percent), Maurice (56 percent) and Sierra Leone (53 percent) suffered from a massive brain drain."

The UN (2005: xii) further underscores that

> "The departure of a skilled migrant signifies a loss of investment in previous education and training for the country of origin as well as a loss of skills and experience that would otherwise provide future contributions to development, including future tax payments. In developing countries, it is important that this phenomenon be counterbalanced by 'earn, learn

and return' strategies to take advantage of the enhanced skills and experience of the expatriate population, with programs to facilitate remittances and encourage migrants to return. In critical employment sectors, such as health and education, governments also need to adopt specific programs and incentives to stem the tide."

And a recent study by Clemens and Pettersson (2007: 13) indicates that

"Approximately 65,000 African-born physicians and 70,000 African-born professional nurses were working overseas in a developed country in the year 2000. This represents about one fifth of African-born physicians in the world, and about one tenth of African-born professional nurses. The fraction of health professionals abroad varies enormously across African countries, from 1% to over 70% according to the according to the occupation and country."

Given the prevailing situation in the civil service in SSA, Corkery et al. (1998: 529) contend that "it is time to look at the experience to try to determine why this is so and what the countries of the region need to do to equip themselves".

In this sub-section, therefore, an attempt is made to present HR training practices and challenges in the SSA by taking into consideration the following nine critical factors (Figure 1).

Presence of Clearly Written and Operational Training Policies:

Experiences of most countries in Africa show that training has not been effective despite the rapid expansion of training institutions mainly due to the absence or inadequacy of the written and operational training policies (Paul, 1983: 34; Kerrigan and Luke, 1987: 204; Tessema et al., 2005: 224). As a consequence, a number of factors which could have contributed positively to the success of training such as needs assessment, monitoring and evaluation, co-ordination of all training related activities, relating training to other personnel functions, etc. are adversely affected. Bennell also notes that "there has been absence of well-specified training policies with a precise strategic focus. Training tends to be isolated and sporadic, and fails to satisfy the learning needs of individual employees" (1994: 10). It should also be acknowledged that the number of SSA countries having written training policies is increasing from time to time (World Bank, 1994; ILO, 1998; Wekita, 2002). However, the most important issue is not only having training policies, but successfully implementing them.

Continuity of Training Needs Assessment (TNA)

Many studies have indicated that mainly due to the absence or ineffective training needs assessment, training efforts have had limited impact in several SSA countries (ILO, 1998)[11]. Training is applied to problems that do not require training as the solution. Civil servants are subjected to programs that are irrelevant to their needs because of lack of skills in assessing trainability (see also ILO, 1998; Thomas & Theresa, 1995). Thomas and Theresa (1995) observe that most training materials are inappropriate since they are not based on clearly

[11] The ILO (1998: 9) indicates that "in many DCs training needs assessments are often lacking or unsatisfactory".

identified training needs[12]. The ILO (1998: 36) also argues that "in Africa, there are examples of donor-driven reform and training activities, which have little chance of success because they are 'blueprints' imposed by the North in the South- and hence inappropriate". What the foregoing quotes demonstrate is that training needs assessment, despite its importance, has not been given the attention it rightly deserves in many SSA countries. Thus, one can argue that poor and inadequate assessment of training needs may lead to an incredible waste of resources that Africa can ill afford.

Presence of Written and Acceptable Trainee-Selection Procedures

Many studies show that many times, civil service organizations in African countries have not selected trainees who could really benefit from particular training programs (ILO, 1998; ECA, 1989). For this reason, training has been done just as 'one's turn to be trained'. The ILO (1998: 9) also indicates that, "at times, it may seem that people are sent to training courses simply because these are available, regardless of training needs".[13] This results in a mis-match between training and the expectation of trainees. This problem may be partly due to the lack of training needs assessment (ILO, 1998; Tessema et al., 2005), and be partly due to the politicization of civil service systems, which in turn affects the kind of civil servants to be selected for training (Das, 1998). Thus, many scholars question the criteria for selection of trainees being used in many countries of SSA. This is because individuals without the required potential have been chosen (even repeatedly) to participate in training, especially if the individuals are to financially benefit from it (Corkery et al., 1998; Tessema et al., 2005).

Linkages of Training Programs to Organizational Objectives

Another key ingredient for effective civil service training is a proper linkage of training programs to organizational objectives. However, many training programs in Africa are not well linked to organizational objectives (Kiggundu, 1989; Cohen & Wheeler, 1997). Many civil service organizations in SSA have not properly specified how many civil servants, in what kind of skills and knowledge (including the kinds of training required to fill the skills gap) have been needed to realize the desired objectives. This problem arises partly due to the lack of effective training needs assessment at individual, organizational and national levels (e.g., Bennell, 1994; ILO, 1998), and partly due to lack of clear organizational objectives (see also Beugre & Offodile, 2001; Das, 1998; Clemens & Pettersson, 2007).

Linkages of Training Programs to Other HR Policies and Programs

It has been argued that linkages of training to other HR programs are vital if training programs are to have the desired impact. However, most SSA countries lack training policies

---

[12] Bennell (1994: 10) underlines that most training courses lack relevance, are too classroom-based, rely mostly on textbooks and other training materials which are out-dated and largely irrelevant, and are taught by people who know little about individual trainees and the organizations they work for.

[13] Ozgediz remarks that, in developing countries, trainees are selected on the basis on training needs assessment, bureaucratic politics, and patronage (1983: 31).

that link training to other personnel programs, such as placement, promotions, salary increment and other incentives (e.g., CAFRAD, 2000; Clemens & Pettersson, 2007; Tessema & Soeters, 2006a)[14]. Grindle (1997: 14) notes that "when newly trained civil servants return home from overseas, their jobs and career opportunities do not always reflect the increased level of skill they have". As a result, frequently many well-trained African civil servants are not well motivated and satisfied (see also Cohen & Wheeler, 1997; Tessema et al., 2005). Prospects of higher rewards in other sectors of the economy have made it increasingly difficult for the government to motivate and retain the trained civil service at the prevailing salary rates. Tessema and Ngoma (2009) state that the salaries of many Eritrean civil servants who got additional long-term training programs were not adjusted or linked to the new skills and knowledge (MA degree) that they acquired. As a result, "public servants tend, once they have obtained better qualifications through training, to move over to the private sector" (ILO, 1998: 35). The prevailing situation has therefore adversely affected the motivation of the ex-trainees as well as the impact of the training. Here, one may argue it is not a question of how many civil servants are trained, but how they are utilized that matters. While many training programs have been given in SSA, little has been achieved in terms of their impact (e.g., Kerrigan & Luke, 1987; CAFRAD, 2000; Cohen & Wheeler, 1997; Ovadje &Ankomah, 2004).

Capacity of a Government to Finance Training Programs

There are varying practices and the proportion of funds allocated by government for training purposes differs widely. Most of the time, training funds in the case of SSA countries, come from two major sources, namely the budgetary allocation by the government and funding by donor agencies or countries (e.g. Cohen & Wheeler, 1997; Corkery et al., 1998).[15] Since budget provisions for training, in most SSA countries, are generally inadequate, it is not possible to meet all the training needs (Ghebregiorgis & Karsten, 2007; Thomas & Theresa, 1995). For this reason, we can argue that in contrast with their counterparts in industrialized countries, only a small amount of money is allocated for training purposes (See also ILO, 1998; Bennell, 1994; Grindle, 1997). This situation has also aggravated recently due to the deteriorating economic[16] situation in most SSA. In the words of Bennell (1994: 10), "with deepening economic crisis, training is one of the first expenditures to be slashed." However, some countries like Nigeria allocated 1 percent of the total federal allocation for every local government to training, which in turn may imply a real commitment of the government to training (ILO, 1998).

[14] As training is usually not followed by reward in terms of salary increment and other incentives, promotion and personal appreciation in most SSA, and is occasionally accompanied by the hazard of losing the previous positions, Senior Civil Servants often come for training only when they cannot successfully avoid it (Hilderbrand & Grindle, 1997).

[15] Most countries of SSA depend upon the assistance of international donor agencies, which in turn affects adversely SSA governments' ability to manage the donated training fund according to their own priority (e.g., ILO, 1998; Cohen and Wheeler, 1997).

[16] Most countries of SSA are increasingly exposed to budgetary constraints, which, in turn, adversely affected the amount of money that is to be invested in training.

Commitment of the Policy Makers and Senior Civil Service Managers to Training

One of the main reasons why training is not effective in many SSA is that there is a lack of strong political and administrative support in the larger environment for training and development in civil service. It is obvious that no book, conference or seminars overlook the need for interest to be shown by ministers, politicians and senior officials in training. Beyond budgetary provision for training, it is rare to find politicians and very senior officers becoming personally involved in training in many SSA (Paul, 1983; Kerrigan & Luke, 1987; ILO, 1998). By the same token, executive training and development programs for senior civil servants have been meagre at best[17]. Despite the importance of training, top management bodies sometimes view it as too costly, and the payoffs too far into the future. Thus, the amount of money invested in training is still very low as compared to other activities, especially in DCs in general and SSA in particular. Moreover, it is regrettable that training should often be the first sector to be affected when economies have to be made in staff expenditure (Bennell, 1994; ILO, 2000; UN, 2005).[18] The environments are characterized instead by a general lack of appreciation for investment in the long-term development strategy (Cohen & Wheeler, 1997). Nevertheless, some countries have made progress in civil service training.[19] For example, Kaul (1997: 26) notes that Ghana tailored civil service training by instituting customized training for staff. The Ghanaian Institute of Management and Public Administration (GIMPA) has expanded its activities to meet the increased demands of training as a result of civil service reforms in Ghana. The government of Botswana has also set up a specialized training centre - Botswana Productivity Centre - for training in productivity and quality improvement programs (see also ILO, 2000).

Conduciveness of the Working Condition (Transfer of Training)

Many scholars have noted that one of the main complaints of former trainees in the civil service of most SSA is a lack of conducive working conditions to practise what they have learned (Cohen & Wheeler, 1997: 146). This is partly due to lack of encouragement by their superiors, who themselves are not willing to participate in training programs and are resistant to the introduction of new ways of doing things (Beugre & Offodile, 2001; Kim & Hong, 2006). Unavailability of the facilities required for the implementation of new ways of doing things is another impediment that civil servants with new knowledge and skills often encounter (Cohen & Wheeler, 1997; Tessema & Ngoma, 2009). Surveying the African scene, one observer noted that,

---

[17] A UN report also notes that: "if senior civil servants were exposed to and convinced of the utility of in-service training, it would have beneficial effects on the desire of lower-echelon staff to participate in in-service training programs" (cited in Paul, 1983: 39).

[18] In our opinion, one factor standing in the way of training is that unlike other development activities it does not show quick or tangible results. It may take many years for the impact of training to become really discernible.

[19] The ILO (1998: 33) points out that training needs were often underestimated in processes of structural change and transition even though some countries gave high priority to training.

> "CAFRAD[20] experience in administrative training in Africa is that the very senior civil servants who need help most are reluctant to come forward for training. This is the commonest complaint our trainees make. What is the use of acquiring new knowledge, skills and attitudes if our bosses are not going to notice, let alone appreciate, the changed performance behaviour" (Paul, 1983: 27).

Continuity of Monitoring and Evaluation of Training Programs

Many civil services in SSA do not properly accomplish monitoring and evaluation (M&E) activities in spite of their contribution to the success of training programs (Kerrigan, 1989; ILO, 1998). Most training institutions in SSA depend mainly on the administration of questionnaires at the end of the training program ("end-of-courses" evaluations) while evaluating the effectiveness of training. However, this is a limited measure of the trainee's satisfaction and, thus, does not measure the training program's effectiveness. While some form of evaluation has generally accompanied the training activities, evaluation usually tends to concentrate on performance during and immediately after the training courses. Efforts to measure the contributions of training to actual or future performance in the work situation have not received much attention. The ILO (1998: 9) also indicates that in many African countries, the evaluation of training impact may also be inadequate or fail to involve the actors concerned. It is paradoxical that although millions of dollars are spent by governments throughout the SSA for training, evaluation of training performance in terms of its contribution to organizations has not kept pace.[21]

What the foregoing discussion suggests is that, providing training is relatively easy, whereas effectively utilizing the expertise of the trained civil servants is more difficult. Hilderbrand & Grindle (1997: 53-54), based on their recent studies on a number of SSA countries (such as the Republic of Central Africa and Tanzania), note that in several of the cases, professionals were very sensitive to whether their jobs were meaningful and appropriate to their level of training. To the extent that they believed they were using their talents to accomplish tasks they considered meaningful, they were more motivated to contribute to the organization. When such people were idle or tied down to routine administrative tasks or kept from their activities because of lack of vehicles or computers, they lost motivation. Cohen and Wheeler (1997: 146) argue that "those trained professionals need to be effectively utilized and productive. Unfortunately this is not the case of Kenya". Hence, one may argue that training may not produce the desired objectives, not because the training process is ineffective but because of the constraints of the administrative system in which the ex-trainees returns to work. As indicated earlier, misuse of trained people is a waste of time, efforts and money. It also provokes demotivation and negative reactions on the part of trainees.

---

[20] CAFRAD refers to African Training and Research Centre in Administration for Development.

[21] Training programmes have been seen as an essential feature of organizational life. However, in spite of the heavy investment in training, organizations often find that they fail to evaluate adequately the value or success of their training programmes.

From the above discussion, it can be deduced that

- high quality training is a goal common to SSA; yet, this simply stated goal is usually not achieved;
- despite the expansion in training activities in the last four decades, impact in improving the performance in the civil service in many SSA has been minimal. This has been due largely to the fact that the factors that are critical for successful civil service training have been inadequate or missing;
- there are many formidable challenges facing governments in SSA in improving the impact of civil service training;
- if there is a real will and commitment on the part of politicians and senior civil servants a real change could come in the impact of civil service training.

Utilization of Civil Servants in Sub-Saharan Africa

Despite the fact that HR utilization is a very crucial aspect of HRM, it is found to be the most problematic area in SSA (Bowen & Ostroff, 2004; ECA, 2005; Grindle, 1997; Hilderbrand & Grindle, 1997; UN, 2005; Tessema et al., 2005). Hilderbrand & Grindle (1997: 53) indicate that "while training and recruitment are important aspects of developing capacity, effective utilization of human resources within organizations is the most important factor in determining whether public officials are productive or not." Therefore, the human resource problem for organizations was often not so much the availability of well-prepared civil servant, but how they were utilized once they were recruited into the organization.

On the one hand, many civil services in SSA countries lack clearly written HR programs and policies (CAFRAD, 2000; Das, 1998; UN, 2005). On the other hand, most civil services in SSA countries lack the ability to successfully put HR programs and policies into action although they are clearly written down (see also ILO, 2000; CAFRAD, 2000). Most SSA countries have been facing economic problems in the last three decades. As a result, their ability to commit the required resources has been adversely affected, which in turn has negatively affected their ability to successfully implement several HR programs and policies. Bearing the above caveats in mind, let us briefly discuss some HR programs and policies, which have important implications for proper utilization civil servants in SSA.

Compensation Management Practices

"Adequate pay is a key component in improving and sustaining the motivation, performance and integrity of public servants" (UN, 2005: x). However, there has been a decline in civil service salaries in SSA. The ILO (1998: 45) states that "real wages in Africa declined by 2 percent annually during the period 1990-1996". This indicates that civil service reforms did not achieve their objective of streamlining the wage structure and raising the level of real wages. Moreover, Adedeji et al. (1995: 16) observe that "civil service salaries in Africa are absolutely not enough". The salaries of senior civil servants in SSA are compressed relative to the minimum pay in the salaries (Das, 1998: 17). For instance in Ghana, the compression ratio was 2.2, which means that the salary of the top-most civil servant was only 2.2 times that of the lowest-paid employee in the government (Numberg, 1994; World Bank, 1994). Severe wage compression however has diminished the incentive to work and induced the more competent staff to leave. The low level of remuneration for senior civil servants has made it difficult for the civil service in most SSA to retain and utilize the best and brightest. Table 1 shows some compensation related reforms introduced in SSA countries.

Table 1. Some compensation related reforms introduced in SSA countries

1. Wage decompression (Ghana has been able to decompose wage from 2.2 to 1 in 1984 to 10.1: 1 in 1991. the target was 13.1: 1 but it slipped to 9.1: 1 in 1995;
2. Monetarisation of benefits (in Tanzania, benefits-in-kind represent 400% of salaries at the top most levels but only 35% at the lowest levels);
3. Raising the general pay level for all civil servants in the hope of paying a minimum living wage (Uganda has been able to raise salaries from 25% to 56% of the government's definition of a minimum living wage between 1990 and 1995);
4. Targeting professionals who are in the greatest demand in the private and public sectors (Ethiopia has devised new salary structure for teachers, doctors and engineers, in order to raise their salaries above others in lower demands);
5. Linking pay to performance and improved productivity of the staff. Performance indicators are being developed and merit systems are replacing automatic hiring in personnel recruitment and seniority in promotion (e.g., Ghana and Botswana); and
6. Improving working conditions and seeking alternative methods of motivating civil servants, e.g., improving benefits in kind and granting awards for commendable performance (e.g., Botswana and Uganda).

Source: Adopted from the ILO, 2000.

Employee Performance Appraisal Practices

Experiences of most SSA countries show that formal performance appraisal measures are rarely developed and implemented in civil service organizations. Thus, employee performance evaluation is not done in most civil services as it should be (CAFRAD, 2000; Thairu, 1999; Ovadje & Ankomah; Tessema & Soeters, 2006a). As a result, different HRM decisions have been taken subjectively. Bennell (1994: 11) notes that appraisal forms are poorly designed with vague and ambiguous rating criteria, many of which have little to do with actual job performance. As Waiguchu (1999: 198) puts it, "in an authoritarian setting, an appraisal system is unavoidably one-sided. In such a case, the supervisor's view of the subordinates' performance prevails". "Frequently, civil servants are not given a chance to discuss their weakness and strengths. Participation by the individual staff member is minimal" (Muneneet et al., 2000: 9).[22]

Promotion Policies and Practices

As long as civil service systems are politicized in many countries of SSA, it is inevitable that promotion would not be based largely on merit. The politicization of the civil service affects promotion practices (Beugre & Offodile, 2001; Tessema & Soeters, 2006b). The career development of the civil servant in many countries in SSA depends more on ascribed criteria than on performance or productivity (Beugre & Offodile, 2001). This situation affects the civil service organization's ability to motivate, retain, and utilize competent civil servants in many SSA (Budhwar & Debrah, 2004; Dirk, 2008; Heady, 1996; Hojnacki, 1996).

Placement and Clarity of Job Descriptions

It has been noted that placement of the right persons in the right positions has not always been realized in SSA countries (Dia, 1996; Hilderbrand & Grindle, 1997; Kiggundu, 1989; Tessema & Ngoma, 2009). Besides, it has been argued that in many SSA, civil servants do not clearly know their responsibilities and duties. For instance, Cohen and Wheeler (1997: 146) note that many Kenyan civil servants lacked any clear understanding of their duties and responsibilities. Department heads and task managers often failed to instigate work programs or meaningful job descriptions for those working under them. Tessema and Soeters (2006b: 367) also noted that "about 38 percent of the respondents did not believe that they are placed on the right positions in the Eritrean civil service". The poor utilization of civil servants with wide-spread mismatching of individual skills and experience with the skill, knowledge, and responsibility requirements of jobs has been affecting the contribution of civil servants in sub-Sahara Africa (Hilderbrand & Grindle, 1997; Dia, 1996; Cohen & Wheeler, 1997).[23]

The foregoing discussion illustrates that:

- the ineffectiveness of the three critical factors for HR utilization [availability of well developed HR programmes and policies, the ability of the civil service to successfully implement HR programmes and policies, and the continuity of monitoring and evaluation of HR programmes and policies] has made utilization of civil servants in the SSA the most problematic area of HRM;
- SSA countries have been experiencing serious HR utilization problems. As a result, continuous warnings have recently been sounded that if development goals are to be

[22] It should also be noted that although there are such cases in the Developed World, they are widely practiced in most SSA countries.

[23] The recent interview with Kenyan returned trainees indicated that they believe they were capable of assuming much greater responsibility and performing much more effectively if given a chance to do so (Cohen & Wheeler, 1997: 142-44).

achieved, the significance of effectively utilizing existing civil servants throughout the total administrative system cannot be overemphasized;

- the prevailing situation has not only affected HR utilization but has also aggravated the turnover of civil servants. Many civil servants trained at the expense of civil service defect to private sector, NGOs, and abroad where salaries and other privileges are often higher.

Concluding Remarks

This chapter leads to the following concluding remarks:

- The case of SSA demonstrates that many of the factors critical for an effective HRM in the civil service (Figure 1) have either been inadequate or missing. Likewise, an analysis of the environmental factors, (mainly economic and political), affecting the way civil servants have been managed in SSA reveals that these factors are not very conducive. On this basis, this study concludes that the unfavourable environmental factors obtaining in SSA countries are the ones that have hindered an effective HRM;
- The circumstances and challenges of most countries in SSA with respect to the management of civil servants are more or less similar. After independence, there was an increase in the size of the civil service to speed up development; then economic slowdown set in, and as a result, salaries in the civil service declined, leading to de-motivation of the employees, a high turnover and the brain-drain. As a remedy, most SSA countries have introduced HRM reforms whose impact has, nonetheless, been limited;
- The cumulative effects of the prevailing HRM challenges have adversely affected civil servants' competence (ability to do), motivation (willingness to work) and retention (willingness to stay). The prevailing situation in most SSA countries contributes to the under-utilization of the limited number of trained personnel. Thus, it is intuitively appealing to support the argument that civil service organizations in SSA are not prestigious places which can attract, motivate and retain qualified and experienced workers;
- Effective HR development programs (training and education) are increasingly important in the development process of DCs. HR development effort emerged as a necessity for countries owing to the shortage of qualified public servants. HR development programs are needed for DCs to maintain an adequate and continuous supply of competent public servants. However, the case of SSA indicates that HR development investments tend to be more easily accomplished than retaining and utilizing trained personnel appropriately;
- The chapter concludes that more than anything else, it is the *personnel crisis* in the civil service organizations in DCs that has to be addressed if meaningful improvements in service delivery are to be realized; and
- Finally, the chapter argues that the *prospects* of effective HRM would be contingent mainly upon the SSA's economic and political conditions (peace and stability as well as good governance). That is, if they improve, there is a high probability of

successfully implementing the three HRM sub-systems (procurement, training and utilization) thereby positively affecting HRM in the SSA civil service.

References

Adamolekun, L. (1993). Note on Civil Service Personnel Policy Reform in Sub-Saharan Africa. *Public Sector Management*, **6(3)**: 38-46.

Adedeji, L, Onimode, B. and Synge, R. (1995). *Issue in African Development.* Ibadan: Heinemann Educational Books.

Ahmad, S. & Schroeder, R. (2003). The impact of HRM practices on operational performance: recognizing country and industry differences. *Journal of Operations Management*, **21**:19-43.

Aredo, D. (2002). *Brain drain reportedly costing $4 billion a year.* Addis Ababa: UN Integrated Regional Information Networks.

Austin, J. (1990). Managing in developing countries: Strategic Analysis and Operating Techniques. New York: The Free Press.

Bennell, P. (1994). Improving the Performance of the Public Sector in LDCs: New approaches to Human Resource Planning and Management. *Occasional Paper* no. **25**. Geneva: ILO.

Berman. E., Bowman, J., West, J., & Van Wart, M. (2001). *Human Resource Management in Public Service: Paradoxes, Processes, and Problems.* London: Sage Publications, Inc.

Beugre, C. and Offodile, O. (2001). Managing for organizational effectiveness in sub-Saharan Africa: A cultural-fit model. *International Journal of Human Resource Management,* **10(4)**: 535-550.

Beyene, A. & Ottobo, E. (1994). Public Administration in Africa: Past Trends and Emerging Challenges. *African Journal of Public Administration and Management,* **3(2)**: 1-30.

Bowen, D. & Ostroff, C. (2004). Understanding HRM-firm performance linkages: The role of the strengths of the HRM system. *Academy of Management Review,* **29(2)**: 203-221.

Boxall, P. (2003). HR strategy and competitive advantage in the service sector. *Human Resource Management Journal,* **13(3)**, 5-20.

Branine, M. (2004). HRM in Algeria. In Pawan S. Budhwar and Yaw A. Debrah. *Human Resource Management in Developing Countries* (pp. 156-174). London: Routledge Research in Employment Relations.

Brewer, G., & Choi, Y. (2007). *Toward a Performing Public Sector: A Cross-Country Study of Democracy's Impact on Government Performance*. Paper presented at the Annual Meeting of the International Research Society for Public Management, Potsdam, Germany, April 2-4.

Budhwar P. S. and Debrah, Y. A. (2004). Introduction. In Pawan S. Budhwar and Yaw A. Debrah. *Human Resource Management in Developing Countries* (pp. 1-15). London: Routledge Research in Employment Relations.

CAFRAD (2000). *Workshop on Management of Human Resources in Africa-Challenges for the third millennium*, Tangier, Morocco, 23 – 27 October. Retrieved September 24, 2008 from
http://unpan1.un.org/intradoc/groups/public/documents/CAFRAD/UNPAN001153.pdf

Clemens, M. A. & Pettersson, G. (2007). New data on African health professionals abroad. *Center Global Development. Working Paper Number* **95**.

Cohen, J. M. & Wheeler, J. R. (1997). Training and retention in African public sectors: Capacity-building lessons from Kenya. In M. S. Grindle (Ed.), *Getting good government: Capacity building in the public sector of developing countries* (pp. 125-153). Cambridge, MA: Harvard University Press.

Corkery, J., Land, A., & Bossuvt, J. (1998). Minding one's own business: Institutional dimensions of Management for capacity development with particular reference to Sub-Saharan Africa. *International Review of Administrative Sciences,* **64(4)***:* 531-552.

Das, S.K. (1998). *Civil Service Reform and Structural Adjustment.* New York: Oxford University Press.

Dessler, G. (2007). *Human Resource Management (11th ed.).* New York: Prentice Hall.

Dia, M. (1996). *Africa's Management in the 1990s and Beyond: Reconciling Indigenous and Transplanted Institutions.* Washington: D.C.: The World Bank.

Dirk, B. (2008). Determinants of democratic successes and failures in Africa. *European Journal of Political Research;* **47(3)**: 269-306.

Economic Commission for Africa (ECA) (2005). Annual Report 2005. Abuja, Nigeria: ECA.

Economic Commission for Africa (ECA). (1989). *Handbook for Manpower Planners in Africa.* Addis Ababa: ECA.

Encyclopaedia Britannica. (2008). Retrieved September 27, 2008 from *http:www.Britannica.com.*

Ghebregiorgis, F. & Karsten, L. (2007). Employee reactions to human resource management and performance in a developing country: Evidence from Eritrea. *Personnel Review,* 36(5), 722-738.

Grindle, M. S. (1997). The good governance imperative: Human resources, organisations, and institutions. In M. S. Grindle (Ed.), *Getting good government: Capacity building in the public sector of developing countries* (pp.3-28). Cambridge, MA: Harvard University Press.

Heady, F. (1996). Configurations of civil service systems. In H. Bekke, J. Perry, and T. Toonen (Eds.), *Civil service systems in comparative perspective* (pp. 207-226). Bloomington: Indiana University Press.

Hilderbrand, M. E. & Grindle, M. S. (1997). Building sustainable capacity in the public sector: What can be done? In M. S. Grindle (Ed.), *Getting good government: Capacity building in the public sector of developing countries* (pp. 31-61). Cambridge, MA: Harvard University Press.

Hiltrop, J. (1996). A Framework for Diagnosing Human Resource Management Practices. *European Management Journal,* **14(3)***:* 243-254.

Hojnacki, W. (1996). Politicization as a Civil service Dilemma. In H. Bekke, J. Perry, and T. Toonen (eds.), *Civil Service Systems in Comparative Perspective* (pp.207-226). Bloomington and Indianapolis: Indiana University Press.

Ingraham, P.W., Selden, S.C. & Moynihan, D.P. (2000). People and Performance: Challenges for the Future Public Service-the Report from the Wye River. *Public Administration Review,* **60(1)***:* 54-60.

Ingraham, P, & Kneedler, A. (2000). Dissecting the Black Box: Toward a Model and Measures of Government Management Performance. In J, Brudney, L. O'toole, and H.

Rainey (eds.), *Advancing Public Management: New Developments in theory, methods, and practice.* Washington, D.C: Georgetown University Press.

International Labour Organization (ILO) (1998). Human Resource Development in the Public service in the context of structural adjustment and transition. Geneva: ILO.

International Labour Organization (ILO). 2000. *Civil Service Reform Training Manual.* Turin: ILO.

Jaeger, A. M., Kanungo, R. N. & Srinvas, N. (1995). A Review of Human Resource Management Success in Developing Countries. In R. N. Kanungo and D. M. Saunders (eds.), *Employee Management in Developing Countries* (pp. pp. 39-54). Greenwich, CT: JAI Press.

Kamoche, K. (2002) Introduction: human resource management in Africa. International *Journal of Human Resource Management*, **13(1)**: 993-997.

Kaul, M. (1997). Civil service reforms: learning from commonwealth experiences. In L. Adamolekun, G. Lusignan, and A. Atomate (eds.), *Civil Service Reform in Francophone Africa: Proceedings of a Workshop,* Abidjan, January 23-26, 1996.

Kerrigan J.E. (1989). Public Administration Education and Training in the Third World: problems and Opportunities. *Policy Studies Review,* **8(4)**: 242-260.

Kerrigan J.E. & Luke, J. S. (1987). *Management Training Strategies for Developing Countries*. USA: Lynne Rienner Publishers.

Kiggundu, M. N. (1989). *Managing organizations in developing countries: An operational and strategic approach.* West Hartford, CT: Kumarian Press, Inc.

Kim, P. S. (2007). Transforming Higher-Level Civil Service in a New Age: A Case Study of a New Senior Civil Service in Korea. Public Personnel Management, Vol. 36.

Kim, P. S. & Hong, K.P. (2006). Searching for effective HRM reform strategy in the public sector: Critical review of WPSR 2005 and suggestions. *Public Personnel Management,* **35(3)**: 199-214

Klingner, D. & Nalbandian, J. (1998). *Public Personnel Management: Context and Strategies.* New Jersey: Prentice Hall.

Maggregor, J., Peterson, S, & Schuftan, C. (1998). Downsizing the civil service in developing countries: The Golden handshake option revisited. *Public Administration and Development,* **19(2)**: 45-63.

Marfouk, A. (2008). *The African Brain Drain: Scope and Determinants.* Retrieved September 10 from http://ideas.repec.org/p/dul/wpaper/08-07rs.html.

Mudhoo, R. (1995). Adjustment in the Public Sector and Management of Human Resources in Mauritania. Working Paper. Geneva: ILO.

Munene, J., Schwartz, S., Smith, P., Akanda, D., & Udwin, M. (2000). Culture and Productivity: exploration into the Cultural Dimensions of African productivity. In K. Prah and A. Ahmed (eds.), *African in transformation: Political and Economic Transformation and Socio-political responses in Africa,* 2: 1-27.

N'dongko, T. (1999). Management Leadership in Africa. In M. Waiguchu, E. Tiagha, and M. Mwaura (eds.), *Management of Organizations in Africa: A Handbook of Reference* (pp. 99-123). Westport, CT: Quorum Books.

Numberg, B. (1994). Experience with Civil Service Pay and Employment Reform: An Overview. In D.L. Lindauer and B. Numberg (eds.), *Rehabilitating Government: Pay and Employment Reform in Africa* (pp. 119-159). Washington D.C: World Bank.

Ovadje F. & Ankomah, A. (2004) HRM in Nigeria. In Pawan S. Budhwar and Yaw A. Debrah. Human Resource Management in Developing Countries (pp. 1-16). London: Routledge Research in Employment Relations.

Ozgediz, S. (1983). *Managing the Public Service in Developing Countries: Issues and Prospects,* Washington, D.C.: The World Bank Staff Working Paper No.583.

Paauwe, J. (2004). *HRM and Performance: Achieving Long-term Value*. Oxford: Oxford University Press.

Paul, S. (1983). *Training for Public Administration and Management in Developing Countries.* World Bank staff Working Paper No. 584, Washington, D.C.: The World Bank.

Pfeffer, J. (1994). Competitive Advantage through People: Unleashing the Power of the Work Force. Boston: Harvard Business School Press.

Polgreen, L. (2006). Africa: Cameroon: 45,000 Fake Civil Servants. *New York Times* (August 12).

Prah, K. (2004). African Wars and Ethnic Conflicts: Rebuilding Failed States. *Human Development Report 2004*. African Regional Background Paper, UNDP.

Rambourg, M., Le Gay, J & Bah, M. (1995). *Administrative Reform Survey in Central African Republic: A Case Study.* Cotonu, African Civil Service Observatory.

Shafritz,J., Rosenbloom, D. & Riccucci, N. (2001). *Personnel Management in Government: Politics and Process.* New York: Marcel and Dekker.

Sills, D (ed.). (1968). *International Encyclopaedia of the Social Science* (Vol.2). The Macmillan Inc.

Stone, R. 1998. *Human Resource Management.* New York: John Wiley and Sons.

Tessema, M. & Alex, N. (2009). Eritrea: Challenges of the brain drain to the public sector. *International Public Management Review*, 9: 2 (forthcoming).

Tessema, M. & Soeters, J. (2006a). Challenges and prospects of HRM in developing countries: Testing the HRM-performance-link: The case of Eritrea. *International Journal of Human Resource Management,* **17(1)***:* 86-105.

Tessema, M. & Soeters, J. (2006b). Practices and challenges of converting former fighters into civil servants: the case of Eritrea. *Public Administration and Development,* **26(4)***:* 359-371.

Tessema, M., Soeters, J. & Abraham, K. (2005). Practices and challenges of training and labour utilisation in Sub-Saharan Africa: The case of Eritrea. *International Journal of Training and Development,* **9(4)**, 214-231

Thomas, K. & Theresa, M. (1995). *Planning for Training and Development: A guide to analysing needs*. London: Save the Children.

Thairu, W. (1999). Team Building and Total Quality Management (TQM) in Africa. In M. J. Waiguchu, E. Tiagha, & M. Mwaura (eds.), *Management of Organizations in Africa: A Handbook of Reference* (pp. 265-280). Westport, CT: Quorum Books.

Tjiptoherijanto, P. (2007). Civil service reform in Indonesia. *International Public Management Review*, **8(2)***:* 31-44.

Turner, M. & Hulme, D. (1997). *Governance, Administration, and Development: Making the State Work.* West Hartford, Conn: Kumarian Press.

UN (2005). Unlocking the Human Potential for Public Sector Performance. World Public Sector Report 2005. Retrieved on September 19, 2008 from http://unpan1.un.org/intradoc/groups/public/documents/UN/UNPAN021617.pdf.

United Nations (1992). *Size and Cost of the Civil Service: Reform Programmes in Africa.* New York: Department of Economic and Social Development.

Waiguchu, M., Tiagha, E., & Mwaura, M. (eds.). (1999). *Management of Organizations in Africa: A Handbook of Reference,* Westport, CT: Quorum Books.

Wekita Consulting Firm (2002). *Consultants reports on human resources development strategy: Medium and long term human resource development and training for the ministry of agriculture.* Asmara, Eritrea.

Wescott, C.G., & Jones, L.R. (2007). Managing for Results and Performance in Asia: Assessing Reform Initiatives in the Public Sector. *International Public Management Review,* **8**(1): 56-102.

World Bank (1997). The State in a Changing World. *World Development Report, 1997.* New York: Oxford University Press.

World Bank (1994). *Adjustment in Africa: Reforms, Results, and the road ahead.* A World Bank Policy Research Report. New York: Oxford University Press.

In: Inflation: Causes and Effects
Editor: Leon V. Schwartz, pp. 27-57
ISBN: 978-1-60741-823-8

Chapter 2

ACCURACY AND RATIONALITY OF JAPANESE CPI FORECASTERS*

Masahiro Ashiya**
Faculty of Economics, Kobe University, 2-1 Rokko-dai, Nada, Kobe, 657-8501, Japan

Abstract

This paper investigates accuracy and rationality of Japanese consumer price index (CPI) forecasts from April 2004 through August 2008. It finds that the majority of zero-month forecasts are inferior to the naïve "last observation" forecast, which is the simple copy of the latest realization of CPI (at the time forecast was made). Moreover, almost all forecasts are irrational in the sense that their forecast errors could be reduced using the latest realization of CPI. These results present a striking contrast to the past literature.

Keywords: Macroeconomic Forecast; Forecast evaluation; Encompassing; Rationality.

1. Introduction

Past few years have experienced dramatic changes of worldwide economic conditions, which rendered economic forecasting tremendously difficult. This paper analyzes accuracy and rationality of macroeconomic forecasts in this tumultuous period. The data we employ is the monthly forecast of Japanese consumer price index (CPI) from April 2004 through August 2008 (Section 2 explains the data in detail).

Section 3 compares the forecast accuracy of the individual forecasts relative to naïve benchmark forecasts. It shows that 86% (48%) of zero-month forecast (two-month forecast) are inferior to the "same-as-the-last-month" forecast (defined in Section 3.1). Furthermore, most forecasters fail to utilize the latest realization of CPI for zero, one, and two-month forecasts.

---

* I gratefully acknowledge financial supports from Grant-in-Aid for Encouragement of Young Scientists from the Japanese Ministry of Education, Science and Culture.
** E-mail address: ashiya@econ.kobe-u.ac.jp

Section 4 reports the results of various rationality tests. Numerous studies have investigated the rationality of individual and institutional forecasters, but the results are somewhat mixed. As for the rationality of forecast errors, Brown and Maital (1981), Batchelor and Dua (1991), Jansen and Kishan (1996), Joutz and Stekler (2000), Ash et al. (2002), and Ashiya (2007) reject the rationality. On the other hand, Zarnowitz (1985), Holden and Peel (1985), Ash et al. (1990 and 1998), Artis (1996), Pons (1999, 2000, and 2001), Öller and Barot (2000), Kreinin (2000), and Ashiya (2005) find that forecasts are generally rational and efficient (See also Fildes and Stekler (2002) and references therein for the related literature). As for the rationality of forecast revisions, Ashiya (2005) finds that 79% of Japanese GDP forecasts pass the martingale tests. However, Berger and Krane (1985), Nordhaus (1987), Batchelor and Dua (1991), Abarbanell and Bernard (1992), Scotese (1994), Clements (1995 and 1997), Ehrbeck and Waldmann (1996), Amir and Ganzach (1998), Loungani (2001), Harvey et al. (2001), and Ashiya (2002, 2003, and 2006a) have shown that forecast revisions are subject to behavioral biases. This paper finds that almost all forecasts are irrational in the sense that their forecast errors could be reduced using the latest realization of CPI.

Section 5 investigates the accuracy and rationality of the consensus forecast, which is defined as the market mean. It shows that the forecast error of the consensus forecast is smaller than that of a typical forecaster, but that it could be reduced using the latest realization of CPI. Section 6 concludes the paper.

2. Data

The Economic Planning Association has conducted a monthly survey of professional forecasters, "ESP Forecast Survey," since April 2004. We use the forecast data of the consumer price index (CPI) through August 2008. We select the data of 42 forecasters (out of 44 forecasters), who participated in 18 surveys or more (The excluded forecasters participated in five surveys).

Let CPI_t be the CPI of month t. Then the rate of change over the year, p_t, is computed by the following equation:

$$p_t \equiv \frac{CPI_t - CPI_{t-12}}{CPI_{t-12}} \times 100.$$

The quarterly average change over the year is calculated as the simple arithmetic mean of p_t. More specifically, the quarterly average change over the year from month $t-2$ to month t, q_t, is defined as

$$q_t \equiv (p_{t-2} + p_{t-1} + p_t)/3.$$

Let $f^i_{t-k,t}$ be the k-month-ahead forecast of forecaster i with respect to q_t, which is released in month $t-k$. The forecast error is defined as $FE^i_{t-k,t} \equiv f^i_{t-k,t} - q_t$. Its absolute value is $AFE^i_{t-k,t} \equiv \left| f^i_{t-k,t} - q_t \right|$.

We analyze zero through five-month-ahead forecasts in this paper. Zero-month forecasts and three-month forecasts are released in March, June, September, and December. One-month forecasts and four-month forecasts are released in February, May, August, and November. Two-month forecasts and five-month forecasts are released in January, April, July, and October. The sample period of each forecast series is as follows: from the first quarter of 2004 through the second quarter of 2008 (18 quarters) for zero-month forecast; from the second quarter of 2004 through the second quarter of 2008 (17 quarters) for one-month forecast; from the second quarter of 2004 through the third quarter of 2008 (18 quarters) for two-month forecast and three-month forecast; from the third quarter of 2004 through the third quarter of 2008 (17 quarters) for four-month forecast and five-month forecast.

3. Relative Accuracy

If forecasters are rational, they should make use of all information available when they release their forecasts. As for CPI, forecasters know p_{t-k-1} and $q_{t-6} \equiv (p_{t-8} + p_{t-7} + p_{t-6})/3$ when they release $f^i_{t-k,t}$ ($k = 0,1,\cdots,5$). Furthermore, they know $q_{t-3} \equiv (p_{t-5} + p_{t-4} + p_{t-3})/3$ when they release $f^i_{t,t}$, $f^i_{t-1,t}$, and $f^i_{t-2,t}$. This section investigates whether the forecasters utilize these latest realizations.

Subsection 3.1 introduces two naïve benchmark forecasts. Subsection 3.2 evaluates relative accuracy using the descriptive statistics. Subsection 3.3 employs the encompassing test. Subsection 3.4 relaxes the assumption of the quadratic loss function and considers the "sign test", which is valid for non-quadratic, asymmetric, or discontinuous loss functions. Subsection 3.5 calculates the correlations of forecast accuracy among different forecast spans. This section will find that the individual forecasters are inferior to the naïve benchmark forecast for zero-month forecast. Moreover, it will find that most of them fail to utilize the latest realization of CPI for zero, one, and two-month forecasts.

3.1. Benchmark Forecasts

We consider the following two naïve forecasts as a benchmark.

(a) Same-as-the-last-month forecast: $f^M_{t-k,t}$

$$f^M_{t-k,t} \equiv p_{t-k-1}.$$

(b) Same-as-the-last-quarter forecast: $f^{Q}_{t-k,t}$

$$f^{Q}_{t-k,t} \equiv \begin{cases} q_{t-3} & \text{for } k = 0,1, \text{ and } 2 \\ q_{t-6} & \text{for } k = 3,4, \text{ and } 5 \end{cases}.$$

These "naïve" forecasts might be optimal if q_t would follow a random walk process. Note that the forecasters have the knowledge of $f^{M}_{t-k,t}$ and $f^{Q}_{t-k,t}$ when they release $f^{i}_{t-k,t}$. Therefore $f^{i}_{t-k,t}$ should be superior to these benchmarks.

3.2. The Descriptive Statistics

Table 1 presents the values of several traditional measures of forecast accuracy for the individual forecasters. The first row in table 1 shows the summary statistics (average, standard deviation, minimum, and maximum) of the mean absolute error (MAE). As for zero-month forecast, the average of the MAE among forecasters is 0.072 percentage points, and the MAE of the best forecaster is zero. The second row shows the summary statistics of the root mean square error (RMSE).

The third and the fourth rows of table 1 show the summary statistics of modified Theil's *U*, constructed as the ratio of the RMSE of each forecaster to the RMSE of the benchmark forecast ($f^{M}_{t-k,t}$ or $f^{Q}_{t-k,t}$). More specifically, define $T^{i}_{t-k,t}$ as the set of quarters in which forecaster *i* released $f^{i}_{t-k,t}$. Let $U^{i}_{t-k,t}\left(f^{B}_{t-k,t}\right)$ ($B = M,Q$) be the Theil's *U* of forecaster *i* for $f^{i}_{t-k,t}$. Then $U^{i}_{t-k,t}\left(f^{B}_{t-k,t}\right)$ is defined as

$$U^{i}_{t-k,t}\left(f^{B}_{t-k,t}\right) \equiv \sqrt{\sum_{t \in T^{i}_{t-k,t}} \left(f^{i}_{t-k,t} - q_t\right)^2} \Big/ \sqrt{\sum_{t \in T^{i}_{t-k,t}} \left(f^{B}_{t-k,t} - q_t\right)^2}$$

$$\text{for } k = 0,1,\cdots,5. \qquad (1)$$

If $U^{i}_{t-k,t}\left(f^{B}_{t-k,t}\right) > 1$, then forecaster *i* is inferior to the benchmark $f^{B}_{t-k,t}$ ($B = M,Q$). Table 1 shows that $U^{i}_{t-k,t}\left(f^{M}_{t-k,t}\right)$ is on average 2.269 for zero-month forecast, which demonstrates that many forecasters are inferior to the naïve "same-as-the-last-month" forecast. The averages of $U^{i}_{t-k,t}\left(f^{M}_{t-k,t}\right)$ for one and two-month forecasts are also larger than unity. On the other hand, the average of $U^{i}_{t-k,t}\left(f^{Q}_{t-k,t}\right)$ is smaller than unity for every forecast span. $U^{i}_{t-k,t}\left(f^{M}_{t-k,t}\right)$ varies significantly among the forecasters, which indicates that forecasting ability is unequal among the forecasters (In comparison, Ashiya (2006b) finds that Japanese GDP forecasters are equal in their forecasting abilities).

Table 1. The descriptive statistics

Zero-month forecast	**Average**	**Std. Dev.**	**Minimum**	**Maximum**
MAE	0.072	0.056	0.000	0.270
RMSE	0.108	0.071	0.000	0.383
$U^i_{t,t}\left(f^M_{t,t}\right)$	2.269	1.522	0.000	8.573
$U^i_{t,t}\left(f^Q_{t,t}\right)$	0.442	0.362	0.000	1.967
One-month forecast	**Average**	**Std. Dev.**	**Minimum**	**Maximum**
MAE	0.107	0.054	0.033	0.325
RMSE	0.149	0.071	0.058	0.453
$U^i_{t-1,t}\left(f^M_{t-1,t}\right)$	1.104	0.899	0.608	5.228
$U^i_{t-1,t}\left(f^Q_{t-1,t}\right)$	0.598	0.403	0.359	2.730
Two-month forecast	**Average**	**Std. Dev.**	**Minimum**	**Maximum**
MAE	0.184	0.072	0.067	0.471
RMSE	0.250	0.090	0.082	0.615
$U^i_{t-2,t}\left(f^M_{t-2,t}\right)$	1.062	0.307	0.577	2.051
$U^i_{t-2,t}\left(f^Q_{t-2,t}\right)$	0.776	0.264	0.497	1.594
Three-month forecast	**Average**	**Std. Dev.**	**Minimum**	**Maximum**
MAE	0.225	0.061	0.100	0.341
RMSE	0.300	0.089	0.114	0.450
$U^i_{t-3,t}\left(f^M_{t-3,t}\right)$	0.959	0.273	0.546	1.874
$U^i_{t-3,t}\left(f^Q_{t-3,t}\right)$	0.618	0.206	0.338	1.486
Four-month forecast	**Average**	**Std. Dev.**	**Minimum**	**Maximum**
MAE	0.268	0.075	0.083	0.380
RMSE	0.361	0.105	0.108	0.501
$U^i_{t-4,t}\left(f^M_{t-4,t}\right)$	0.811	0.200	0.510	1.519
$U^i_{t-4,t}\left(f^Q_{t-4,t}\right)$	0.720	0.176	0.393	1.200
Five-month forecast	**Average**	**Std. Dev.**	**Minimum**	**Maximum**
MAE	0.362	0.122	0.133	0.817
RMSE	0.478	0.151	0.183	0.979
$U^i_{t-5,t}\left(f^M_{t-5,t}\right)$	0.962	0.170	0.558	1.395
$U^i_{t-5,t}\left(f^Q_{t-5,t}\right)$	0.912	0.226	0.583	2.028

MAE: mean absolute error.

RMSE: root mean square error.

$U^i_{t-k,t}\left(f^B_{t-k,t}\right) \equiv \sqrt{\sum_{t\in T^i_{t-k,t}} \left(f^i_{t-k,t} - q_t\right)^2} \Big/ \sqrt{\sum_{t\in T^i_{t-k,t}} \left(f^B_{t-k,t} - q_t\right)^2}$ for $k = 0,1,\cdots,5$ and $B = M, Q$.

Table 2 classifies the forecasters by the value of $U^i_{t-k,t}\left(f^B_{t-k,t}\right)$. The first column shows that 6 out of 42 forecasters are superior to $f^M_{t-k,t}$ for zero-month forecast. The second column, however, shows that 36 forecasters (86%) are inferior to $f^M_{t-k,t}$ for zero-month forecast. Similarly, 13 forecasters (31%) are inferior to $f^M_{t-k,t}$ for one-month forecast, and 20 forecasters (48%) are inferior to $f^M_{t-k,t}$ for two-month forecast. The third column of Table 2 shows that the majority of forecasters are superior to $f^Q_{t-k,t}$.

Since every forecaster had known the value of $f^M_{t-k,t}$ when she released $f^i_{t-k,t}$, her forecast should have been better than $f^M_{t-k,t}$. The above result demonstrates that the majority of forecasters fail to utilize even the latest realization of CPI.

Table 2. Comparison of forecast accuracy by Theil's U

k	$U^i_{t-k,t}\left(f^M_{t-k,t}\right)\le 1$	$U^i_{t-k,t}\left(f^M_{t-k,t}\right)>1$	$U^i_{t-k,t}\left(f^Q_{t-k,t}\right)\le 1$	$U^i_{t-k,t}\left(f^Q_{t-k,t}\right)>1$
0	6	36	39	3
1	29	13	40	2
2	22	20	36	6
3	25	17	40	2
4	39	3	38	4
5	26	16	32	10

3.3. The Encompassing Test

This subsection evaluates relative accuracy by the encompassing test. This test is proposed by Chong and Hendry (1986), and employed by Cooper and Nelson (1975), Mizon and Richard (1986), Ericsson (1992), Jansen and Kishan (1996), Romer and Romer (2000), and Ashiya (2005 and 2007).

The encompassing test evaluates two forecasting systems, f^1 and f^2, by the following regression:

$$q_t = \delta f^1_{t-k,t} + (1-\delta) f^2_{t-k,t} + u_t$$

If δ is positive and significantly different from zero, it indicates that f^1 provides some information concerning q_t, which information is excluded from f^2. In this case f^1 is said to "encompass" f^2. Similarly, if $1-\delta$ is positive and significantly different from zero, then f^2 is said to encompass f^1.

Ericsson (1992, p.485, l.1) argues, however, that "the forecast-encompassing test may have no power when the dependent variable is $I(1)$." Hence we follow Ericsson (1992) and Jansen and Kishan (1996), and estimate the transformed encompassing test:

$$q_t - f^2_{t-k,t} = \delta\left(f^1_{t-k,t} - f^2_{t-k,t}\right) + u_t \qquad (2)$$

If δ is significantly larger than zero, then f^1 encompasses f^2. If δ is significantly smaller than unity, then f^2 encompasses f^1. If $\delta = 0$ ($\delta = 1$), then f^1 (f^2) provides no additional information useful in forecasting q_t given f^2 (f^1). When $\delta < 0$ ($\delta > 1$), f^1 (f^2) is so inaccurate that the minimum squared error composite requires "short selling" of it (Cooper and Nelson, 1975, p.8).

We substitute $f^i_{t-k,t}$ for f^1 and $f^M_{t-k,t}$ (or $f^Q_{t-k,t}$) for f^2 in equation (2). We eliminate the data of forecasters who have released $f^i_{t-k,t}$ for less than 14 quarters. Table 3 shows the regression result. The first column shows the number of forecasters who have released *k*-month forecasts ($f^i_{t-k,t}$) for 14 quarters or more. The second (third) column shows the number of forecasters for whom the null of $\delta \leq 0$ is rejected at the 0.025 (0.05) significance by the one-tailed test. The fourth (fifth) column shows the number of forecasters for whom the null of $\delta \geq 1$ is rejected at the 0.025 (0.05) significance by the one-tailed test.

The first through the sixth rows of table 3 show the results of substituting $f^M_{t-k,t}$ for f^2. As for zero-month forecast, the first row shows that $f^i_{t-k,t}$ encompasses $f^M_{t-k,t}$ at the 0.05 significance for 24 out of 32 forecasters. However, $f^M_{t-k,t}$ encompasses $f^i_{t-k,t}$ at the 0.05 significance for 29 out of 32 forecasters (88%). This means that 88% of forecasters fail to exploit useful information contained in $f^M_{t-k,t}$ when they make zero-month forecasts. Namely, their zero-month forecasts could be improved by simply taking account of the latest realization of CPI.

The second and the third rows show the results for one and two-month forecasts: $f^M_{t-k,t}$ encompasses $f^i_{t-k,t}$ at the 0.05 significance for 11 forecasters. Namely, one-third of forecasters did not fully utilize the latest realization for one and two-month forecasts. On the other hand, $f^M_{t-k,t}$ encompasses $f^i_{t-k,t}$ for less than seven forecasters for three, four, and five-month forecasts.

The lower half of table 3 presents the results of substituting $f^Q_{t-k,t}$ for f^2. It shows that almost every forecaster encompasses $f^Q_{t-k,t}$ and at most one forecaster is encompassed by $f^Q_{t-k,t}$ for every forecast span. It demonstrates that $f^i_{t-k,t}$ contains all information in $f^Q_{t-k,t}$.

Table 3. The encompassing test

Model: (2) $q_t - f_{t-k,t}^2 = \delta\left(f_{t-k,t}^1 - f_{t-k,t}^2\right) + u_t$

		$H_0 : \delta \le 0$		$H_0 : \delta \ge 1$	
$\left(f_{t-k,t}^1, f_{t-k,t}^2\right)$	Obs.	$p<0.025$ [a]	$p<0.05$ [b]	$p<0.025$ [a]	$p<0.05$ [b]
$\left(f_{t,t}^i, f_{t,t}^M\right)$	32	21	24	28	29
$\left(f_{t-1,t}^i, f_{t-1,t}^M\right)$	33	21	23	8	11
$\left(f_{t-2,t}^i, f_{t-2,t}^M\right)$	31	13	17	9	11
$\left(f_{t-3,t}^i, f_{t-3,t}^M\right)$	32	16	17	5	6
$\left(f_{t-4,t}^i, f_{t-4,t}^M\right)$	33	22	28	0	1
$\left(f_{t-5,t}^i, f_{t-5,t}^M\right)$	30	13	16	3	4
$\left(f_{t,t}^i, f_{t,t}^Q\right)$	32	32	32	0	1
$\left(f_{t-1,t}^i, f_{t-1,t}^Q\right)$	33	33	33	0	0
$\left(f_{t-2,t}^i, f_{t-2,t}^Q\right)$	31	26	29	0	1
$\left(f_{t-3,t}^i, f_{t-3,t}^Q\right)$	32	32	32	0	0
$\left(f_{t-4,t}^i, f_{t-4,t}^Q\right)$	33	32	33	0	0
$\left(f_{t-5,t}^i, f_{t-5,t}^Q\right)$	30	20	24	1	1

Obs.: The number of forecasters who have released *k*-month forecasts for 14 quarters or more.
[a] The number of forecasters for whom the null is rejected at the 0.025 significance (by the one-tailed test).
[b] The number of forecasters for whom the null is rejected at the 0.05 significance (by the one-tailed test).

We also conduct the generalized encompassing test;

$$q_t = \alpha + \delta_1 \cdot f_{t-k,t}^1 + \delta_2 \cdot f_{t-k,t}^2 + u_t . \tag{3}$$

Regression (3) relaxes the restrictions of $\alpha = 0$ and $\delta_1 + \delta_2 = 1$ in (2). If δ_i ($i = 1,2$) is significantly larger than zero, then f^i contains useful information not in the constant term and f^j ($j \neq i$). If $\delta_i = 0$, f^i provides no additional information useful in forecasting q_t given f^j. This test is also employed by Cooper and Nelson (1975), Fair and Shiller (1990), Joutz and Stekler (2000), Romer and Romer (2000), Batchelor (2001), and Ashiya (2007).

The estimation results are summarized in table 4, which gives us a clearer picture than Table 3. The third column shows that δ_1 is significant for 16 out of 32 forecasters for zero-month forecast. Namely, given $f_{t-k,t}^M$, only 50% of zero-month forecasts provide useful information. In contrast to this, the fifth column shows that δ_2 is significant for 28 forecasters (88%) for zero-month forecast. It indicates that $f^{M}_{t-k,t}$ is useful for predicting q_t given $f^{i}_{t-k,t}$. In other words, 88% of forecasters neglect information contained in $f^{M}_{t-k,t}$.

Table 4. The generalized encompassing test

Model: (3) $q_t = \alpha + \delta_1 \cdot f^{1}_{t-k,t} + \delta_2 \cdot f^{2}_{t-k,t} + u_t$

		$H_0 : \delta_1 \le 0$		$H_0 : \delta_2 \le 0$	
$\left(f^{1}_{t-k,t}, f^{2}_{t-k,t}\right)$	Obs.	$p<0.025$[a]	$p<0.05$[b]	$p<0.025$[a]	$p<0.05$[b]
$\left(f^{i}_{t,t}, f^{M}_{t,t}\right)$	32	13	16	28	28
$\left(f^{i}_{t-1,t}, f^{M}_{t-1,t}\right)$	33	16	21	23	25
$\left(f^{i}_{t-2,t}, f^{M}_{t-2,t}\right)$	31	11	18	15	23
$\left(f^{i}_{t-3,t}, f^{M}_{t-3,t}\right)$	32	18	20	7	9
$\left(f^{i}_{t-4,t}, f^{M}_{t-4,t}\right)$	33	19	20	2	5
$\left(f^{i}_{t-5,t}, f^{M}_{t-5,t}\right)$	30	11	14	4	5
$\left(f^{i}_{t,t}, f^{Q}_{t,t}\right)$	32	32	32	1	1
$\left(f^{i}_{t-1,t}, f^{Q}_{t-1,t}\right)$	33	32	32	0	0
$\left(f^{i}_{t-2,t}, f^{Q}_{t-2,t}\right)$	31	24	26	4	4
$\left(f^{i}_{t-3,t}, f^{Q}_{t-3,t}\right)$	32	32	32	0	0
$\left(f^{i}_{t-4,t}, f^{Q}_{t-4,t}\right)$	33	27	30	1	1
$\left(f^{i}_{t-5,t}, f^{Q}_{t-5,t}\right)$	30	17	20	2	3

Obs.: The number of forecasters who have released k-month forecasts for 14 quarters or more.

[a]: The number of forecasters for whom the null is rejected at the 0.025 significance (by the one-tailed test).

[b]: The number of forecasters for whom the null is rejected at the 0.05 significance (by the one-tailed test).

We have the same results for one-month and two-month forecasts: δ_1 is insignificant for 12 out of 33 (13 out of 31) forecasters for one-month (two-month) forecast (We can obtain these numbers by subtracting the number in the third column from the number in the first column). These forecasters provide little additional information useful in forecasting q_t given $f^{M}_{t-k,t}$. Furthermore, the fifth column shows that around three-quarter of forecasters did not make good use of $f^{M}_{t-k,t}$ for one-month and two-month forecasts.

The fourth through the sixth rows show the results for three to five-month forecasts: δ_2 is significant for only 5 to 9 forecasters. It implies that $f^M_{t-k,t}$ is not useful given $f^i_{t-k,t}$ when the forecast span is three months or longer.

The seventh through the twelfth rows present the results of substituting $f^Q_{t-k,t}$ for f^2. We have the same result as Table 3. δ_1 is significant for almost all forecasters for zero to four-month forecasts. δ_2 is significant for four or less forecasters for every forecast span. These results indicate that the forecasters fully utilize information contained in $f^Q_{t-k,t}$.

3.4. Generalized Loss Function

Diebold and Mariano (1995, p253) argue that "realistic economic loss functions frequently do not conform to stylized textbook favorites like mean squared prediction error." Therefore this subsection relaxes the assumption that the loss associated with a particular forecast error is proportional to its square. More specifically, we evaluate relative accuracy using the "sign test" explained below.

Let T be the sample size, and let n be the number of quarters the individual forecaster "wins", i.e., its absolute forecast error is smaller than that of the benchmark forecast. Then

$$Z \equiv \frac{n - 0.5T}{\sqrt{0.25T}} \tag{4}$$

is asymptotically distributed according to $N(0,1)$. If Z is significantly larger (smaller) than zero, then the individual forecaster is superior (inferior) to the benchmark forecast. Note that this test is valid for non-quadratic, asymmetric, or discontinuous loss functions.

Table 5 shows the result. The statistics is significant for very few forecasters, because the sample size is small (18 or less) and many quarters ended in a tie. As for zero-month forecast, however, five forecasters are beaten by $f^M_{t-k,t}$.

Table 5. The sign test

	vs. $f^M_{t-k,t}$	vs. $f^Q_{t-k,t}$
k	**win [a] / lose [b]**	**win [a] /lose [b]**
0	0 / 5	2 / 0
1	0 / 0	2 / 0
2	1 / 0	0 / 0
3	0 / 0	3 / 0
4	0 / 0	3 / 0
5	1 / 0	0 / 0

[a]: The number of forecasters for whom the null of $Z \leq 0$ is rejected at the 0.05 significance (by the one-tailed test).

[b]: The number of forecasters for whom the null of $Z \geq 0$ is rejected at the 0.05 significance (by the one-tailed test).

Table 6. Correlations of forecast accuracy among different forecast spans

(a) Correlations of $U^i_{t-k,t}\left(f^M_{t-k,t}\right)$	$U^i_{t,t}\left(f^M_{t,t}\right)$	$U^i_{t-1,t}\left(f^M_{t-1,t}\right)$	$U^i_{t-2,t}\left(f^M_{t-2,t}\right)$	$U^i_{t-3,t}\left(f^M_{t-3,t}\right)$	$U^i_{t-4,t}\left(f^M_{t-4,t}\right)$
$U^i_{t,t}\left(f^M_{t,t}\right)$	1.000				
$U^i_{t-1,t}\left(f^M_{t-1,t}\right)$	0.727	1.000			
$U^i_{t-2,t}\left(f^M_{t-2,t}\right)$	0.600	0.451	1.000		
$U^i_{t-3,t}\left(f^M_{t-3,t}\right)$	0.636	0.686	0.632	1.000	
$U^i_{t-4,t}\left(f^M_{t-4,t}\right)$	0.477	0.738	0.506	0.795	1.000
$U^i_{t-5,t}\left(f^M_{t-5,t}\right)$	0.320	0.203	0.763	0.548	0.394
(b) Correlations of $U^i_{t-k,t}\left(f^Q_{t-k,t}\right)$					
	$U^i_{t,t}\left(f^Q_{t,t}\right)$	$U^i_{t-1,t}\left(f^Q_{t-1,t}\right)$	$U^i_{t-2,t}\left(f^Q_{t-2,t}\right)$	$U^i_{t-3,t}\left(f^Q_{t-3,t}\right)$	$U^i_{t-4,t}\left(f^Q_{t-4,t}\right)$
$U^i_{t,t}\left(f^Q_{t,t}\right)$	1.000				
$U^i_{t-1,t}\left(f^Q_{t-1,t}\right)$	0.873	1.000			
$U^i_{t-2,t}\left(f^Q_{t-2,t}\right)$	0.615	0.733	1.000		
$U^i_{t-3,t}\left(f^Q_{t-3,t}\right)$	0.676	0.730	0.761	1.000	
$U^i_{t-4,t}\left(f^Q_{t-4,t}\right)$	0.491	0.684	0.700	0.801	1.000
$U^i_{t-5,t}\left(f^Q_{t-5,t}\right)$	0.194	0.325	0.713	0.573	0.608

3.5. Correlations of Forecast Accuracy among Different Forecast Spans

Table 6 shows the correlations of forecast accuracy among different forecast spans. The second row of Table 6 (a) shows that the correlation between $U^i_{t-1,t}\left(f^M_{t-1,t}\right)$ and $U^i_{t,t}\left(f^M_{t,t}\right)$ is 0.727. It indicates that relative accuracy of $f^i_{t-1,t}$ (the one-month forecast of forecaster i) is positively correlated with that of $f^i_{t,t}$ (the zero-month forecast of forecaster i). The correlation is 0.7 or higher between $U^i_{t-1,t}\left(f^M_{t-1,t}\right)$ and $U^i_{t,t}\left(f^M_{t,t}\right)$, $U^i_{t-4,t}\left(f^M_{t-4,t}\right)$ and $U^i_{t-1,t}\left(f^M_{t-1,t}\right)$, $U^i_{t-4,t}\left(f^M_{t-4,t}\right)$ and $U^i_{t-3,t}\left(f^M_{t-3,t}\right)$, and $U^i_{t-5,t}\left(f^M_{t-5,t}\right)$ and $U^i_{t-2,t}\left(f^M_{t-2,t}\right)$. The fact that accuracy of $f^i_{t-4,t}$ ($f^i_{t-5,t}$) is highly correlated with $f^i_{t-1,t}$ ($f^i_{t-2,t}$) is interesting because forecasters release four-month (five-month) forecast and one-month (two-month) forecast simultaneously.

Table 6 (b) shows the correlations of $U^i_{t-k,t}\left(f^Q_{t-k,t}\right)$. The results are similar to Table 6 (a): forecast accuracy is positively correlated among different forecast spans.

4. Rationality

A rational forecast should not be biased, and should use available information efficiently. This section analyzes unbiasedness and efficiency of the individual forecasts based on the properties of their forecast errors and forecast revisions. It will find that almost all forecasts are inefficient: they fail to use the information contained in the latest realization efficiently.

4.1. Tests for Unbiasedness

A forecast is unbiased if its average deviation from the outcome is zero. Holden and Peel (1990) suggest a simple regression of the forecast error on a constant term as the test for unbiasedness. We estimate

$$FE^i_{t-k,t} = \alpha^i + u^i_t, \tag{5}$$

where $FE^i_{t-k,t} \equiv f^i_{t-k,t} - q_t$. The null hypothesis is $\alpha^i = 0$: forecaster i could reduce her forecast error by changing her forecast to $f^i_{t-k,t} - \alpha^i$ if α^i is significantly different from zero. We also check serial correlation in u^i_t for zero, one, and two-month forecasts. The reason is forecasts could be improved if there is serial correlation in the error term. We allow serial correlation in u_t for three, four, and five-month forecasts because forecasters do not know the forecast errors of their last forecasts (Their forecasts might exhibit a first-order moving average error).

Table 7 presents the result of the unbiasedness test. The first row is the result of zero-month forecast, and the second row is that of one-month forecast. The first column shows the number of forecasters who have released k-month forecasts for 14 quarters or more. The second column shows the number of forecasters for whom the null of no bias and no serial correlation are not rejected at the 0.10 significance (We allow serial correlation in u_t for three, four, and five-month forecasts). We check serial correlation in u_t^i up to fourth order by the Ljung-Box Q-statistic. The third column shows the number of forecasters for whom either the null of no bias or the null of no serial correlation is rejected at the 0.10 significance.

Table 7 shows that 44% of zero-month forecasts, 33% of one-month forecasts, 87% of two-month forecasts, 31% of three-month forecasts, 30% of four-month forecasts, and 23% of five-month forecasts are biased. Since unbiasedness is a necessary condition for efficiency, these forecasts are considered to be inefficient and hence irrational. Namely, they violate the weakest form of the rational expectations hypothesis.

Table 7. The test for unbiasedness

Model: (5) $FE_{t-k,t}^i = \alpha^i + u_t^i$					
k	**Obs.**	**Pass** [a]	**Fail** [b]	$\alpha^i \neq 0$ [c]	**autocorrelation** [d]
0	32	18	14	5	9
1	33	22	11	2	9
2	31	4	27	12	25
3	32	22 [e]	10 [e]	10	(28) [e]
4	33	23 [e]	10 [e]	10	(30) [e]
5	30	23 [e]	7 [e]	7	(30) [e]

Obs.: The number of forecasters who have released k-month forecasts for 14 quarters or more.

a: The number of forecasters for whom the null of no bias and no serial correlation are not rejected at the 0.10 significance.

b: The number of forecasters for whom either the null of no bias or the null of no serial correlation is rejected at the 0.10 significance.

c: The number of forecasters whose forecasts are biased at the 0.10 significance..

d: The number of forecasters whose forecast errors have serial correlation of first, second, third, or fourth order at the 0.10 significance..

e: We allow serial correlation in u_t for three, four, and five-month forecasts.

4.2. Tests for Efficiency

A rational forecaster should use available information efficiently. Thus its forecast error should not be related to information available when the forecast was made, and its forecast revision should not be related to information available when the earlier forecast was made. This sub-section tests the efficiency of the forecast error, and the next sub-section tests the efficiency of the forecast revision.

A test of weak efficiency is represented by the following equation:

$$FE_{t-k,t}^i = \alpha^i + \beta^i \cdot X_{t-k}^i + u_{t-k}^i , \tag{6}$$

where X^i_{t-k} is the information available when the forecast was made. Each forecaster must know own forecast ($f^i_{t-k,t}$), and each forecaster should check the latest realization ($f^M_{t-k,t}$ and $f^Q_{t-k,t}$). Hence we substitute $f^i_{t-k,t}$, $f^M_{t-k,t}$, and $f^Q_{t-k,t}$ for X^i_{t-k}. The null hypothesis is $\alpha^i = \beta^i = 0$ (Otherwise the forecast could be improved using X^i_{t-k}). Since $f^i_{t-k,t}$, $f^M_{t-k,t}$, and $f^Q_{t-k,t}$ are found to be non-stationary, we conduct the ADF tests for cointegration.

Table 8 reports the results. The first column shows the variable substituted for X^i_{t-k}. The second column shows the number of forecasters who have released *k*-month forecasts for 14 quarters or more. The third column shows the number of forecasters for whom the null of $\alpha^i = 0$, $\beta^i = 0$, and $\alpha^i = \beta^i = 0$ are not rejected at the 0.10 significance. The fourth column shows the number of failed forecasters, i.e., those for whom at least one of the null hypotheses is rejected at the 0.10 significance. We also tabulated the number of forecasters who have failed in any of the three regressions for the given forecast span (These numbers are summarized in Table 11). The eighth column shows the number of forecasters whose forecast errors are cointegrated with X^i_{t-k} at the 0.10 significance. The ninth (tenth) column shows the number of forecasters who pass (fail) the efficiency test and whose forecast errors are cointegrated with X^i_{t-k}.

The first row of the Table 8 shows the estimation result of zero-month forecast when we substitute $f^i_{t-k,t}$ for X^i_{t-k}. The nulls are rejected for 11 forecasters (34%). These forecasters are irrational in the sense that their forecast errors could be reduced by their own forecasts. The result is the same for the forecasters whose forecast errors are cointegrated with $f^i_{t-k,t}$: the nulls are rejected for 9 out of 24 forecasters (37.5%). The second row shows the result when we substitute $f^M_{t,t}$ for X^i_{t-k}: 19 forecasters (59%) fail to use $f^M_{t,t}$ efficiently. As for the forecasters whose forecast errors are cointegrated with $f^M_{t,t}$, the nulls are rejected for 14 out of 25 forecasters (56%). The third row shows that 9 forecasters (28%) fail to use $f^Q_{t,t}$ efficiently. As for the forecasters whose forecast errors are cointegrated with $f^Q_{t,t}$, the nulls are rejected for 7 out of 22 forecasters (32%). In all, 19 forecasters (59%) have failed in any of these three regressions. As for the forecasters whose forecast errors are cointegrated with $f^i_{t-k,t}$, $f^M_{t-k,t}$, and $f^Q_{t-k,t}$, 13 out of 22 forecasters (59%) have failed in any of these three regressions.

We obtain the same results for one-month forecast. The number of forecasters who have failed in any regression is 19 (58%). As for the forecasters whose forecast errors are cointegrated with $f^i_{t-k,t}$, $f^M_{t-k,t}$, and $f^Q_{t-k,t}$, 13 out of 19 forecasters (68%) have failed in any of these three regressions.

Table 8. The test for efficiency

Model: (6) $FE^i_{t-k,t} = \alpha^i + \beta^i \cdot X^i_{t-k} + u^i_{t-k}$										
k	X^i_{t-k}	**Obs.**	**Pass** [a]	**Fail** [b]	$\alpha^i \neq 0$ [c]	$\beta^i \neq 0$ [d]	***F*-test** [e]	**Cointg.**	**Pass** [f]	**Fail** [g]
0	$f^i_{t,t}$	32	21	11	3	7	5	24	15	9
0	$f^M_{t,t}$	32	13	19	3	17	11	25	11	14
0	$f^Q_{t,t}$	32	23	9	2	6	5	22	15	7

* 19 forecasters (59%) have failed in any of these three regressions.

* As for the forecasters whose forecast errors are cointegrated with $f^i_{t-k,t}$, $f^M_{t-k,t}$, and $f^Q_{t-k,t}$, 13 out of 22 forecasters (59%) have failed in any of these three regressions.

k	X^i_{t-k}	**Obs.**	**Pass** [a]	**Fail** [b]	$\alpha^i \neq 0$ [c]	$\beta^i \neq 0$ [d]	***F*-test** [e]	**Cointg.**	**Pass** [f]	**Fail** [g]
1	$f^i_{t-1,t}$	33	21	12	2	10	4	23	14	9
1	$f^M_{t-1,t}$	33	14	19	2	18	14	21	8	13
1	$f^Q_{t-1,t}$	33	27	6	1	5	3	19	17	2

* 19 forecasters (58%) have failed in any of these three regressions.

* As for the forecasters whose forecast errors are cointegrated with $f^i_{t-k,t}$, $f^M_{t-k,t}$, and $f^Q_{t-k,t}$, 13 out of 19 forecasters (68%) have failed in any of these three regressions.

Table 8. Continued

k	X^i_{t-k}	Obs.	Pass [a]	Fail [b]	$\alpha^i \neq 0$ [c]	$\beta^i \neq 0$ [d]	*F*-test [e]	Cointg.	Pass [f]	Fail [g]
2	$f^i_{t-2,t}$	31	19	12	3	7	8	7	3	4
2	$f^M_{t-2,t}$	31	12	19	2	13	17	9	3	6
2	$f^Q_{t-2,t}$	31	19	12	3	8	9	7	3	4

* 20 forecasters (65%) have failed in any of these three regressions.

* As for those whose forecast errors are cointegrated with $f^i_{t-k,t}$, $f^M_{t-k,t}$, and $f^Q_{t-k,t}$, 5 out of 7 forecasters (71%) have failed in any of these three regressions.

k	X^i_{t-k}	Obs.	Pass [a]	Fail [b]	$\alpha^i \neq 0$ [c]	$\beta^i \neq 0$ [d]	*F*-test [e]	Cointg.	Pass [f]	Fail [g]
3	$f^i_{t-3,t}$	32	8	24	2	22	23	6	0	6
3	$f^M_{t-3,t}$	32	4	28	1	27	26	5	0	5
3	$f^Q_{t-3,t}$	32	14	18	5	13	16	5	3	2

* 28 forecasters (88%) have failed in any of these three regressions.

* As for those whose forecast errors are cointegrated with $f^i_{t-k,t}$, $f^M_{t-k,t}$, and $f^Q_{t-k,t}$, 3 out of 3 forecasters (100%) have failed in any of these three regressions.

k	X^i_{t-k}	Obs.	Pass [a]	Fail [b]	$\alpha^i \neq 0$ [c]	$\beta^i \neq 0$ [d]	*F*-test [e]	Cointg.	Pass [f]	Fail [g]
4	$f^i_{t-4,t}$	33	8	25	1	24	24	5	3	2
4	$f^M_{t-4,t}$	33	5	28	1	28	28	2	1	1
4	$f^Q_{t-4,t}$	33	10	23	6	20	20	2	2	0

* 29 forecasters (88%) have failed in any of these three regressions.

* As for those whose forecast errors are cointegrated with $f^i_{t-k,t}$, $f^M_{t-k,t}$, and $f^Q_{t-k,t}$, 1 out of 2 forecasters (50%) have failed in any of these three regressions.

Table 8. Continued

k	X^i_{t-k}	Obs.	Pass [a]	Fail [b]	$\alpha^i \neq 0$ [c]	$\beta^i \neq 0$ [d]	*F*-test [e]	Cointg.	Pass [f]	Fail [g]
5	$f^i_{t-5,t}$	30	20	10	3	5	9	2	1	1
5	$f^M_{t-5,t}$	30	17	13	3	9	10	3	1	2
5	$f^Q_{t-5,t}$	30	20	10	3	4	9	1	1	0

* 14 forecasters (47%) have failed in any of these three regressions.

* As for those whose forecast errors are cointegrated with $f^i_{t-k,t}$, $f^M_{t-k,t}$, and $f^Q_{t-k,t}$, 0 out of 1 forecaster (0%) has failed in any of these three regressions.

Obs.: The number of forecasters who have released *k*-month forecasts for 14 quarters or more.

a: The number of forecasters for whom the null of $\alpha^i = 0$, $\beta^i = 0$, and $\alpha^i = \beta^i = 0$ are not rejected at the 0.10 significance.

b: The number of forecasters for whom at least one of the null hypotheses is rejected at the 0.10 significance.

c: The number of forecasters for whom *t*-test rejects the null of $\alpha^i = 0$ at the 0.10 significance.

d: The number of forecasters for whom *t*-test rejects the null of $\beta^i = 0$ at the 0.10 significance.

e: The number of forecasters for whom *F*-test rejects the null of $\alpha^i = \beta^i = 0$ at the 0.10 significance.

Cointg.: The number of forecasters whose forecast errors are cointegrated with X^i_{t-k} at the 0.10 significance.

f: The number of forecasters who pass the efficiency test and whose forecast errors are cointegrated with X^i_{t-k}.

g: The number of forecasters who fail the efficiency test and whose forecast errors are cointegrated with X^i_{t-k}.

The results are similar for other forecast spans, but the forecast error and X_{t-k}^{i} are not cointegrated in the bulk of the regressions. Hence the following results are not as robust as those of zero and one-month forecasts. The percentage of forecasters who have failed in any regression is 65% (20 out of 31 forecasters) for two-month forecast, 88% (28 out of 32 forecasters) for three-month forecast, 88% (29 out of 33 forecasters) for four-month forecast, and 47% (14 out of 30 forecasters) for five-month forecast. These figures are almost the same for those whose forecast errors are cointegrated with X_{t-k}^{i}. As for the forecasters whose forecast errors are cointegrated with $f_{t-k,t}^{i}$, $f_{t-k,t}^{M}$, and $f_{t-k,t}^{Q}$, the percentage of forecasters who have failed in any regression is 71% (5 out of 7 forecasters) for two-month forecast, 100% (3 out of 3 forecasters) for three-month forecast, 50% (1 out of 2 forecasters) for four-month forecast, and 0% (0 out of 1 forecaster) for five-month forecast.

4.3. Tests for Martingale

This sub-section examines the rationality of forecast revisions. Batchelor and Dua (1991, p.695) argue that, if a forecaster is rational, her forecast revision must be uncorrelated with variables known at the time of the earlier forecast. They propose the following regression as the martingale test:

$$f_{t-k+1,t}^{i} - f_{t-k,t}^{i} = \alpha^{i} + \beta^{i} \cdot X_{t-k}^{i} + u_{t-k}^{i}, \tag{7}$$

where $f_{t-k+1,t}^{i}$ is $k-1$ month forecast of forecaster i and X_{t-k}^{i} is the information available when $f_{t-k,t}^{i}$ was made. X_{t-k}^{i} will be substituted by $f_{t-k,t}^{i}$, $f_{t-k,t}^{M}$, $f_{t-k,t}^{Q}$, and $f_{t-k,t}^{i} - f_{t-k-1,t}^{i}$ (the previous revision). The null hypothesis is $\beta^{i} = 0$. We allow a nonzero intercept because average forecast revision can be positive (negative) when the economy continually experiences positive (negative) shocks to prices.

Table 9 presents the results. We do not have the result of zero-month forecast because $f_{t-k+1,t}^{i}$ does not exist for $k = 0$. The first column shows the variable substituted for X_{t-k}^{i}. The second column indicates the number of forecasters who have released the forecast set $\left(f_{t-k+1,t}^{i}, f_{t-k,t}^{i}\right)$ 14 times or more. The third column shows the number of forecasters for whom the null of $\beta^{i} = 0$ is not rejected at the 0.10 significance. We also tabulated the number of forecasters who have failed in any of the three regressions for the given forecast span (These numbers are summarized in Table 11). The fifth column shows the number of forecasters whose forecast revisions are cointegrated with X_{t-k}^{i} at the 0.10 significance. The sixth (seventh) column shows the number of forecasters who pass (fail) the martingale test and whose forecast revisions are cointegrated with X_{t-k}^{i}.

Table 9. The test for martingale (1)

Model: (7) $f^{i}_{t-k+1,t} - f^{i}_{t-k,t} = \alpha^{i} + \beta^{i} \cdot X^{i}_{t-k} + u^{i}_{t-k}$							
k	X^{i}_{t-k}	**Obs.**	**Pass** [a]	$\beta^{i} \neq 0$ [b]	**Cointg.**	**Pass** [c]	**Fail** [d]
1	$f^{i}_{t-1,t}$	32	22	10	22	17	5
1	$f^{M}_{t-1,t}$	32	13	19	21	9	12
1	$f^{Q}_{t-1,t}$	32	27	5	21	19	2

* 19 forecasters (59%) have failed in any of these three regressions.

* As for the forecasters whose forecast revisions are cointegrated with $f^{i}_{t-k,t}$, $f^{M}_{t-k,t}$, and $f^{Q}_{t-k,t}$, 12 out of 21 forecasters (57%) have failed in any of these three regressions.

k	X^{i}_{t-k}	**Obs.**	**Pass** [a]	$\beta^{i} \neq 0$ [b]	**Cointg.**	**Pass** [c]	**Fail** [d]
2	$f^{i}_{t-2,t}$	28	26	2	10	10	0
2	$f^{M}_{t-2,t}$	28	25	3	12	12	0
2	$f^{Q}_{t-2,t}$	28	27	1	12	12	0

* 5 forecasters (18%) have failed in any of these three regressions.

* As for the forecasters whose forecast revisions are cointegrated with $f^{i}_{t-k,t}$, $f^{M}_{t-k,t}$, and $f^{Q}_{t-k,t}$, 0 out of 10 forecasters (0%) have failed in any of these three regressions.

k	X^{i}_{t-k}	**Obs.**	**Pass** [a]	$\beta^{i} \neq 0$ [b]	**Cointg.**	**Pass** [c]	**Fail** [d]
3	$f^{i}_{t-3,t}$	30	12	18	14	6	8
3	$f^{M}_{t-3,t}$	30	8	22	16	6	10
3	$f^{Q}_{t-3,t}$	30	11	19	9	5	4

* 22 forecasters (73%) have failed in any of these three regressions.

* As for the forecasters whose forecast revisions are cointegrated with $f^{i}_{t-k,t}$, $f^{M}_{t-k,t}$, and $f^{Q}_{t-k,t}$, 3 out of 8 forecasters (38%) have failed in any of these three regressions.

k	X^{i}_{t-k}	**Obs.**	**Pass** [a]	$\beta^{i} \neq 0$ [b]	**Cointg.**	**Pass** [c]	**Fail** [d]
4	$f^{i}_{t-4,t}$	32	21	11	24	19	5
4	$f^{M}_{t-4,t}$	32	14	18	23	11	12
4	$f^{Q}_{t-4,t}$	32	19	13	22	14	8

* 20 forecasters (63%) have failed in any of these three regressions.

* As for the forecasters whose forecast revisions are cointegrated with $f^{i}_{t-k,t}$, $f^{M}_{t-k,t}$, and $f^{Q}_{t-k,t}$, 15 out of 22 forecasters (68%) have failed in any of these three regressions.

Table 9. Continued

k	X^i_{t-k}	Obs.	Pass [a]	$\beta^i \neq 0$ [b]	Cointg.	Pass [c]	Fail [d]
5	$f^i_{t-5,t}$	28	27	1	15	14	1
5	$f^M_{t-5,t}$	28	24	4	16	13	3
5	$f^Q_{t-5,t}$	28	23	5	15	13	2

* 5 forecasters (18%) have failed in any of these three regressions.

* As for the forecasters whose forecast revisions are cointegrated with $f^i_{t-k,t}$, $f^M_{t-k,t}$, and $f^Q_{t-k,t}$, 3 out of 15 forecasters (20%) have failed in any of these three regressions.

Obs.: The number of forecasters who have released the forecast set $\left(f^i_{t-k+1,t}, f^i_{t-k,t}\right)$ 14 times or more.

a: The number of forecasters for whom the null of $\beta^i = 0$ is not rejected at the 0.10 significance.

b: The number of forecasters for whom *t*-test rejects the null of $\beta^i = 0$ at the 0.10 significance.

Cointg.: The number of forecasters whose forecast revisions are cointegrated with X^i_{t-k} at the 0.10 significance.

c: The number of forecasters who pass the martingale test and whose forecast revisions are cointegrated with X^i_{t-k}.

d: The number of forecasters who fail the martingale test and whose forecast revisions are cointegrated with X^i_{t-k}.

Table 10. The test for martingale (2)

Model: (8) $f^i_{t-k+1,t} - f^i_{t-k,t} = \alpha^i + \beta^i \cdot \left(f^i_{t-k,t} - f^i_{t-k-1,t}\right) + u^i_{t-k}$						
k	Obs.	Pass [a]	$\beta^i \neq 0$ [b]	Cointg.	Pass [c]	Fail [d]
1	26	23	3	15	14	1
2	26	25	1	9	9	0
3	29	22	7	14	10	4
4	26	21	5	16	12	4

Obs.: The number of forecasters who have released the forecast set $\left(f^i_{t-k+1,t}, f^i_{t-k,t}, f^i_{t-k-1,t}\right)$ 14 times or more.

a: The number of forecasters for whom the null of $\beta^i = 0$ is not rejected at the 0.10 significance.

b: The number of forecasters for whom *t*-test rejects the null of $\beta^i = 0$ at the 0.10 significance.

Cointg.: The number of forecasters for whom $f^i_{t-k+1,t} - f^i_{t-k,t}$ is cointegrated with $f^i_{t-k,t} - f^i_{t-k-1,t}$ at the 0.10 significance.

c: The number of forecasters who pass the martingale test and $f^i_{t-k+1,t} - f^i_{t-k,t}$ is cointegrated with $f^i_{t-k,t} - f^i_{t-k-1,t}$.

d: The number of forecasters who fail the martingale test and $f^i_{t-k+1,t} - f^i_{t-k,t}$ is cointegrated with $f^i_{t-k,t} - f^i_{t-k-1,t}$.

Table 11. Summary of the rationality tests

k	Obs.	Fail (5)	Fail (6)	Fail (7)	Fail (8)	Pass (5) & (6)	Pass all
0	32	14	19	---	----	9	---
1	33	11	19	19	3	11	6
2	31	27	20 [a]	5 [a]	1 [a]	3	2
3	32	10	28 [a]	22 [a]	7 [a]	4	2
4	33	10	29 [a]	20	5	4	2
5	30	7	14 [a]	5	---	16	15

Obs.: The number of forecasters who have released k-month forecasts for 14 quarters or more.
a: This number is not robust because more than half of the regressions have failed the cointegration test.

The first row of Table 9 shows the result of one-month forecast when we substitute $f^i_{t-k,t}$ for X^i_{t-k}. Again we find significant inefficiency: the null is rejected for 10 forecasters (31%). The result is the same for the forecasters whose forecast revisions are cointegrated with $f^i_{t-k,t}$: the null is rejected for 5 out of 22 forecasters (23%). The second row shows the result when we substitute $f^M_{t,t}$ for X^i_{t-k}. The null is rejected for 19 forecasters (59%). It indicates that 59% of forecasters fail to utilize $f^M_{t,t}$ in their forecast revisions. As for those whose forecast revisions are cointegrated with $f^M_{t,t}$, the null is rejected for 12 out of 21 forecasters (57%). The third row shows that 5 forecasters fail to utilize $f^Q_{t,t}$ in their forecast revisions. In all, 19 forecasters (59%) have failed in any of these three martingale tests. As for those whose forecast revisions are cointegrated with $f^i_{t-k,t}$, $f^M_{t-k,t}$, and $f^Q_{t-k,t}$, 12 out of 21 forecasters (57%) have failed in any of these three regressions.

We obtain the same results for other forecast spans. The percentage of forecasters who have failed in any regression is 18% (5 out of 28 forecasters) for two-month forecast, 73% (22 out of 30 forecasters) for three-month forecast, 63% (20 out of 32 forecasters) for four-month forecast, and 18% (5 out of 28 forecasters) for five-month forecast. These figures are almost the same for those whose forecast revisions are cointegrated with X^i_{t-k}. As for those whose forecast revisions are cointegrated with $f^i_{t-k,t}$, $f^M_{t-k,t}$, and $f^Q_{t-k,t}$, the percentage of forecasters who have failed in any regression is 0% (0 out of 10 forecasters) for two-month forecast, 38% (3 out of 8 forecasters) for three-month forecast, 68% (15 out of 22 forecasters) for four-month forecast, and 20% (3 out of 15 forecasters) for five-month forecast.

Table 10 shows the results of the following regression, in which X^i_{t-k} of equation (7) is substituted by $f^i_{t-k,t} - f^i_{t-k-1,t}$:

$$f^i_{t-k+1,t} - f^i_{t-k,t} = \alpha^i + \beta^i \cdot \left(f^i_{t-k,t} - f^i_{t-k-1,t}\right) + u^i_{t-k}. \qquad (8)$$

Berger and Krane (1985, p.130) argue that "if forecasts are formed in a consistent fashion, then current forecast revisions should not be at all predictable from past revisions."

Namely, $f^i_{t-k+1,t} - f^i_{t-k,t}$ should not be correlated with $f^i_{t-k,t} - f^i_{t-k-1,t}$. The null hypothesis of rationality is $\beta^i = 0$. Equation (8) evaluates the serial correlation of forecast revisions for a fixed *future realization*. Rejection of the null indicates that the forecaster fails to utilize the information she previously used to revise her forecast for the same realization. Nordhaus (1987), Clements (1995), Loungani (2001), and Ashiya (2006a) also consider this regression.

The first column of Table 10 shows the number of forecasters who have released the forecast set $\left(f^i_{t-k+1,t}, f^i_{t-k,t}, f^i_{t-k-1,t}\right)$ 14 times or more. We do not have the result of zero-month forecast and five-month forecast because $f^i_{t-k+1,t}$ does not exist for $k = 0$ and $f^i_{t-k-1,t}$ does not exist for $k = 5$. The second column shows the number of forecasters for whom the null of $\beta^i = 0$ is not rejected at the 0.10 significance. The fourth column shows the number of forecasters for whom $f^i_{t-k+1,t} - f^i_{t-k,t}$ is cointegrated with $f^i_{t-k,t} - f^i_{t-k-1,t}$ at the 0.10 significance. The fifth (sixth) column shows the number of forecasters who pass (fail) the martingale test among them.

Table 10 shows that more than three-quarter of the forecasters pass the test of equation (8) for each forecast span. We obtain similar results for those $f^i_{t-k+1,t} - f^i_{t-k,t}$ and $f^i_{t-k,t} - f^i_{t-k-1,t}$ are cointegrated.

4.4. Summary of the Rationality Tests

Table 11 summarizes the results of equations (5) through (8). The first column shows the number of forecasters who have released *k*-month forecasts for 14 quarters or more. The second through the fifth columns shows the number of forecasters who have failed in each test.

The sixth column shows the number of forecasters who pass both the unbiasedness tests of equation (5) and the efficiency tests of equation (6). The percentage of the forecasters who pass (5) and (6) is 28% for zero-month forecast, 33% for one-month forecast, 10% for two-month forecast, 13% for three-month forecast, 12% for four-month forecast, and 53% for five-month forecast. These percentages are significantly lower than that of other studies (usually 60-80%), although our results for two, three, four, and five-month forecasts are not robust because the majority of the regressions have failed the cointegration test.

The seventh column shows the number of forecasters who pass all tests in all of equations (5) through (8). The percentage of those who pass all is 18% for one-month forecast, 6% for two-month forecast, 6% for three-month forecast, 6% for four-month forecast, and 50% for five-month forecast.

5. Consensus Forecast

This section investigates accuracy and rationality of the consensus forecast, i.e., the mean forecast of 42 forecasters. More precisely, the consensus forecast $\bar{f}_{t-k,t}$ is defined as

$$\bar{f}_{t-k,t} \equiv \frac{1}{42}\sum_{i=1}^{42} f_{t-k,t}^{i}\,.$$

Its forecast error is $FE_{t-k,t} \equiv \bar{f}_{t-k,t} - q_t$.

5.1. Forecast Accuracy

Past literature such as Clemen (1989) has noted that the consensus forecast outperforms a typical forecaster. Table 12 presents the descriptive statistics of the consensus forecast. $U_{t-k,t}\left(f_{t-k,t}^{B}\right)$ ($B = M, Q$) is calculated by substituting $\bar{f}_{t-k,t}$ for $f_{t-k,t}^{i}$ in equation (1). $Z\left(f_{t-k,t}^{B}\right)$ is the *Z*-statistics (of the sign test) calculated by equation (4).

The first column of Table 12 shows that the MAE of the consensus forecast is 0.050 for zero-month forecast, 0.088 for one-month forecast, and 0.164 for two-month forecast. On the other hand, Table 1 has shown that the market average of the MAE of the individual forecasters is 0.072 for zero-month forecast, 0.107 for one-month forecast, and 0.184 for two-month forecast. Therefore the consensus forecast is better than the average forecaster when the forecast span is short. However, the difference is insignificant for longer forecast spans: the MAE of the consensus forecast is 0.208, 0.262, and 0.356 for three, four, and five-month forecasts, whereas the market average of the MAE is 0.225, 0.268, and 0.362 for three, four, and five-month forecast.

As for the relative accuracy, the consensus forecast is inferior to $f_{t-k,t}^{M}$ for zero-month forecast: $U_{t-k,t}\left(f_{t-k,t}^{M}\right) = 1.366$ and $Z\left(f_{t-k,t}^{M}\right)$ is -2.828, which is significant at the 0.01 level. On the other hand, the consensus forecast is superior to $f_{t-k,t}^{M}$ for five-month forecast: $U_{t-k,t}\left(f_{t-k,t}^{M}\right) = 0.937$ and $Z\left(f_{t-k,t}^{M}\right)$ is positive at the 0.10 significance. The sign test shows that the consensus forecast is superior to $f_{t-k,t}^{Q}$ for one, three, and four-month forecast (the sixth column).

Table 12. The descriptive statistics of the consensus forecast

k	MAE	RMSE	$U_{t-k,t}\left(f_{t-k,t}^{M}\right)$	$U_{t-k,t}\left(f_{t-k,t}^{Q}\right)$	$Z\left(f_{t-k,t}^{M}\right)$	$Z\left(f_{t-k,t}^{Q}\right)$
0	0.050	0.064	1.366	0.238	-2.828 ***	1.414
1	0.088	0.112	0.682	0.403	-0.243	1.698 *
2	0.164	0.226	0.947	0.643	0.471	0.000
3	0.208	0.286	0.834	0.516	0.000	1.886 *
4	0.262	0.366	0.733	0.645	0.243	2.183 **
5	0.356	0.488	0.937	0.843	1.698 *	1.213

***: Significant at the 0.01 level. **: Significant at the 0.05 level. *: Significant at the 0.10 level.

5.2. The Encompassing Test for the Consensus Forecast

Table 13 shows the result of the encompassing test. We substitute $\bar{f}_{t-k,t}$ for f^1 and $f^M_{t-k,t}$ (or $f^Q_{t-k,t}$) for f^2 in equation (2). The third column shows the significance levels for the null of $\delta = 0$, and the fifth column shows the significance levels for the null of $\delta = 1$. The first row shows that δ is significantly smaller than one for zero-month forecast. This indicates that $f^M_{t,t}$ contains useful information given the consensus forecast. On the other hand, the null of $\delta = 1$ is not rejected for other forecast spans of $f^M_{t-k,t}$ and all forecast spans of $f^Q_{t-k,t}$. This indicates that the consensus forecast for these forecast spans covers all information contained in the latest realizations.

Table 14 shows the result of the generalized encompassing test (equation (3)). We obtain the same result as that of table 13.

Table 13. The encompassing test for the consensus forecast

Model: (2) $q_t - f^2_{t-k,t} = \delta\left(f^1_{t-k,t} - f^2_{t-k,t}\right) + u_t$					
$\left(f^1_{t-k,t}, f^2_{t-k,t}\right)$	**Obs.**	δ	***P*-value**	$1-\delta$	***P*-value**
$\left(\bar{f}_{t,t}, f^M_{t,t}\right)$	18	0.361	0.003 ***	0.639	0.000 ***
$\left(\bar{f}_{t-1,t}, f^M_{t-1,t}\right)$	17	1.136	0.000 ***	-0.136	0.610 [a]
$\left(\bar{f}_{t-2,t}, f^M_{t-2,t}\right)$	18	0.661	0.114	0.339	0.404
$\left(\bar{f}_{t-3,t}, f^M_{t-3,t}\right)$	18	1.523	0.008 ***	-0.523	0.319 [a]
$\left(\bar{f}_{t-4,t}, f^M_{t-4,t}\right)$	17	2.069	0.000 ***	-1.069	0.016 [a]
$\left(\bar{f}_{t-5,t}, f^M_{t-5,t}\right)$	17	1.229	0.146	-0.229	0.779 [a]
$\left(\bar{f}_{t,t}, f^Q_{t,t}\right)$	18	1.180	0.000 ***	-0.180	0.004 [a]
$\left(\bar{f}_{t-1,t}, f^Q_{t-1,t}\right)$	17	1.417	0.000 ***	-0.417	0.001 [a]
$\left(\bar{f}_{t-2,t}, f^Q_{t-2,t}\right)$	18	1.563	0.000 ***	-0.563	0.048 [a]
$\left(\bar{f}_{t-3,t}, f^Q_{t-3,t}\right)$	18	1.739	0.000 ***	-0.739	0.000 [a]
$\left(\bar{f}_{t-4,t}, f^Q_{t-4,t}\right)$	17	2.043	0.000 ***	-1.043	0.001 [a]
$\left(\bar{f}_{t-5,t}, f^Q_{t-5,t}\right)$	17	2.290	0.003 ***	-1.290	0.071 [a]

***: Significant at the 0.01 level. **: Significant at the 0.05 level. *: Significant at the 0.10 level.

[a]: This value is meaningless for the encompassing test because $\delta > 1$.

Table 14. The generalized encompassing test for the consensus forecast

Model: (3) $q_t = \alpha + \delta_1 \cdot f^1_{t-k,t} + \delta_2 \cdot f^2_{t-k,t} + u_t$					
$\left(f^1_{t-k,t}, f^2_{t-k,t}\right)$	**Obs.**	δ_1	***P*-value**	δ_2	***P*-value**
$\left(\bar{f}_{t,t}, f^M_{t,t}\right)$	18	0.323	0.046 **	0.670	0.000 ***
$\left(\bar{f}_{t-1,t}, f^M_{t-1,t}\right)$	17	0.756	0.019 **	0.439	0.198
$\left(\bar{f}_{t-2,t}, f^M_{t-2,t}\right)$	18	0.731	0.048 **	0.442	0.211
$\left(\bar{f}_{t-3,t}, f^M_{t-3,t}\right)$	18	1.464	0.003 ***	-0.087	0.837 [a]
$\left(\bar{f}_{t-4,t}, f^M_{t-4,t}\right)$	17	1.815	0.001 ***	-0.302	0.560 [a]
$\left(\bar{f}_{t-5,t}, f^M_{t-5,t}\right)$	17	1.617	0.094 *	-0.055	0.945 [a]
$\left(\bar{f}_{t,t}, f^Q_{t,t}\right)$	18	1.209	0.000 ***	-0.231	0.020 [a]
$\left(\bar{f}_{t-1,t}, f^Q_{t-1,t}\right)$	17	1.490	0.000 ***	-0.477	0.011 [a]
Model: (3) $q_t = \alpha + \delta_1 \cdot f^1_{t-k,t} + \delta_2 \cdot f^2_{t-k,t} + u_t$					
$\left(\bar{f}_{t-2,t}, f^Q_{t-2,t}\right)$	18	1.271	0.001 ***	-0.144	0.731 [a]
$\left(\bar{f}_{t-3,t}, f^Q_{t-3,t}\right)$	18	1.747	0.000 ***	-0.631	0.045 [a]
$\left(\bar{f}_{t-4,t}, f^Q_{t-4,t}\right)$	17	2.080	0.000 ***	-0.713	0.111 [a]
$\left(\bar{f}_{t-5,t}, f^Q_{t-5,t}\right)$	17	2.203	0.011 **	-0.719	0.370 [a]

***: Significant at the 0.01 level. **: Significant at the 0.05 level. *: Significant at the 0.10 level.

[a]: This value is meaningless for the encompassing test because $\delta_2 < 0$.

5.3. Rationality of the Consensus Forecast

Table 15 presents the result of the unbiasedness test (equation (5)). Two-month forecast is found to be biased at the 0.10 level.

Table 16 shows the result of the efficiency test (equation (6)). Note that the forecast error is not cointegrated with X_{t-k} when the forecast span is two months or longer. Hence the results for these forecast spans are not reliable. When we substitute $\bar{f}_{t-k,t}$ for X_{t-k}, the null of $\beta = 0$ is rejected for one through five-month forecasts. When we substitute $f^M_{t-k,t}$ for X_{t-k}, the null of $\beta = 0$ is rejected for zero through four-month forecasts. When we substitute $f^Q_{t-k,t}$ for X_{t-k}, the null of $\beta = 0$ is rejected for two, three, and four-month forecasts. These results show that the forecast error of the consensus forecast could be reduced by the information available when the forecast was made.

Table 15. The unbiasedness test for the consensus forecast

Model: (5) $FE_{t-k,t} = \alpha + u_t$					
k	**α (P-value)**	**P-value of Q(1)**	**P-value of Q(2)**	**P-value of Q(3)**	**P-value of Q(4)**
0	-0.011 (0.502)	0.537	0.800	0.853	0.265
1	-0.020 (0.489)	0.213	0.397	0.463	0.177
2	-0.091 (0.090) *	0.007 ***	0.014 **	0.031 **	0.009 ***
3	-0.097 (0.157)	0.004 [a]	0.005	0.013	0.006
4	-0.128 (0.156)	0.007 [a]	0.009	0.024	0.017
5	-0.170 (0.158)	0.012 [a]	0.015	0.036	0.020

***: Significant at the 0.01 level. **: Significant at the 0.05 level. *: Significant at the 0.10 level.

$Q(r)$ is the Ljung-Box *Q*-statistic, which tests serial correlation in u_t up to *r*-th order.

a: We allow serial correlation in u_t for three, four, and five-month forecasts.

Table 16. The efficiency test for the consensus forecast

Model: (6) $FE_{t-k,t} = \alpha + \beta \cdot X_{t-k} + u_{t-k}$					
k	X_{t-k}	α (***P*-value**)	β (***P*-value**)	***F*-test (*P*-value)** [a]	**Cointg.**
0	$\bar{f}_{t,t}$	-0.000 (0.893)	-0.056 (0.126)	1.563 (0.240)	Yes
0	$f^M_{t,t}$	0.000 (0.971)	-0.065 (0.045) **	2.662 (0.100) *	Yes
0	$f^Q_{t,t}$	-0.010 (0.559)	-0.020 (0.688)	0.307 (0.740)	Yes
1	$\bar{f}_{t-1,t}$	0.000 (0.983)	-0.133 (0.049) **	2.602 (0.107)	Yes
1	$f^M_{t-1,t}$	-0.003 (0.913)	-0.168 (0.027) **	3.356 (0.062) *	Yes
1	$f^Q_{t-1,t}$	-0.015 (0.594)	-0.081 (0.356)	0.703 (0.511)	No
2	$\bar{f}_{t-2,t}$	-0.055 (0.286)	-0.161 (0.068) *	3.806 (0.044) **	No
2	$f^M_{t-2,t}$	-0.051 (0.302)	-0.181 (0.037) **	4.617 (0.026) **	No
2	$f^Q_{t-2,t}$	-0.061 (0.245)	-0.185 (0.096) *	3.380 (0.060) *	No
3	$\bar{f}_{t-3,t}$	-0.015 (0.787)	-0.380 (0.002) ***	8.495 (0.003) ***	No
3	$f^M_{t-3,t}$	-0.034 (0.547)	-0.364 (0.004) ***	7.256 (0.006) ***	No
3	$f^Q_{t-3,t}$	-0.079 (0.220)	-0.347 (0.092) *	2.849 (0.087) *	No
4	$\bar{f}_{t-4,t}$	-0.004 (0.946)	-0.574 (0.002) ***	8.751 (0.003) ***	No
4	$f^M_{t-4,t}$	-0.069 (0.361)	-0.581 (0.011) **	5.810 (0.014) **	No
4	$f^Q_{t-4,t}$	-0.101 (0.219)	-0.511 (0.048) **	3.664 (0.051)*	No
5	$\bar{f}_{t-5,t}$	-0.074 (0.540)	-0.558 (0.080) *	3.038 (0.078) *	No

Table 16. Continued

Model: (6) $FE_{t-k,t} = \alpha + \beta \cdot X_{t-k} + u_{t-k}$					
k	X_{t-k}	α (*P*-value)	β (*P*-value)	*F*-test (*P*-value)[a]	Cointg.
5	$f^M_{t-5,t}$	-0.116 (0.318)	-0.454 (0.107)	2.700 (0.100) *	No
5	$f^Q_{t-5,t}$	-0.133 (0.268)	-0.414 (0.216)	1.978 (0.173)	No

***: Significant at the 0.01 level. **: Significant at the 0.05 level. *: Significant at the 0.10 level.
The significance levels for the null are given in parentheses.

[a]: The null is $\alpha = \beta = 0$.

Cointg.: Yes if and only if the forecast error is cointegrated with X_{t-k} at the 0.10 significance.

Table 17. The martingale test for the consensus forecast (1)

Model: (7) $\bar{f}_{t-k+1,t} - \bar{f}_{t-k,t} = \alpha + \beta \cdot X_{t-k} + u_{t-k}$			
k	X_{t-k}	β (*P*-value)	Cointg.
1	$\bar{f}_{t-1,t}$	0.078 (0.012) **	Yes
1	$f^M_{t-1,t}$	0.093 (0.007) ***	No
1	$f^Q_{t-1,t}$	0.059 (0.151)	No
2	$\bar{f}_{t-2,t}$	0.054 (0.585)	No
2	$f^M_{t-2,t}$	0.080 (0.356)	No
2	$f^Q_{t-2,t}$	0.033 (0.749)	No
3	$\bar{f}_{t-3,t}$	0.185 (0.000) ***	No
3	$f^M_{t-3,t}$	0.193 (0.000) ***	No
3	$f^Q_{t-3,t}$	0.235 (0.004) ***	No
4	$\bar{f}_{t-4,t}$	0.153 (0.001) ***	Yes
4	$f^M_{t-4,t}$	0.158 (0.004) ***	Yes
4	$f^Q_{t-4,t}$	0.165 (0.005) ***	No
5	$\bar{f}_{t-5,t}$	0.094 (0.314)	No
5	$f^M_{t-5,t}$	0.080 (0.328)	No
5	$f^Q_{t-5,t}$	0.078 (0.417)	No

***: Significant at the 0.01 level. **: Significant at the 0.05 level. *: Significant at the 0.10 level.
The significance levels for the null are given in parentheses.

Cointg.: Yes if and only if the forecast revision is cointegrated with X_{t-k} at the 0.10 significance.

Table 17 shows the result of the martingale test of equation (7). One, three, and four-month forecasts fail the test, but two-month forecast and five-month forecast pass the test for all three regressions.

Table 18 shows the estimation result of equation (8). One, three, and four-month forecasts fail the test, but two-month forecast passes it.

Table 18. The martingale test for the consensus forecast (2)

Model: (8) $\bar{f}_{t-k+1,t} - \bar{f}_{t-k,t} = \alpha + \beta \cdot \left(\bar{f}_{t-k,t} - \bar{f}_{t-k-1,t}\right) + u_{t-k}$		
k	β **(*P*-value)**	**Cointg.**
1	0.255 (0.004) ***	Yes
2	0.172 (0.706)	No
3	1.190 (0.000) ***	Yes
4	0.486 (0.000) ***	Yes

***: Significant at the 0.01 level. **: Significant at the 0.05 level. *: Significant at the 0.10 level.
The significance levels for the null are given in parentheses.
Cointg.: Yes if and only if $\bar{f}_{t-k+1,t} - \bar{f}_{t-k,t}$ is cointegrated with $\bar{f}_{t-k,t} - \bar{f}_{t-k-1,t}$ at the 0.10 significance.

6. Conclusions

This paper has used the monthly survey of the Economic Planning Association, "ESP Forecast Survey," and investigated accuracy and rationality of Japanese consumer price index (CPI) forecasts. The sample period is from April 2004 to August 2008, and the number of participants is 42.

Section 3 defined the naïve "same-as-the-last-month" forecast as the simple copy of the latest realization of CPI (at the time forecast was made). It found that 86% of the individual forecasts were inferior to the "same-as-the-last-month" forecast for zero-month forecast, and 31% (48%) of one-month (two-month) forecasts were inferior to this benchmark forecast. The generalized encompassing test demonstrated that most forecasters fail to utilize the latest realization of CPI for the short-span forecasts (88% for zero-month forecast, 76% for one-month forecast, and 74% for two-month forecast). Moreover, more than one-third of forecasts were useless given the latest realization of CPI (50% for zero-month forecast, 36% for one-month forecast, 42% for two-month forecast, 38% for three-month forecast, 39% for four-month forecast, and 53% for five-month forecast).

Section 4 tested the rationality of the forecasts and found that almost all forecasts were irrational in the sense that their forecast error could have been reduced using the latest realization of CPI. More concretely, the percentage of either biased or inefficient forecasts was 72% for zero-month forecast, 67% for one-month forecast, 90% for two-month forecast, 87% for three-month forecast, 88% for four-month forecast, and 47% for five-month forecast. The percentage of forecasts which failed in the unbiasedness test, the efficiency test, or the martingale test was 72% for zero-month forecast, 82% for one-month forecast, 94% for two/three/four-month forecast, and 50% for five-month forecast.

Section 5 evaluated the accuracy and rationality of the consensus forecast. The consensus forecast was inferior to the "same-as-the-last-month" forecast for zero-month forecast.

To sum up, almost all forecasters are found to be inaccurate and irrational. This result is contrary to the result obtained in the analysis of the Japanese GDP forecasters. However, this conclusion relies on the crucial assumption that forecasters aim to minimize expected squared forecast errors. There are various reasons for rational forecasters to announce forecasts different from the conditional expected value. Ashiya (2009) finds that the Japanese GDP forecasters in industries that emphasize publicity tend to make less accurate but more extreme forecasts in order to gain publicity for their firms. Whether this "publicity effect" can explain the results of this paper is an important topic for future research.

References

Abarbanell, J.S., and Bernard, V.L. (1992) "Tests of Analysts' Overreaction/Underreaction to Earnings Information as an Explanation for Anomalous Stock Price Behavior." *Journal of Finance,* **47**, 1181-1207.

Amir, E., and Ganzach, Y. (1998) "Overreaction and Underreaction in Analysts' Forecasts." *Journal of Economic Behavior and Organization,* **37**, 333-347.

Artis, M.J. (1996) "How Accurate are the IMF's Short-term Forecasts? Another Examination of the World Economic Outlook." *International Monetary Fund Working Paper,* WP/96/89.

Ash, J.C.K., Easaw, J.Z., Heravi, S.M., and Smith, D.J. (2002) "Are Hodrick-Prescott 'Forecasts' Rational?" *Empirical Economics,* **27**, 631-643.

Ash, J.C.K., Smyth, D.J., and Heravi, S.M. (1990) "The Accuracy of OECD Forecasts of the International Economy." *International Journal of Forecasting,* **6**, 379-392.

Ash, J.C.K., Smyth, D.J., and Heravi, S.M. (1998) "Are OECD Forecasts Rational and Useful?: A Directional Analysis." *International Journal of Forecasting,* **14**, 381-391.

Ashiya, M. (2002) "Accuracy and Rationality of Japanese Institutional Forecasters." *Japan and the World Economy,* **14**, 203-213.

Ashiya, M. (2003) "Testing the Rationality of Japanese GDP Forecasts: The Sign of Forecast Revision Matters." *Journal of Economic Behavior and Organization,* **50**, 263-269.

Ashiya, M. (2005) "Twenty-two Years of Japanese Institutional Forecasts." *Applied Financial Economics Letters,* **1**, 79-84.

Ashiya, M. (2006a) "Testing the Rationality of Forecast Revisions Made by the IMF and the OECD." *Journal of Forecasting,* **25**, 25-36.

Ashiya, M. (2006b) "Forecast Accuracy and Product Differentiation of Japanese Institutional Forecasters." *International Journal of Forecasting,* **22**, 395-401.

Ashiya, M. (2007) "Forecast Accuracy of the Japanese Government: Its Year-Ahead GDP Forecast Is Too Optimistic." *Japan and the World Economy,* **19**, 68-85.

Ashiya, M. (2009) "Strategic Bias and Professional Affiliations of Macroeconomic Forecasters." *Journal of Forecasting,* **28**, 120-130.

Batchelor, R. (2001) "How Useful Are the Forecasts of Intergovernmental Agencies? The IMF and OECD versus the Consensus." *Applied Economics,* **33**, 225-235.

Batchelor, R., and Dua, P. (1991) "Blue Chip Rationality Tests." *Journal of Money, Credit, and Banking,* **23**, 692-705.

Berger, A.N., and Krane, S.D. (1985) "The Informational Efficiency of Econometric Model Forecasts." *Review of Economics and Statistics,* **67**, 667-674.

Brown, W.B., and Maital, S. (1981) "What Do Economists Know? An Empirical Study of Experts' Expectations." *Econometrica,* **49**, 491-504.

Chong, Y.Y., and Hendry, D.F. (1986) "Econometric Evaluation of Linear Macro- Economic Models." *Review of Economic Studies,* **53**, 671-690.

Clemen, R.T. (1989) "Combining Forecasts: A Review and Annotated Bibliography." *International Journal of Forecasting,* **5**, 559-583.

Clements, M.P. (1995) "Rationality and the Role of Judgement in Macroeconomic Forecasting." *Economic Journal,* **105**, 410-420.

Clements, M.P. (1997) "Evaluating the Rationality of Fixed-event Forecasts." *Journal of Forecasting,* **16**, 225-239.

Cooper, J.P., and Nelson, C.R. (1975) "The Ex Ante Prediction Performance of the St. Louis and FRB-MIT-PENN Econometric Models and Some Results on Composite Predictors." *Journal of Money, Credit, and Banking,* **7**, 1-32.

Diebold, F.X., and Mariano, R.S. (1995) "Comparing Predictive Accuracy." *Journal of Business and Economic Statistics,* **13**, 253-263.

Ehrbeck, T., and Waldmann, R. (1996) "Why Are Professional Forecasters Biased? Agency versus Behavioral Explanations." *Quarterly Journal of Economics,* **111**, 21-40.

Ericsson, N.R. (1992) "Parameter Constancy, Mean Square Forecast Errors, and Measuring Forecast Performance: An Exposition, Extensions, and Illustration." *Journal of Policy Modeling,* **14**, 465-495.

Fair, R.C., and Shiller, R.J. (1990) "Comparing Information in Forecasts from Econometric Models." *American Economic Review,* **80**, 375-389.

Fildes, R., and Stekler, H. (2002) "The State of Macroeconomic Forecasting." *Journal of Macroeconomics,* **24**, 435-468.

Harvey, D.I., Leybourne, S.J., and Newbold, P. (2001) "Analysis of a Panel of UK Macroeconomic Forecasts." *Econometrics Journal,* **4,** S37-S55.

Holden, K., and Peel, D.A. (1985) "An Evaluation of Quarterly National Institute Forecasts." *Journal of Forecasting,* **4**, 227-234.

Holden, K., and Peel, D.A. (1990) "On Testing for Unbiasedness and Efficiency of Forecasts." *The Manchester School,* **58**, 120-127.

Jansen, D.W., and Kishan, R.P. (1996) "An Evaluation of Federal Reserve Forecasting." *Journal of Macroeconomics,* **18**, 89-109.

Joutz, F., and Stekler, H.O. (2000) "An Evaluation of the Predictions of the Federal Reserve." *International Journal of Forecasting,* **16**, 17-38.

Kreinin, M.E. (2000) "Accuracy of OECD and IMF Projection." *Journal of Policy Modeling,* **22**, 61-79.

Loungani, P. (2001) "How Accurate Are Private Sector Forecasts? Cross-country Evidence from *Consensus Forecasts* of Output Growth." *International Journal of Forecasting,* **17**, 419-432.

Mizon, G. E., and Richard, J.F. (1986) "The Encompassing Principle and Its Application to Testing Non-Nested Hypotheses." *Econometrica,* **54**, 657-678.

Nordhaus, W.D. (1987) "Forecasting Efficiency: Concepts and Applications." *Review of Economics and Statistics*, **69**, 667-674.

Öller, L.E., and Barot, B. (2000) "The Accuracy of European Growth and Inflation Forecasts." *International Journal of Forecasting,* **16**, 293-315.

Pons, J. (1999) "Evaluating the OECD's Forecasts for Economic Growth." *Applied Economics,* **31**, 893-902.

Pons, J. (2000) "The Accuracy of IMF and OECD Forecasts for G7 Countries." *Journal of Forecasting,* **19**, 53-63.

Pons, J. (2001) "The Rationality of Price Forecasts: A Directional Analysis." *Applied Financial Economics,* **11**, 287-290.

Romer, C.D., and Romer, D.H. (2000) "Federal Reserve Information and the Behavior of Interest Rates." *American Economic Review,* **90**, 429-457.

Scotese, C.A. (1994) "Forecast Smoothing and the Optimal Under-Utilization of Information at the Federal Reserve." *Journal of Macroeconomics,* **16**, 653-670.

Zarnowitz, V. (1985) "Rational Expectations and Macroeconomic Forecasts." *Journal of Business and Economic Statistics,* **3**, 293-311.

In: Inflation: Causes and Effects
Editor: Leon V. Schwartz, pp. 59-84

ISBN: 978-1-60741-823-8

Chapter 3

THE NONPARAMETRIC TIME-DETRENDED FISHER EFFECT

Heather L.R. Tierney
Department of Economics and Finance, College of Charleston, Charleston SC, USA

Abstract

This paper uses frontier nonparametric VARs techniques to investigate whether the Fisher Effect holds in the U.S. The Fisher Effect is examined taking into account structural breaks and nonlinearities between nominal interest rates and inflation, which are trend-stationary in the two samples examined. The nonparametric time-detrended test for the Fisher Effect is formed from the cumulative orthogonal dynamic multiplier ratios of inflation to nominal interest rates. If the Fisher Effect holds, this ratio statistically approaches one as the horizon goes to infinity. The nonparametric techniques developed in this paper conclude that the Fisher Effect holds for both samples examined.

Keywords: Fisher Effect, nonparametrics, dynamic multipliers, monetary policy, trend-stationarity.

JEL Classification Code: E40, E52, E58

1. Introduction

The dynamics of nominal interest rates and inflation are fundamental forces at the core of economic and financial decisions. The Fisher Effect, which relates these two variables, has several consequences on market rationality and efficiency, option pricing, portfolio allocation, monetary policy, and international trade just to name a few illustrations.[1]

---

[1] The Fisher Effect is a theoretical proposition based on the Fisher Equation, which defines nominal interest rates as being equal to the ex ante real interest rate plus expected inflation. According to the Fisher Effect in the long run, the real interest rate is constant, which means that there should be a long run one-to-one relationship between inflation and nominal interest rates that is referred to as the Fisher Hypothesis.

Some economic and financial models implicitly assume constancy of the real interest rate (e.g. the capital asset pricing model, CAPM). Thus, the legitimacy of the decisions based on these models is tied to the assumption that the Fisher Effect holds. Monetary policy is also closely related to the Fisher Effect. For instance, if the Fisher Effect holds, short-term changes to nominal interest rates can be made to adjust for changes in inflation and unemployment without impacting the long-term real interest rate.

This paper investigates whether the Fisher Effect holds in the U.S. for two sample periods: for the first quarter of 1960 to the third quarter of 1995 and for the first quarter of 1960 to the second quarter of 2004. These long samples are necessary to investigate the long run relationship between nominal interest rates and inflation. The latter sample encompasses a period in which there is a substantial decrease in the volatility of nominal interest rates. This has allowed markets to have a more perceptible signal of likely future monetary policy action by the Federal Reserve, especially since 1995.

Frontier nonparametric techniques are used to investigate whether the Fisher Effect holds. In particular, the local linear least squares nonparametric method (LLLS) is applied to investigate the effect. This method is better equipped to deal with outliers, since each nonparametric estimator is locally estimated with more weight given to observations closer to the data point. This methodology is applied to study the dynamics of nominal interest rates and inflation in bivariate VARs, and the results are compared with the ones obtained from parametric techniques.

The advantage of using nonparametric over parametric VARs is that the nonparametric version yields cumulative dynamic multipliers obtained from nominal interest rates and inflation that capture the nonlinearities present in these series. The consideration of nonlinearities in the nonparametric VAR permits a more efficient use of information as evidenced by the smaller variance-covariance matix.

The related literature examining the time series properties of nominal interest rates and inflation do not present a consensus on whether or not the Fisher Effect holds. In addition, the literature is also divided into two broad groups: those who find a cointegration relationship between nominal interest and inflation and those who find that the series are not integrated.

There are several possible explanations for the divergence of these conclusions. The possible econometric reasons could be related to not taking into consideration the potential non-stationarity and/or nonlinearities in the individual series or breaks in the relationship between nominal interest rates and inflation. These statistical features may arise from changes in the structure of the economy, such as different monetary policy regimes over time, or breaks in the level of inflation and in inflation expectations amongst other things.

Along the lines of the cointegration examination of the Fisher Effect, Mishkin (1992) finds a cointegration relationship through the use of the Engle and Granger (1987) model, which indicates that the long run Fisher Effect exists. Wallace and Warner (1993) have some reservations that inflation is integrated of order one, I(1), but nonetheless proceed with the cointegration model as proposed by Johansen (1988) and Johansen and Juselius (1990). Upon establishing cointegration between the nominal interest rate and inflation, they conclude that the long run Fisher Effect holds. Crowder and Hoffman (1996) and Daniels, Nourzad, and Toutkoushian (1996) report similar findings for nominal interest rates and inflation. In particular, Crowder and Hoffman find that inflation is an I(1) moving average process, and Daniels et al. find that inflation is I(1), based on the Dickey and Pantula (1987) test for unit roots. These two papers report that inflation Granger-causes nominal interest rates, and since cointegration exists between the series, the conclusion is that the long run Fisher Effect holds. King and Watson (1997) use a bivariate model projecting the nominal interest rate onto inflation and vice-versa. The model produces an estimated coefficient less than one, which indicates that the long run Fisher Effect does not hold.

In regards to the non-cointegration literature, the seminal work of Fama (1975) examines the Fisher Effect with the purpose of determining market efficiency. Fama finds that the Fisher Effect does hold. Garcia and Perron (1996) study the constancy of the ex ante real interest rate under the assumption of rational expectations in order to investigate the Fisher Effect. Non-stationarity is accounted for by allowing changes in the mean and variance through the use of Hamilton's (1989) Markov Switching model. The conclusion is that the Fisher Effect sporadically holds if infrequent breaks in the mean are permitted. Another non-cointegration technique to study the Fisher Effect is proposed by Malliaropulos (2000), which uses dynamic multipliers from a bivariate VAR with the assumption that inflation and nominal interest rates are trend-stationary once structural breaks and deterministic trends have been taken into account.

The main difficulty in determining the Fisher Effect in a cointegration framework is the low power of unit root and cointegration tests, which tend to erroneously fail to reject the null of non-stationarity too frequently. The power of these tests is further weaken if structural breaks are not taken into account or if the model is also misspecified due to erroneous number of lags lengths, etc.

In this paper, the Fisher Effect is further studied, taking into account possible misspecifications, the presence of potential structural breaks, and nonlinearities. The results of parametric and nonparametric techniques are compared, and the nonparametric time-detrended relationship between nominal interest rates and inflation is presented as an alternative tool to examine the 'traditional' Fisher Effect.

The key to investigating the Fisher Effect lies in the time series properties of nominal interest rates and inflation. This paper attempts to resolve the economic and econometric issues of testing for the Fisher Effect by first undertaking a careful investigation of the univariate properties of inflation and nominal interest rates. The findings are that these series present structural changes in the early 1980s. When these breaks are taken into account, nonstationarity tests indicate that they are trend-stationary.

In the second stage, the residuals from the detrending regressions of nominal interest rates and inflation are used to form a stationary, nonparametric, time-detrended VAR with either median or averaged coefficients. This framework allows for the investigation of nonlinearities in the relationship between nominal interest rates and inflation through the study of the dynamic multipliers of the impulse response functions. The nonparametric time-detrended test for the Fisher Effect is formed from the cumulative dynamic multiplier ratios of inflation to nominal interest rates inflation, under a shock to nominal interest rates. If this ratio statistically approaches one as the horizon goes to infinity, this signifies that, even with the removal of the time component, the changes in nominal interest rate are being matched by the changes in inflation in the long run, and hence, the Fisher Effect holds.

Two variations of the relationship between nominal interest rates and inflation are investigated in this paper: a nonparametric time-detrended Fisher effect using standardized data for the first sample period, and a nonparametric time-detrended Fisher effect using level data for the second sample period. Both techniques conclude that the Fisher effect holds. In particular, using a median, nonparametric, time-detrended VAR(3), the nonparametric time-detrended Fisher Effect statistically holds at approximately the twelfth quarter for the first sample period (1960:Q1-1995:Q3) using standardized detrended nominal interest rates and inflation. Using level detrended inflation and nominal interest rates in a nonparametric VAR(4) with averaged coefficients for the second period (1960:Q1-2004:Q2), the nonparametric time-detrended Fisher Effect is statistically achieved at approximately the fifteenth quarter.

The recent widespread use of inflation targeting rules by different countries has spurred some debate as to whether the Federal Reserve should follow a monetary policy rule or discretionary monetary policy. The question of the validity of the Fisher Effect can be applied to assess inflation targeting rules. For example, a proposed rule would be to implement tight or loose monetary policy depending on whether inflation is above or below the long run equilibrium given by the Fisher Effect. That is, the monetary policy rule could be implemented based on investigating whether or not the movements in inflation exceed the movements in nominal interest rates in the long run – changes in policy would be warranted in order to maintain the long run equilibrium between these series, as reflected in the Fisher Effect. The findings that the Fisher Effect holds, especially for the more recent period, suggest that current monetary policy can be implemented based on minor discrete changes vis-à-vis discrete changes in nominal interest rates in order to maintain the long run equilibrium between nominal interest rates and inflation.

The structure of this paper is as follows: Section 2 investigates the univariate dynamic properties of inflation and nominal interest rates. Section 3 presents the parametric and nonparametric techniques and the VAR models used to test for the Fisher Effect. The empirical results are presented in Section 4, and Section 5 concludes.

2. Univariate Analysis – Modeling Inflation and Nominal Interest Rates

A first important step before composing the VAR(p) models is to study the individual dynamics of each time series to be used in the system. This section investigates univariate model specifications of inflation and nominal interest rates, including nonstationarity tests in the presence of structural breaks.

The data are analyzed in annualized quarterly frequency. The three-month Treasury bill rate is used as the nominal interest rate, whereas the log of the first difference of the seasonally adjusted Consumer Price Index (CPI) is used as a measure of inflation.[2] The analysis is carried out for two sample periods: from the second quarter of 1960 to the third quarter of 1995 (142 observations), and from the second quarter of 1960 to the second quarter of 2004 (177 observations).[3]

Each series, inflation and nominal interest rates, is first tested in order to identify potential time intervals containing structural breaks. The recursive residuals test, CUSUM test, CUSUMQ test, and the recursive coefficients test are applied to an AR(1) model of the

[2] The data are obtained from the St. Louis F.R.E.D. For CPI (CPIAUCSL) and the 3-month T-Bill rates (TB3MS), monthly data are converted to quarterly data.

[3] The first quarter of 1960 is lost due to the construct of inflation.

series.[4] Once an interval containing a potential structural break is identified by at least one of the previously mentioned tests, the log likelihood ratio of the Chow breakpoint test and the Chow forecast test is then applied to specific times within the indicated periods. Based upon agreement of the two Chow tests for both sample periods, a structural break is found in 1981:Q3 for inflation and in 1980:Q2 for nominal interest rates.

The optimal univariate model for each time series is chosen taking into consideration the parsimony of lag length using the Akaike Information Criteria (AIC) and the Schwartz's Bayesian Criteria (SBC) and the statistical significance of each regressor as well as the whiteness of the residuals.

The Augmented Dickey-Fuller (ADF) test is used to test for stationarity of inflation and nominal interest rates. The test indicates that inflation and nominal interest rates do not have unit roots for the first sample period (1960:Q2-1995:Q3); it fails to reject the hypothesis of nonstationarity in these series for the second sample period (1960:Q2 and 2004:Q2). A summary of the results is reported in Tables 1A and 1B.

The conflicting results in the unit root tests across samples point to a possible model misspecification, which could lead the ADF test to erroneously fail to reject the null of nonstationarity. Hence, the dynamics of the series are further investigated by including an appropriate deterministic trend. Based on the findings of breakpoints in these series, Perron's test (1989) for nonstationarity against the alternative of a deterministic trend in the presence of sudden structural changes is used in the next step.

Table 1A. INFLATION (π_t)—Results of the ADF Test

Sample Period	*Model*	**Estimated Coefficient of ϕ**	***Estimated* t-statistic of $\hat{\phi}$**	**ADF Critical Value**	**Result Unit Root Process (Yes or No)**
1960:Q2 - 1995:Q3	Intercept Only (3 lags $\Delta\pi_t$) Removing $\Delta\pi_{t-1}$	-0.137	-3.2733	-2.882	No
1960:Q2 - 2004:Q2	Intercept Only (3 lags $\Delta\pi_t$)	-0.111	-2.758	-2.878	Yes
1960:Q2 - 1979:Q1	Trend & Intercept; Eliminating $\Delta\pi_{t-1}$ and $\Delta\pi_{t-2}$, (4 lags $\Delta\pi_t$)	-0.338	*-4.117*	-3.473	No
1984:Q4 - 1995:Q3	Intercept Only (0 lags $\Delta\pi_t$)	-0.596	*-4.167*	-2.929	No
1984:Q4 - 2004:Q2	Intercept Only (0 lags $\Delta\pi_t$)	-0.538	*-5.277*	-2.898	No

[4] All hypotheses are tested at the 5% significance level.

Table 1B. NOMINAL INTEREST RATES (i_t)—Results of the ADF Test

Sample Period	*Model*	Estimated Coefficient of ϕ	*Estimated* t-statistic of $\hat{\phi}$	ADF Critical Value	Result Unit Root Process (Yes or No)
1960:Q2 - 1995:Q3	Intercept Only (5 lags Δi_t) Removing Δi_{t-4}	-0.083	-3.241	-2.882	No
1960:Q2 - 2004:Q2	Intercept Only (5 lags Δi_t) Removing Δi_{t-4}	-0.111	-2.815	-2.878	Yes
1960:Q2 - 1979:Q1	Trend & Intercept (3 lags Δi_t) Removing Δi_{t-2}	-0.237	-3.952	-3.471	No
1984:Q4 - 1995:Q3	Trend & Intercept (6 lags Δi_t) Removing Δi_{t-2}, Δi_{t-3}, Δi_{t-4}, Δi_{t-5}	-0.227	-4.746	-3.514	No
1984:Q4 - 2004:Q2	Trend & Intercept (6 lags Δi_t) Removing Δi_{t-2}, Δi_{t-3}, Δi_{t-4}, Δi_{t-5}	-0.159	-4.691	-3.467	No

The inclusion of a time trend is just as important in Perron's test since otherwise it could also mistakenly lead to failing to reject the null of nonstationarity. The test is estimated under the alternate hypothesis of trend stationarity in the residuals of the detrended series. For this reason, three specific types of deterministic time trends are considered as alternate hypotheses: Model A – taking into account a break in the mean (intercept); Model B – taking into account a break in the drift (slope); and Model C – taking into account a break in the mean and in the drift. Model C, which encompasses Models A and B, is:

$$x_t = a_0 + a_2 t + \mu_2 D_L + \mu_3 D_T + x_t^a \qquad (1)$$

where x_t is either nominal interest rates or inflation, t refers to the time trend, and x_t^a are the residuals of the detrended series. D_L is a dummy variable that takes a value of *0* for $t < T_B$ and a value of *1* for $t \geq T_B$, where T_B is the time of the structural break. D_T is the dummy variable, which is D_L multiplied by the time trend that takes on a value of *0* for $t < T_B$, and a value of the time trend, t, for any $t \geq T_B$.[5]

The results of Perron's test are reported in Tables 2A and 2B. The test selects Model C as the best specification for both series and for both sample periods. This result is illustrated in

[5] A more complete report of the results for Perron's test can be found in Tables 2A and 2B.

Graphs 1A and 1B. Since the residuals of the detrended regressions of inflation and nominal interest rates, x_t^a, are found to be trend stationary, these detrended residuals – which take into account the structural breaks found in the individual series – will be used in the VAR in the next section.

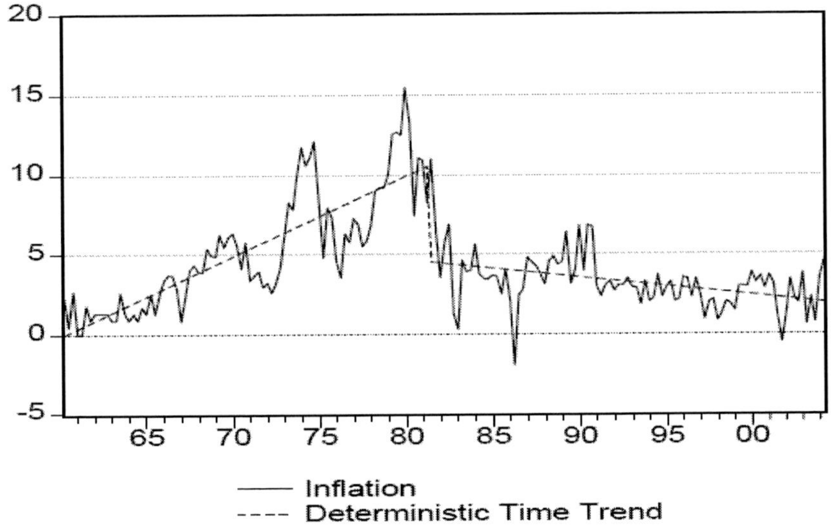

Graph 1A. Inflation; 1960:Q2 to 2004:Q2.

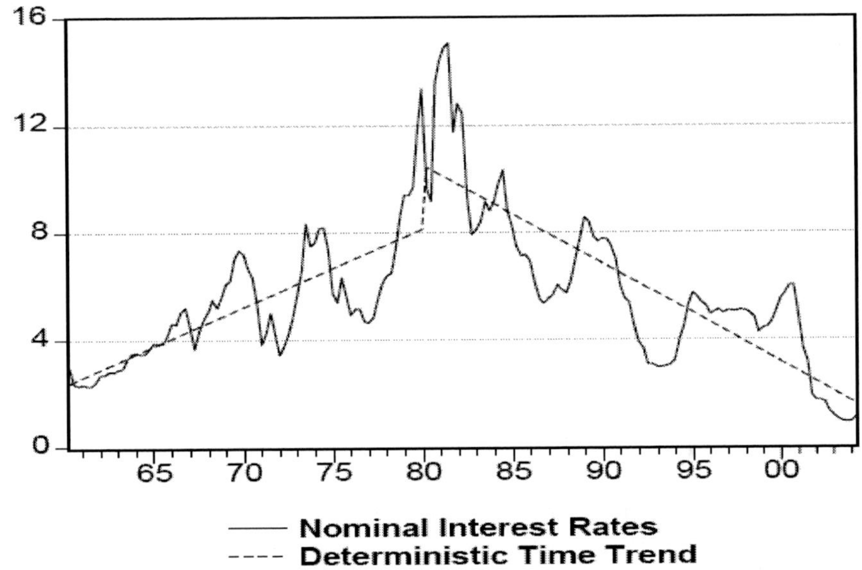

Graph 1B. Nominal Interest Rates; 1960:Q2 to 2004:Q2.

Table 2A. DETRENDED INFLATION (π_t^a)

Results of the Perron Test for Structural Change

Sample Period	Time Series	Model	Break Fraction[1] λ	Estimated Coefficient of a_1	Estimated t-statistic of $\hat{a}_1$	Perron Critical Value	Result: Unit Root (Yes or No)
1960:Q2 to 1995:Q3	π_t^a	Model A; Eliminating $\Delta\pi_{t-1}^a$ (3 lags $\Delta\pi_t^a$)	0.60	0.715	-4.775	-3.76	No
1960:Q2 to 1995:Q3	π_t^a	Model B; Eliminating $\Delta\pi_{t-1}^a$, & $\Delta\pi_{t-2}^a$ (3 lags $\Delta\pi_t^a$)	0.60	0.572	-6.381	-3.95	No
1960:Q2 to 1995:Q3	π_t^a	Model C; Eliminating $\Delta\pi_{t-1}^a$, & $\Delta\pi_{t-2}^a$ (3 lags $\Delta\pi_t^a$)	0.60	0.550	-6.622	-4.24	No
1960:Q2 to 2004:Q2	π_t^a	Model A (3 lags $\Delta\pi_t^a$)	0.50	0.853	-3.015	-3.76	Yes

[1] The break fraction, λ, is rounded off to the tenths since only these critical values are provided in Perron (1989). For the sample period of 1960:Q2 to 1995:Q3 for inflation, λ = 85/142 =0.598, and for nominal interest rates, λ = 80/142 =0.563. For the sample period of 1960:Q2 to 1995:Q3 for inflation, λ = 85/177 =0.480, and for nominal interest rates, λ = 80/177 =0.452.

Table 2A. Continued

Sample Period	Time Series	Model	Break Fraction[2] λ	Estimated Coefficient of a_1	Estimated t-statistic of $\hat{a}_1$	Perron Critical Value	Result: Unit Root (Yes or No)
1960:Q2 to 2004:Q2	π_t^a	Model B; Eliminating $\Delta\pi_{t-1}^a$, & $\Delta\pi_{t-2}^a$ (3 lags $\Delta\pi_t^a$)	0.50	0.609	-6.755	-3.96	No
1960:Q2 to 2004:Q2	π_t^a	Model C Eliminating $\Delta\pi_{t-1}^a, \Delta\pi_{t-2}^a$ (3 lags $\Delta\pi_t^a$)	0.50	0.529	-7.525	-4.24	No

Table 2B. Detrended Nominal Interest Rates (i_t^a)

Results of the Perron Test for Structural Change

Sample Period	Time Series	Model	Break Fraction λ	Estimated Coefficient of a_1	Estimated t-statistic of $\hat{a}_1$	Perron Critical Value	Result: Unit Root (Yes or No)
1960:Q2 to 1995:Q3	i_t^a	Model A; Eliminating Δi_{t-4}^a (5 lags Δi_t^a)	0.50	0.908	-3.090	-3.76	Yes

[2] The break fraction, λ, is rounded off to the tenths since only these critical values are provided in Perron (1989). For the sample period of 1960:Q2 to 1995:Q3 for inflation, λ = 85/142 =0.598, and for nominal interest rates, λ = 80/142 =0.563. For the sample period of 1960:Q2 to 1995:Q3 for inflation, λ = 85/177 =0.480, and for nominal interest rates, λ = 80/177 =0.452.

Table 2B. Continued

Sample Period	Time Series	Model	Break Fraction λ	Estimated Coefficient of a_1	Estimated t-statistic of $\hat{a}_1$	Perron Critical Value	Result: Unit Root (Yes or No)
1960:Q2 to 1995:Q3	i_t^a	Model B; Eliminating Δi_{t-4}^a (5 lags Δi_t^a)	0.50	0.906	-3.487	-3.95	Yes
1960:Q2 to 1995:Q3	i_t^a	Model C; Eliminating Δi_{t-4}^a (5 lags Δi_t^a)	0.50	0.691	-5.005	-4.24	No
1960:Q2 to 2004:Q2	i_t^a	Model A; Eliminating Δi_{t-4}^a 5 lags Δi_t^a)	0.50	0.917	-2.987	-3.76	Yes
1960:Q2 to 2004:Q2	i_t^a	Model B; Eliminating Δi_{t-4}^a , Δi_{t-5}^a , & Δi_{t-6}^a (7 lags Δi_t^a)	0.50	0.953	-2.139	-3.96	Yes
1960:Q2 to 2004:Q2	i_t^a	Model C Eliminating Δi_{t-4}^a (5 lags Δi_t^a)	0.50	0.775	-5.237	-4.24	No

3. Parametric and Nonparametric VAR Models

The methodology followed in this paper to test for the Fisher Effect consists of first determining the best model specification for the univariate series. Since trend stationarity has been determined for both series, the next step is to set up a bivariate VAR of inflation and nominal interest rates. The residuals from the detrending regression, x_t^a, which include a break in the mean and in the drift as specified in Equation (1), are used in the VAR, and the analysis of the Fisher Effect is carried out using parametric and nonparametric techniques.

The cumulative sums of the orthogonalized dynamic multipliers are used to study the long run behavior of the VAR. These sums capture the long run effect of a shock to a variable in the system. The time-detrended Fisher Effect can be investigated using the ratio of the sum of the orthogonalized dynamic multipliers of the responses of inflation to the sum of the responses of nominal interest rates due to a shock in nominal interest rates. If this ratio converges to unity, the Fisher Effect holds, which indicates that the changes in detrended nominal interest rates and detrended inflation are in synchronization in the long run. This section presents the theoretical VAR models used to examine the Fisher Effect.

3.1. The Parametric Model

The Fisher Effect essentially relates the long run movement of nominal interest rates and inflation. A linear, stationary, bivariate VAR(p) framework can be used to study the interaction between the variables in the system, without the complications that arise from estimating and testing a non-stationary system.

The impulse response functions use the history of the system in order to capture the average behavior of a variable to an isolated shock in the system. Orthogonalizing the impulse response functions results in dynamic multipliers that are not history or shock-dependent when the size of the shock is standardized to one standard deviation.

Hence, a one-standard-deviation shock has no direct impact on the dynamic multipliers. Furthermore, the orthogonalization of the impulse response functions removes the composition effect by not including the impact of the shock on the other variables in the VAR when the covariances are different from zero.

In forming the VAR(p) to be used to test the Fisher Effect, the lag p and the order of causality are determined based on statistical tests and economic theory. Inflation is found to follow nominal interest rates, based on the persistence of inflation and on the Granger causality test. This test finds that nominal interest rates uni-directionally causes inflation for both sample periods. The optimal lag length of the VAR(p) is determined using the AIC, SBC, and the stationarity of the VAR(p). The structural breaks of inflation and nominal interest rates are taken into account indirectly in the VAR(p) through the residuals of the detrending regressions obtained from Equation (1), which are stationary.

Concerning the variables in the system, the regressand matrix is denoted as $Y = \begin{pmatrix} y_1 & \cdots & y_t & \cdots & y_{t-1} & y_T \end{pmatrix}'$, which is an $((n \times T) \times 1)$ matrix, where $t = 1, \ldots, T$ with T equaling the total number of observations in the VAR. For *each* iteration of the VAR, the regressand is denoted as $y_t = \begin{pmatrix} y_{1t} & \cdots & y_{rt} & \cdots & y_{n-1t} & y_{nt} \end{pmatrix}'$ with n being the total number of equations in each iteration of the VAR, r representing the rth regressand of the VAR with $r = 1, \ldots r', \ldots, n$, and t referring to the tth observation where $t = 1, \ldots, T$. For this paper, y_{rt} represents the regressand, which is either detrended nominal interest rates $\left(i_t^a\right)$ or detrended inflation $\left(\pi_t^a\right)$. The set of regressors for each equation in the VAR is identical for each iteration of the VAR and is denoted as $X = \left(Z \quad X_1 \quad \cdots \; X_m \quad \cdots \quad X_{k-1} \quad X_k\right)$, which is of dimensions $\left(\left(n \times T\right) \times q\right)$ where $q = (k+1)$.[1] Z is a scalar column matrix with the dimensions of $\left(\left(n \times T\right) \times 1\right)$, and X_m is a column matrix with the dimensions of $\left(\left(n \times T\right) \times 1\right)$ with $m = 1, \ldots, k$.[2] In regards to the stability of the system, this can be verified by converting the VAR(p) to a VAR(1), which is weakly-stationary, if the modulus of each eigenvalue of the system is less than one, i.e., $\left|\lambda_j\right| < 1$.

The parametric VAR(p) model is represented by:

$$\Phi(L)\, y_t = \varepsilon_t \tag{2}$$

where y_t is a vector $y_t = \left(i_t^a \quad \pi_t^a\right)'$ containing the detrended series of nominal interest rates and inflation, $\Phi(L)$ is a $(n \times p)$ matrix of the pth order polynomials in the lag operator, and $\varepsilon_t = \left(\varepsilon_{it} \quad \varepsilon_{\pi t}\right)'$ is the residual vector which are $\varepsilon_t \sim N(0, \Sigma)$.

In order to test for the existence of the time-detrended Fisher Effect, the coefficients of the VAR(p) are used to form its MA(∞) representation, which are orthogonalized through the application of the Choleski decomposition. Specifically,

$$y_t = M(L) v_t \tag{3}$$

where $M(L) \equiv \Psi(L)P \equiv \Phi(L)^{-1}P$, P is the lower triangular Choleski matrix that satisfies $\Sigma = PP'$ and $v_t = (v_{\pi t} \; v_{it})' = P^{-1}\varepsilon_t$, with $E(v_t) = 0$, $Var(v_t) = I$. The orthogonalized MA(∞) coefficients are used to form the dynamic multiplier ratios, which will be discussed in more detail in Section 3.3. Concerning the implementation of the theoretical model, if the error terms, u_t, are uncorrelated with the set of regressors, then the VAR can be consistently estimated by n ordinary least squares (OLS) equations.

3.2. The Nonparametric Model

The nonparametric model uses an empirical kernel density, which is a weighted smoothing function. The nonparametric model presented in this paper is estimated using the local linear least squares nonparametric method (LLLS). LLLS is a kernel weighted least

[1] The set of regressors can either be lag operators of y_t or exogenous variables.
[2] When using standardized data, the scalar matrix is not included.

squares regression model, which locally fits a straight line conditionally on each data point, with more weight given to observations close to the conditioning data point and less weight to observations farther away.

As opposed to other nonparametric methodologies, such as using the Nadaraya-Watson estimator, the LLLS is better able to utilize the information in the tail regions. Hence, we have a more efficient use of information, particularly when compared to a linear parametric model. Since the nonparametric model does not specify a functional form of the model, the LLLS is capable of exploiting the non-linearity present in the model to produce large stationary coefficients, which are important in testing for the Fisher Effect. Another benefit of using LLLS is that the coefficients can be analyzed using standard regression methods such as ordinary least squares (OLS) by using the average or median coefficients.

As in the parametric VAR(*p*), the nonparametric VAR can be estimated equation-by-equation provided that there are no contemporaneous variables in the set of regressors, and the error terms of each equation are not correlated with the set of regressors.[3]

The implementation of the nonparametric VAR(*p*) requires an equation-by-equation methodology that begins with the kernel. For this paper, the Gaussian kernel, which has the Rosenblatt-Parzen properties of being a probabilistic, symmetrical, and bounded function, is used (Pagan and Ullah 1999). The Gaussian kernel measures the distance between the ith observation in each regressor to the jth conditioning element of each regressor where both $i = 1, \ldots, T$ and $j = 1, \ldots, T$. A weight is assigned to each distance measure with more weight being given to the ith observations closer to the jth conditioning element and progressively less weight to distance measures farther away. The form of the Gaussian kernel is as follows:

$$K = \sum_{i=1}^{T} K(\psi_{ij}), \tag{4}$$

where

$$K(\psi_{ij}) = \frac{1}{(2\pi)^{\frac{k}{2}}} exp\left(-\frac{1}{2}\left(\left(\frac{x_{1i} - x_{1j}}{h_1}\right)^2 + \cdots \left(\frac{x_{mi} - x_{mj}}{h_m}\right)^2 + \cdots + \left(\frac{x_{ki} - x_{kj}}{h_k}\right)^2\right)\right)$$

with

$$\psi_{ij} = \left(\frac{x_{1i} - x_{1j}}{h_1} \quad \cdots \quad \frac{x_{mi} - x_{mj}}{h_m} \quad \cdots \quad \frac{x_{ki} - x_{kj}}{h_k}\right).$$

In order to prevent over-smoothing, which results in a loss of information, or under-smoothing, which causes too much 'noise' in the empirical density, the window width, h_m, for $m = 1 \ldots, k$, is chosen based on a pre-asymptotic approach that relies only on the available data and not on the estimation of some unknown parameter. Based on Marron (1988) but adapting it to a VAR system, the window width that minimizes the residual sum of squares is chosen. Regarding this paper, each of the two equations of the VAR produces a slightly different window width, but the window width that produces the smaller residual sum of

[3] If this were not the case, the Seemingly Unrelated Regression (SUR) method would need to be used.

squares is chosen in order to keep the set of regressors identical.[4] Robustness of the window widths is also examined by using one and a half times the selected window width, which did not affect the findings.

In matrix notation, the $(q \times 1)$ vector of nonparametric coefficients for the rth regressand and t^{th} iteration of the VAR(p) is denoted as

$$\beta_{rt} = \left(X'KX\right)^{-1} X'Ky_{rt} \tag{5}$$

Using Equation (5) to calculate all T iterations for each rth regressand, the compilation of the transpose of the VAR(p) coefficients results in a $(T \times q)$ matrix of nonparametric coefficients.

Once the nonparametric coefficients for the rth regressand is obtained, the VAR(p) can be re-written as a linear combination of the coefficients and regressors since the LLLS nonparametric method fits a line within the window width:

$$y_{rt} = X\beta_{rt} + \omega_{rt}, \tag{6}$$

where the regressand y_{rt} and the residual ω_{rt} are scalars, with $\omega_{rt} \sim \left(0, \sigma_{rt}^2\right)$.

The median or average of each column is used to form the aggregated nonparametric version of vector $\Phi(L)$, an $(n \times p)$ matrix of the pth order polynomials in the lag operator. The aggregate nonparametric coefficients could consist of either the mean or median measures. The nonparametric orthogonalized MA(∞) representation of the VAR(p), which is best described by Equation (3), is used to form the dynamic multipliers used to test for the Fisher Effect. This is presented in the next section.

3.3. Testing for the Fisher Effect

The time-detrended Fisher Effect holds statistically if the cumulative orthogonalized dynamic multiplier ratios converge to one as g – the lag length of the impulse response function – goes to infinity. The orthogonalized MA(∞) coefficients are used to form the nonparametric conditional orthogonalized impulse response functions. For instance, the form of the orthogonalized dynamic multiplier of the $(t+s)$ response of the $(r')^{th}$ regressand caused by a shock to the rth regressand at time t is:

$$\frac{d\left(y_{r't+s}\right)}{dw\left(x_t\right)_r} = M_{r'r}. \tag{7}$$

[4] The VAR has also been estimated using different window widths for each equation of the VAR, but the results did not statistically differ.

The gth cumulative dynamic multiplier ratio is referred to as Γ_g, where Γ_g is the sum of the responses of detrended inflation caused by a shock to detrended nominal interest rates $(M_{\pi i})$ to the sum of the responses of detrended nominal interest rates caused by a shock to detrended nominal interest rates (M_{ii}). Specifically for this paper, for each sample period, the gth ratio of nonparametric orthogonalized cumulative dynamic multipliers, which is denoted as Γ_g, is of the general form of:

$$\Gamma_g = \frac{\sum_{s=0}^{g} M_{\pi i,s}}{\sum_{s=0}^{g} M_{ii,s}}, \tag{8}$$

where $g = 1, 2, \ldots, \infty$.

For both the parametric and nonparametric models, up to one hundred lag lengths of the impulse response functions are calculated in order to determine whether the dynamic multiplier ratios converge to unity. This is needed since potential non-stationarity can mistakenly indicate an early appearance of the Fisher Effect in the medium run, which may break down in the very long run. The convergence to unity signifies that the changes in detrended nominal interest rate are being matched by the changes in detrended inflation, which indicates that the Fisher Effect holds.

Three different methodologies to compute the orthogonal dynamic multipliers are presented in order to test for the Fisher Effect. One is based on the parametric VAR and the orthogonal dynamic multiplier ratios described in Equation (8). The other two methods are based on the nonparametric VAR. Methods 2 and 3 can be computed using the median nonparametric and the average nonparametric coefficients. The three techniques are as follows:

METHOD 1: The parametric VAR of detrended nominal interest rates and inflation is estimated equation-by-equation, in order to obtain the sum of the orthogonalized dynamic multipliers of the responses of inflation divided by the responses of nominal interest rates to a shock in nominal interest rates.

METHOD 2: The orthogonal dynamic multiplier ratios of the Fisher Effect are obtained from the local nonparametric estimation of the VAR using the median of the T estimated coefficients for each regressor as a measure of central tendency. The median coefficients are used to form the MA(∞) coefficients, which are then used to form the dynamic multipliers. The error terms from the T local nonparametric equations of the VAR are used to obtain the (2×2) unconditional variance-covariance matrix of the error terms. The Choleski decomposition can then be calculated in order to form the orthogonalized impulse responses – the orthogonal dynamic multipliers.

METHOD 3: The orthogonal dynamic multiplier ratios of the Fisher Effect are obtained from the nonparametric estimation of the VAR. The median of T estimated coefficients for each regressor is obtained. The median nonparametric coefficients are used to form the

MA(∞) coefficients that comprises the dynamic multiplier ratios of the Fisher Effect. As indicated by Equation (9), the error terms of each equation in the VAR are then obtained from the regression:

$$\varepsilon_{np} = Y - X\beta_{np\_med}, \tag{9}$$

which is then used to obtain the (2×2) variance-covariance matrix of the error terms. Once the variance-covariance matrix of the error terms is obtained, the Choleski decomposition can then be calculated to form orthogonal dynamic multipliers.[5]

The average, orthogonal, nonparametric dynamic multiplier ratios of the time-detrended Fisher Effect are obtained by replacing the median nonparametric coefficients in the formation of the MA(∞) version of the VAR(p) with the average nonparametric coefficients. If the orthogonal dynamic multiplier ratios of the Fisher Effect converge to unity and are within the 95% bootstrapped confidence band, the Fisher Effect statistically holds. For each test of the Fisher Effect, the bootstrapped confidence band is constructed from the empirical density based on five thousand iterations of re-sampling with replacement. For each run, the VAR is estimated, and the test for the Fisher Effect is formed using the bootstrapped data with the average used to construct the confidence band.

By definition, the Fisher Effect means that the real interest rate is constant in the long run and is not impacted by either the short-term movements of nominal interest rates or inflation. Hence, if the Fisher Effect holds, the convergent movement of nominal interest rates should match the convergent movement of inflation. Intuitively, where δ is some constant, that is:

$$r_{t+s} = i_{t+s} - \pi_{t+s} = \delta \tag{10}$$

$$\frac{d\sum_{s=0}^{g} \pi^{a}_{t+s}}{dw_{it}} = \frac{d\sum_{s=0}^{g} i^{a}_{t+s}}{dw_{it}} \tag{11}$$

$$\left(\frac{d\sum_{s=0}^{g} \pi^{a}_{t+s}}{dw_{it}} \right) \Bigg/ \left(\frac{d\sum_{s=0}^{g} i^{a}_{t+s}}{dw_{it}} \right) = 1. \tag{12}$$

For monetary policy purposes, examining Equation (12) can be an informative tool for inflation-targeting regimes, since an inequality indicates that inflation and nominal interest rates are in disequilibria. If the orthogonal dynamic multiplier ratios are greater than unity, the

[5] In most instances, the cumulative multiplier ratio of Equation (8) converges to approximately the same level regardless of whether Method 2 or Method 3 as is shown in Tables 6A and 6B.

cumulative responses of inflation are greater than the cumulative responses of nominal interest rates, which would act as a signal to the monetary authorities that anti-inflationary measures in the form of tight monetary policies might be needed. This is particularly the case if the ratio exceeds unity by a preset amount. Alternatively, if the orthogonal dynamic multiplier ratios are less than unity, then the monetary authorities might consider implementing loose monetary policies that could bring inflation and nominal interest rates back into synchronization, given that the Fisher Effect holds in the long run.

4. Empirical Results

4.1. First Sample Period

The first sample period is from the second quarter of 1960 to the third quarter of 1995. In order to show the advantages of the nonparametric model, the parametric model is used as a benchmark. The data used in the estimated parametric and nonparametric VAR(p) models are the standardized detrended residuals of nominal interest rates and inflation generated from the estimation of Equation (1).

In choosing the lag length of the VAR(p), the estimated parametric VAR(3) has a higher AIC but a lower SBC, when compared to the parametric VAR(4). Due to the conflicting results of the AIC and SBC, various lag lengths of the VAR(p) were tested in an attempt to obtain a more parsimonious model. As is shown in Tables 6A and 6B, the optimal estimated model is selected based upon the stationarity of the VAR, as indicated by the moduli of the eigenvalues (whether they are less than unity). Even though the detrended series of inflation and nominal interest rates are stationary, the VAR(p) is not necessarily stationary as indicated by the moduli of the eigenvalues of the VAR. This is due to the dynamic interaction of the two series in the VAR(p).

Concerning the estimation of the nonparametric models, the choice of window width is critical since too large of a window width over-smoothes the data, which decreases the variance and increases the bias of the estimated coefficients. If the window width is too small, the variance increases and the bias of the estimated coefficients decreases (Pagan and Ullah 1999). For this paper, the optimal window width is chosen by minimizing the residual sum of squares as calculated by Method 2. The optimal window width for the VAR(3) with median nonparametric coefficients is 0.40 while the optimal window width for the VAR(4) with median nonparametric coefficients is 0.48.

The nonparametric VAR(3) and VAR(4) models, which are able to produce the dynamic multiplier ratios of the Fisher Effect, have the characteristics that the sum of the AR coefficients and the modulus of the eigenvalue of each variable of the system are not very close to unity (i.e., not equal to 0.99 or exceed unity). As shown in Table 3A, the majority of the estimated nonparametric coefficients is larger than their parametric counterparts, and the non-linearity can be seen in Graph 2A.[6] The moduli of the eigenvalues are, on average, larger than their analogous parametric versions (Table 4A).

[6] The intent of Graphs 2A and 2B are to demonstrate the non-linearity present in both sample periods. Hence for demonstration purposes, four nonparametric coefficients greater than |9| were removed in order to make the scaling of the graphs more homogeneous in Graphs 2A and 2B.

As illustrated in Graph 3A, the Fisher Effect holds in the case of the nonparametric VAR models, since they are able to exploit the non-linearity in the system, which produces larger estimated coefficients while maintaining stationarity (i.e., they do not exceed unity).

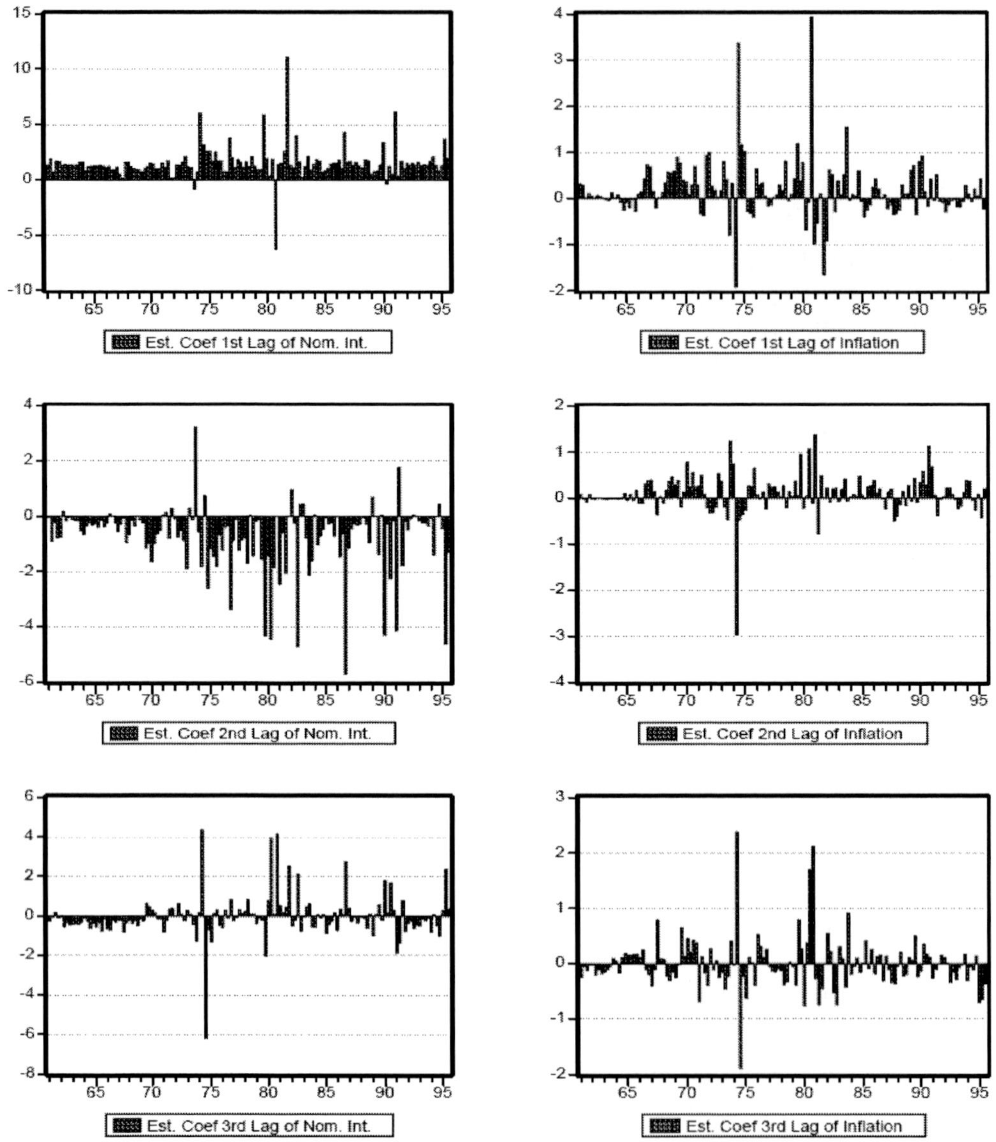

Graph 2A. Graphs of Estimated Nonparametric Coefficients with Detrended Inflation as the Regressand Sample Period: 1960:Q2 to 1995:Q3.

In the nonparametric case, using both Methods 2 and 3, the VAR(3) model statistically produces the Fisher Effect when using standardized data with median nonparametric coefficients while the counterpart parametric model is unable to produce the Fisher Effect.[7]

[7] For the first sample period, using Methods 2 and 3 and a nonparametric VAR(4) using standardized data with either mean or median nonparametric coefficients, the test for the Fisher Effect converges to 1.05. Regarding

Table 3A. Sample Period—1960:Q2 to 1995:Q3 Parametric and Median Nonparametric Estimated Coefficients of a VAR(3)[8]

Estimated Coefficients	Parametric Method 1		Nonparametric Method 2		Nonparametric Method 3	
	EQ 1 of VAR	EQ 2 of VAR	EQ 1 of VAR	EQ 2 of VAR	EQ 1 of VAR	EQ 2 of VAR
i^a_{t-1}	1.1377 (0.0847)	0.6940 (0.1123)	1.3139 (0.0029)	0.7644 (0.0034)	1.3139 (0.0067)	0.7644 (0.0101)
i^a_{t-2}	-0.6132 (0.1196)	-0.4627 (0.1587)	-0.3561 (0.0057)	-0.3146 (0.0069)	-0.3561 (0.0133)	-0.3146 (0.0202)
i^a_{t-3}	0.2834 (0.0951)	0.0785 (0.1262)	-0.1661 (0.0036)	-0.0625 (0.0043)	-0.1661 (0.0084)	-0.0625 (0.0127)
π^a_{t-1}	-0.0956 (0.0651)	0.2972 (0.0864)	0.0796 (0.0017)	0.3209 (0.0020)	0.0796 (0.0039)	0.3209 (0.0060)
π^a_{t-2}	0.2609 (0.0675)	0.0085 (0.0896)	0.07523 (0.0018)	0.0558 (0.0022)	0.07523 (0.0042)	0.0558 (0.0064)
π^a_{t-3}	-0.1617 (0.0657)	0.1494 (0.0871)	-0.0505 (0.0017)	0.1779 (0.0021)	-0.0505 (0.0040)	0.1779 (0.0061)

Table 3B. Sample Period—1960:Q2 to 2004:Q3 Parametric and Median Nonparametric, Estimated Coefficients of a VAR(4)

Estimated Coefficients	Parametric Method 1		Nonparametric Method 2		Nonparametric Method 3	
	EQ 1 of VAR	EQ 2 of VAR	EQ 1 of VAR	EQ 2 of VAR	EQ 1 of VAR	EQ 2 of VAR
i^a_{t-1}	1.2377 (0.0771)	0.8517 (0.1357)	1.3051 (0.0108)	0.8192 (0.0014)	1.3051 (0.0043)	0.8192 (0.0108)
i^a_{t-2}	-0.6849 (0.1179)	-0.7110 (0.2073)	-0.4290 (0.0252)	-0.5161 (0.0033)	-0.4290 (0.0101)	-0.5161 (0.0251)
i^a_{t-3}	0.5050 (0.1201)	0.4318 (0.2113)	0.2711 (0.0262)	0.1981 (0.0035)	0.2711 (0.0105)	0.1981 (0.0261)
i^a_{t-4}	-0.1990 (0.0838)	-0.4247 (0.1474)	-0.1605 (0.0127)	-0.0895 (0.0017)	-0.1605 (0.0051)	-0.0895 (0.0127)
π^a_{t-1}	-0.0701 (0.0429)	0.3814 (0.0754)	0.1179 (0.0033)	0.4008 (0.0004)	0.1179 (0.0013)	0.4008 (0.0033)
π^a_{t-2}	0.1461 (0.0446)	-0.0554 (0.0784)	0.0199 (0.0036)	-0.0661 (0.0005)	0.0199 (0.0015)	-0.0661 (0.0036)
π^a_{t-3}	-0.0994 (0.0455)	0.2864 (0.0801)	-0.0446 (0.0038)	0.3062 (0.0005)	-0.0446 (0.0015)	0.3062 (0.0037)
π^a_{t-4}	-0.0169 (0.0437)	-0.1041 (0.0770)	-0.1047 (0.0035)	-0.0902 (0.0005)	-0.1047 (0.0014)	-0.0902 (0.0035)

the parametric counterpart model, the test for the Fisher Effect converges 0.57. Hence the Fisher Effect is statistically achieved in the nonparametric VAR(4) models and not in the parametric VAR(4) model.

[8] For both sample periods, the nonparametric estimated coefficients of the VAR(p) using Method 2 and Method 3 are the same, but the methods of obtaining the estimated standard deviations are different and are discussed in Section 3.3.

Table 4A. Sample Period—1960:Q2 to 1995:Q3

Eigenvalues of Parametric VAR(4)	Modulus	Eigenvalues of Median Nonparametric VAR(3)	Modulus
-0.1974+0.6373i	0.6671	-0.2331+0.4848i	0.5379
-0.1974-0.6373i	0.6671	-0.2331-0.4848i	0.5379
0.1727+0.4422i	0.4747	0.7583+0.2575i	0.6237
0.1727-0.4422i	0.4747	0.7583-0.2575i	0.6237
0.7925	0.7925	0.8038	0.8038
0.6918	0.6918	-0.2193	0.2193

Table 4B. Sample Period—1960:Q2 to 2004:Q2

Eigenvalues of Parametric VAR(4)	Modulus	Eigenvalues of Median Nonparametric VAR(4)	Modulus
-0.3428+0.6761i	0.7580	-0.2820+0.6519i	0.7103
-0.3428-0.6761i	0.7580	-0.2820-0.6519i	0.7103
-0.0330+0.6432i	0.6440	-0.1363+0.4234i	0.4448
-0.0330-0.6432i	0.6440	-0.1363-0.4234i	0.4448
0.7117+0.2555i	0.7562	0.9393+0.0727i	0.9421
0.7117-0.2555i	0.7562	0.9393-0.0727i	0.9421
0.8275	0.8275	0.5609	0.5609
0.1199	0.1199	0.1029	0.1029

Table 5A. Sample Period—1960:Q2 to 1995:Q3

	Parametric Method 1		Nonparametric Method 2		Nonparametric Method 3	
Variance-Covariance	02992	0.1007	0.5554	-0.0701	0.4785	0.1507
Matrix	0.1007	0.5263	-0.0701	0.8448	0.1507	0.5731
Choleski Decomposition	0.5468	0.0000	0.7452	0.0000	0.6917	0.0000
Matrix	0.1841	0.7017	-0.0941	0.9143	0.2179	0.7250

Table 5B. Sample Period—1960:Q2 to 2004:Q2

	Parametric Method 1		Nonparametric Method 2		Nonparametric Method 3	
Variance-Covariance	0.5482	0.1613	1.9859	0.0054	0.8007	0.2416
Matrix	0.1613	1.6956	0.0054	0.2621	0.2416	1.9826
Choleski Decomposition	0.7405	0.0000	1.4092	0.0000	0.8948	0.0000
Matrix	0.2177	1.2838	0.0038	0.5119	0.2700	1.3819

As shown in Table 6A, the dynamic multiplier ratios of the nonparametric VAR(3), using standardized data and median nonparametric coefficients, statistically converge to 0.97 at approximately the ninth quarter using Method 2. Using Method 3, the dynamic multiplier ratios statistically converge to 1.02 using Method 3 at approximately the sixth quarter, and the dynamic multiplier ratios converge to 1.0 at approximately the twelfth quarter as demonstrated in Graph 3A and Table 6A.

While the Fisher Effect statistically holds for Methods 2 and 3, Method 3 is better representative of the Fisher Effect due to the smaller variances as is shown in Table 5A. The smaller variances produce a smaller bootstrap confidence band, which leads to more reliable results of the test for the Fisher Effect. Thus, the nonparametric VAR(3), using standardized detrended data and median coefficients, from this point forward will be referred to as the optimal nonparametric VAR(3).

The optimal nonparametric VAR(3) produces orthogonalized dynamic multiplier ratios that statistically converge to 1.02 at approximately the twelfth quarter, while the parametric VAR(3) using standardized data produces orthogonalized dynamic multiplier ratios that converge to 0.77. Hence, the time-detrended Fisher Effect holds in the very long run, which can be explained by the sluggish nature of inflation as well as by the long implementation lag that monetary policy takes to go into effect.

Table 6A. Sample Period—1960:Q2 to 1995:Q3

Parametric/ Nonparametric Coefficients	**No. of Lags**	**Window Width**	**Stationary (Yes/No)**	**Convergence of Γ_k**	**Existence of Fisher Effect (Yes/No)**
Parametric --Level Data	3	N/A	Yes	0.83	No
Parametric --Standardized Data	3	N/A	Yes	0.77	No
Parametric --Level Data	4	N/A	Yes	1.57	No
Parametric --Standardized Data	4	N/A	Yes	0.57	No
Nonparametric --Level Data (Median)	3	0.78	Yes	Method 2 → -3.64 Method 3 → -0.36	No
Nonparametric --Level Data (Mean)	3	0.73	Yes	Method 2 → 0.33 Method 3 → 0.48	No
Nonparametric -- Standardized Data (Median)	3	0.40	Yes	Method 2 → 0.97 Method 3 → 1.02	Yes
Nonparametric -- Standardized Data (Mean)	3	0.43	Yes	Method 2 → 0.71 Method 3 → 0.74	No
Nonparametric --Level Data (Median)	4	0.90	Yes	Method 2 → 0.69 Method 3 → 0.69	No
Nonparametric --Level Data (Mean)	4	0.92	Yes	Method 2 → 0.40 Method 3 →0.40	No
Nonparametric -- Standardized Data (Median)	4	0.48	Yes	Method 2 → 1.01 Method 3 →0.93	Yes
Nonparametric -- Standardized Data (Mean)	4	0.52	Yes	Method 2 → 1.05 Method 3 → 1.05	Yes

Table 6B. Sample Period—1960:Q2 to 2004:Q2

Parametric/ Nonparametric Coefficients	No. of Lags	Window Width	Stationary (Yes/No)	Convergence of Γ_k	Existence of Fisher Effect (Yes/No)
Parametric --Level Data	3	N/A	Yes	0.58	No
Parametric --Standardized Data	3	N/A	Yes	0.51	No
Parametric --Level Data	4	N/A	Yes	1.35	No
Parametric --Standardized Data	4	N/A	Yes	0.48	No
Nonparametric --Level Data (Median)	3	0.95	Yes	Method 2 →0.54 Method 3 → 0.56	No
Nonparametric --Level Data (Mean)	3	0.90	Yes	Method 2 → 0.17 Method 3 → 0.21	No
Nonparametric -- Standardized Data (Median)	3	0.46	Yes	Method 2 → 0.07 Method 3 → 0.10	No
Nonparametric – Standardized Data (Mean)	3	0.53	Yes	Method 2 →0.34 Method 3 → 0.33	No
Nonparametric --Level Data (Median)	4	0.87	Yes	Method 2 → 0.94 Method 3 → 0.95	Yes
Nonparametric --Level Data (Mean)	4	0.99	Yes	Method 2 → 0.83 Method 3 → 0.67	No
Nonparametric -- Standardized Data (Median)	4	0.45	Yes	Method 2 → 1.09 Method 3 → 1.08	Yes
Nonparametric -- Standardized Data (Mean)	4	0.54	Yes	Method 2 → 0.52 Method 3 → 0.51	No

4.2. Second Sample Period

As in the case of the first sample period, the results of the nonparametric model are compared to the corresponding parametric model. The data used in the parametric and nonparametric VAR(p) models for the second time period (from the second quarter of 1960 to the second quarter of 2004) are the level detrended residuals of nominal interest rates and inflation as generated by the estimated detrending regression of Equation (1).

Various lag lengths are tested which produced conflicting AIC and SBC results in the second sample period as it does in the first sample period. Unlike the first sample period, the

Fisher Effect is only able to be produced by the VAR(4) model, which is an indicator of changing dynamics with respect to the first sample period.[9]

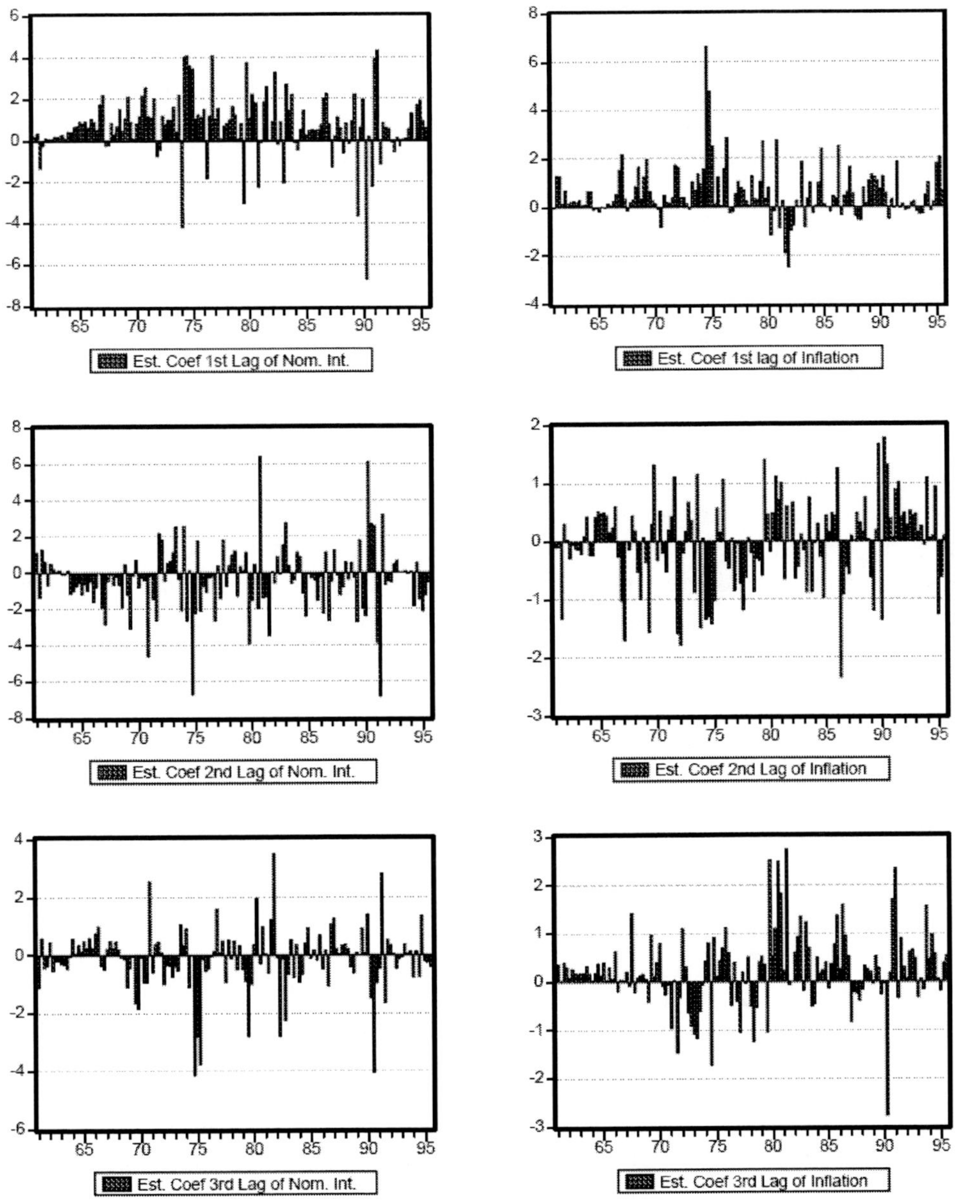

Graph 2B. Graphs of Estimated Nonparametric Coefficients with Detrended Nominal Interest Rates as the Regressand Sample Period: 1960:Q2 to 1995:Q3.

The level nonparametric VAR(4) model, in which the Fisher Effect statistically holds, is able to exploit the non-linearity in the system to generate larger estimated coefficients whose sum does not exceed unity (Graph 2B and Table 3B). Furthermore, the VAR(4) produces

[9] In the first sample period, various versions of the VAR(3) and VAR(4) model are able to produce the Fisher

moduli of the eigenvalues that are large but do not exceed unity (Table 4B). Concerning, the window width, which produces the smallest sum of squared residuals, as calculated by Method 2 for the VAR(4) with median nonparametric coefficients, is 0.45 while the optimal window with for the VAR(4) with mean nonparametric coefficients is 0.54.

By using Method 2, the dynamic multiplier ratios statistically converges to 0.94 at approximately the fifteenth quarter. As is shown in Table 5B, Method 2 also produces a smaller estimated variance-covariance matrix, which produces a smaller bootstrap confidence band thereby making the results of the test for the Fisher Effect more reliable when compared to the results obtained by using Method 3 (Graph 3B). Alternatively, Method 3 produces dynamic multiplier ratios that statistically converge to 0.95 at approximately the twenty-fifth quarter (Table 6B). Hence the nonparametric VAR(4) using level data and median nonparametric coefficients is the optimal model that produces the Fisher Effect.[10]

The difference in results between the first and second samples indicates that some changes have taken place in the dynamics of nominal interest rates and inflation. In particular, the use of level detrended data is necessary to create a stable VAR(p) with large enough coefficients in the second sample, which permits investigation of the Fisher Effect in a stationary setting. Furthermore, the Fisher Effect statistically takes a longer time to go into effect in the second sample period when compared to the first sample period. These changes are partially related to the decreased volatility in nominal interest rates. In regards to the inflation-targeting rule, the results of the second sample period indicate that there is a one-to-one movement between nominal interest rates and inflation. Consequently, the Fisher Effect still holds, which indicates that monetary policy should only follow discrete movements in inflation.

In summary, the results are that the Fisher Effect statistically holds, regardless of the use of standardized detrended data or level detrended data, even with the noticeable decrease in the volatility of nominal interest rates during the second period.

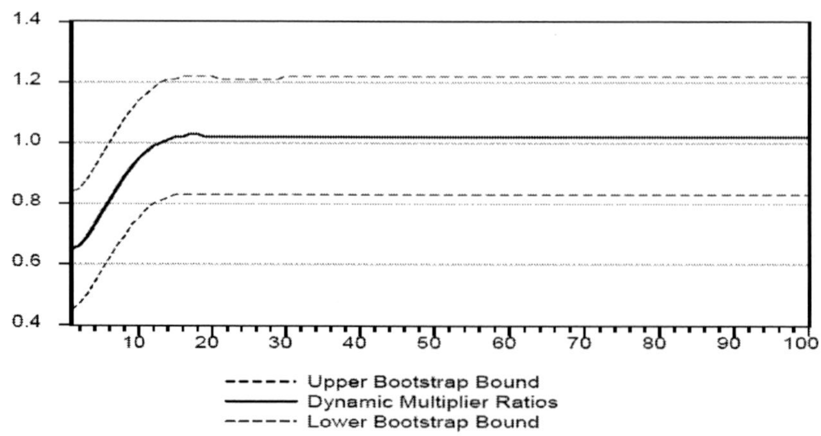

Graph 3A. Graph of the Fisher Effect for the First Sample Period.

Effect, but this is not the case in the second sample period.

[10] For the second sample period, a VAR(4) using standardized data and median nonparametric estimated coefficients is able to produce the Fisher Effect while the parametric VAR(4) with standardized data is unable to produce the Fisher Effect. For the nonparametric model converges to 1.09 using Method 2 and 1.08 using Method 3. The parametric model converges to 0.48.

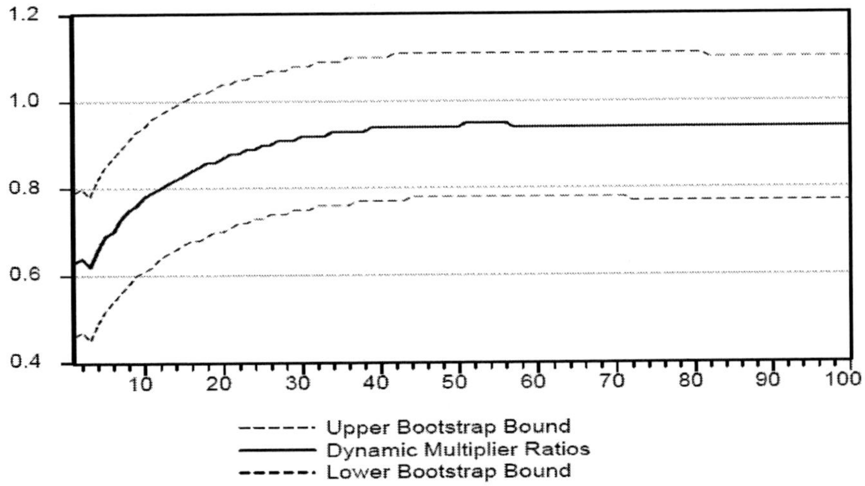

Graph 3B. Graph of the Fisher Effect for the Second Sample Period.

5. Conclusion

This paper investigates the Fisher Effect for two sample periods: for the first quarter of 1960 to the third quarter of 1995, and for the first quarter of 1960 to the second quarter of 2004. Nonparametric techniques are used to investigate whether the Fisher Effect holds. The methodology is applied to study the dynamics of nominal interest rates and inflation in bivariate VARs, and the results are compared with the ones obtained from parametric techniques. The advantages of using nonparametric over parametric techniques are that the nonparametric version is better equipped to deal with outliers and is able to capture nonlinearities in the underlying system. The empirical investigation of the Fisher Effect pursued in this paper also takes into account possible misspecifications and the presence of potential structural breaks.

The first findings are that nominal interest rates and inflation have structural changes in the early 1980s. When these breaks are taken into account, nonstationarity tests indicate that both time series are trend-stationary. Thus, a time-detrended Fisher Effect is warranted to measure the long run relationship of nominal interest rates to inflation. Notice that if these breaks are not taken into account, this could lead to the erroneous conclusion that the respective time series contain a stochastic trend due to the low power of unit root and cointegration tests.

In the second stage, the residuals from the detrending regressions of inflation and nominal interest rates are used to form a stationary, nonparametric, time-detrended VAR with median or mean coefficients. This framework permits the investigation of nonlinearities in the relationship between nominal interest rates and inflation through the study of the estimated coefficients and the dynamic multipliers of the orthogonalized impulse response functions. The nonparametric time-detrended test for the Fisher Effect is formed from the cumulative orthogonalized dynamic multiplier ratios of inflation to nominal interest rates pursuant to a shock to nominal interest rates. If the Fisher Effect holds, this ratio statistically approaches one as the horizon goes to infinity, which means that the changes in detrended nominal interest rates are matched by the changes in detrended inflation in the long run.

Two variations of the relationship between inflation and nominal interest rates are investigated in this paper: a nonparametric time-detrended Fisher Effect using standardized data for the first sample period, and a nonparametric time-detrended Fisher Effect using level data for the second sample period. Thus, both nonparametric techniques conclude that the Fisher Effect holds.

A monetary policy rule could be implemented based on investigating whether or not movements in inflation exceed movements in nominal interest rates in the long run – changes in policy would be warranted in order to maintain the long run equilibrium between these series, as reflected in the Fisher Effect. The findings that the Fisher Effect holds, especially for the more recent period, suggest that current monetary policy can be implemented based on minor discrete changes vis-à-vis discrete changes in nominal interest rates, in order to maintain the long run equilibrium between nominal interest rates and inflation.

References

Crowder, W. J. and D. L. Hoffman, 1996, The long run relationship between nominal interest rates and inflation: the Fisher equation revisited, *Journal of Money, Credit, and Banking,* **28**, 103-118.

Daniels, J. P., Nourzad, F. and R. K. Toutkoushian, 1996, Testing the Fisher Effect as a long-run equilibrium relation, *Applied Financial Economics,* **6,** 115-120.

Engle, R. F., and C. W. Granger, 1987, Co-integration and error correction: representation, estimation and testing, *Econometrica,* **55**, 251-276.

Fama, E. F., 1975, Short-term interest rates as predictors of inflation, *American Economic Review,* 65, 269-282.

Garcia, R. and P. Perron, 1996, An analysis of the real interest rate under regime shifts, *Review of Economics and Statistics,* **78**, 111-125.

Hamilton, J. D., 1989, A new approach to the economic analysis of nonstationary time series and the business cycle, *Econometrica,* **57**, 357-384.

King, R. G. and M. W. Watson, 1997, Testing long run neutrality, *Economic Quarterly*, **83**, 69-101.

Malliaropulos, D., 2000, A note on non-stationarity, structural breaks, and the Fisher Effect, *Journal of Banking and Finance,* **24**, 695-707.

Marron, J.S. (1988), "Automatic Smoothing Parameter Selection: A Survey," *Empirical Economics*, **13**, 187-208.

Mishkin, F., 1992, Is the Fisher Effect for real a re-examination of the relationship between inflation and interest rates, *Journal of Monetary Economics,* **30**, 95-215.

Pagan, A. and Ullah, A. (1999), *Nonparametric Econometrics*, Cambridge: Cambridge University Press.

Perron, P., 1989, The great crash, the oil price shock, and the unit root hypothesis, *Econometrica,* **6**, 1361-1401.

Wallace, M.S. and J.T. Warner, 1993, The Fisher Effect and the term structure of interest rates: tests of cointegration. *Review of Economics and Statistics,* **75**, 320-324.

In: Inflation: Causes and Effects
Editor: Leon V. Schwartz, pp. 85-101

ISBN: 978-1-60741-823-8

Chapter 4

FORECASTING INFLATION USING SIGNAL PLUS NOISE MODELS

Khurshid M. Kiani[1]

Department of Finance, Bang College of Business, Kazakhstan Institute of Management, Economics and Strategic Research (KIMEP), Republic of Kazakhstan

Abstract

This paper employs implicit gross domestic product (GDP) deflator and consumer price index (CPI) for forecasting inflation in Canada and USA. Inflation in these countries is modeled using non-Gaussian signal plus noise models that incorporate non-normality and conditional heteroskedasticity that may be present in the series. Inflation forecast from unrestricted non-Gaussian signal plus noise models and their restricted versions are compared with the inflation forecasts obtained from the Gaussian signal plus noise models for all the series.

The non-Gaussian signal plus noise models are estimated using filtering algorithm due to Sorenson and Alspach (1971). The results show that non-normality cannot be rejected in all the series even when the conditional heteroskedasticity is excluded from the models. When compared to the Gaussian signal plus noise models, the non-Gaussian models employed are able to take into account the outliers and level shifts in the inflation series.

The results from the present empirical exercise show statistically significant evidence of predictability of inflation in Canada and the USA series. The results obtained from non-Gaussian signal plus noise models show that there does not appears much disparity among the mean inflation forecasts for Canada using GDP Deflator and CPI series. However, substantial disparity does exist among the results for USA inflation forecasts obtained using CPI and GDP deflator.

Key phrases: signal plus noise model, stable distribution, non-normality, GDP deflator, inflation.

JEL codes: C22, C53, E31, E37.

---

[1] E-mail addresses: mkkiani@yahoo.com, or, kkiani@kimep.kz. Tel: + 7 (727) 270 44 40 Ext. 2320, Fax: + 7 (727) 270 44 63. Address for Correspondence: Department of Finance, Bang College of Business, Kazakhstan Institute of Management, Economics and Strategic Research (KIMEP), Room #305, Dostyk Building, 2 Abai Avenue, Almaty 050010, Republic of Kazakhstan.

1. Introduction

Although it is arduous to capture public's belief on the future changes in the inflation rates, the role of the inflation expectations on the behavior of nominal and real interest rates have long been the focus of finance. The inflation forecast being pivotal to economic analysis and economic decision making, most investment decisions require forecasts of ex-ante real interest rates that are based on inflation forecasts. Irving Fisher (1930) assumed that the erratic behavior of real interest rates emerges from money illusion. This assumption was also supported by Friedman and Schwartz (1963), and Summers (1983), however, the views of Barsky (1987) on it are in sharp contrast.

Fisher (1928-30) showed that there was one-for-one relationship between inflation and nominal interest rates; however, he assumed that inflation forecasts are subject to systematic bias which is too low during the upswing of the inflation whereas it would be high during its downturn. This paradigm was supported by Summers (1987) who showed that there was hardly any evidence that would support a relationship between inflation and the real interest rates. On the other hand Sargent (1973) showed statistically significant evidence of a link between nominal interest rate and inflation. In addition, Fama (1975) showed that interest rates help forecasting inflation and also maintained that the movements in the interest rates presumably reflect fluctuations in expected inflation rather than changes in real interest rates. Nelson and Schwert (1977), Mishkin (1981), and Fama and Gibbon (1982) also support this paradigm.

Researchers developed various proxies for forecasting inflation. For instance, Friedman and Schwartz (1963) noted that the proxies used for inflation forecasts included the difference between the two types of assets, and the difference between stocks and bonds etc. Therefore, for forecasting inflation, stocks and bonds are considered to be the close substitutes of each other and the ex-ante real interest rates are considered to be the equilibrium interest rates in the capital market.

A varying performance of traditional models such as term structure models and Phillips curves was noted by Mehra (1988) and Stockton and Glassman (1987) although Robertson (1992), Carleton and Cooper (1976), and Mishkin (1990, a and b) showed that the term structure model was adequate for forecasting inflation. This means that the slope of the yield curve would be an indicator of the future path of inflation (deflation). Alternately, Stock and Watson (1999) showed that the Philips curve was the superior model for forecasting inflation.

Davis and Fagan (1997) showed that financial spreads were useful for forecasting inflation. Fama (1975), Mishkin (1989), Jorion and Mishkin (1991), Browne and Manasse (1989) employed yield spread for forecasting inflation because the nominal interest rate was composed mainly of the real interest rates and inflation. It is because under certain restrictive assumptions such as constancy of real interest rates over time, perfect substitutability between assets of different maturities, and existence of the expectation theory of the term structure, and the slope of the yield curve would offer a relatively fair forecast of inflation since Schiller and McCulloch (1987) maintained that monetary policy was unable to manipulate the slope of the yield curve. However, contrary to Fisher (1930) the link between the inflation and the nominal interest rate appears to be less accurate than what is expected due to the restricted assumptions mentioned above.

A declining slope of the yield curve signals a future decline in the economic activity which is consistent with theoretical macroeconomics assumptions where short-term rate could be higher due to a contractionary monetary policy. However, as mentioned by Laurant (1988) a positive shift in the yield curve would cause bankers to purchase long term securities which boost the economic activity. However, Mishkin (1991) maintained that the short term maturity does not encompass substantial information to unveil the future path of inflation.

Barsky (1987) agreed that inflation rates are often subject to changes in level shift, therefore, Markov Switching models due to Hamilton (1989) and Lam (1990) would be recommended for forecasting inflation. However, Markov Switching models limit the use of the number of states when compared to state space models that are capable of accounting for a range of state values.

Empirical research shows that both univariate as well as multivariate models have been employed for forecasting inflation. Fama and Gibbons (1984), and Hafer and Hein (1990) compare forecast performance of these models. However, Hamilton (1985) and Burmeister, Wall and Hamilton (1986) employed multivariate state space models that were developed to work with interest rates and inflation rates assuming that errors follow a normal process. However, Nelson (1972), and Bidarkota and McCulloch (1998) noted that more parsimonious univariate models do a better job in forecasting inflation when compared to the complex structural multivariate models.

Fama (1975) employed short term interest rates for forecasting inflation. However, Darin and Hetzel (1995) employed quarterly data on GDP deflator for forecasting United States of America (USA) inflation and claimed that their inflation forecasts were comparable with those of Data Resources Inc. (DRI). This was the motivation for employing GDP deflator for Canada and USA as against employing the consumer price index (CPI) for predicting future movements in price level in these highly developed industrialized neighboring countries. Nevertheless, CPI series are also employed for Inflation forecasts of both the countries, although Bidarkota and McCulloch (1998) reported that the long CPI series for USA were flawed.

Most studies that are focused on forecasting inflation employed models that assumed disturbances to come from normal family, however, because of the generalized central limit theorem due to Zolotarev (1986) the economic disturbances being a multitude of unobserved contributions could also have non-Gaussian distributions encompassing fat tails. This paradigm was confirmed by Blanchard and Watson (1986), Balke and Fomby (1994) and Baillie et al. (1996). Inefficient estimation of inflation forecast would result when non-normality is not included in the models employed for forecasting inflation for the series that encompass fat tails (Batchelor 1981). McCulloch (1996) provided a summary of financial application of stable distributions and Bidarkota and McCulloch (1998) employed models incorporating stable distributions to account for fat tails in the data for forecasting inflation.

The preliminary data analysis reveals non-normality and presence of autoregressive conditional heteroskedasticity in the series employed motivated to incorporate conditional heteroskedasticity in the models employed for forecasting inflation volatility in all the series. Indeed, if the series encompass persistent signal, an unobserved component model provides a convenient description of the observed series signal and random noise. Harvey (1989) and Watson (1986) used state space or unobserved component models with the assumptions that the underlying errors were normal. This is because the powerful Kalman Filter is operable efficiently only with the normal disturbances. However, as in Oh (1994), and Bidarkota and

McCulloch (1988), the normality assumption is relaxed here in favor of stable distribution. Further, in order to account for non-Gaussian data, inflation is modeled with the framework of Paretian Stable distributions. Mantangna and Stanley (1995), Buckel (1995), and McCulloch (1997) used stable distributions to model returns series. The present work also uses GARCH-like models that are employed here to explicitly encompass volatility persistence in all the series.

The remaining study is organized as follows. First the most general model used in the present work as well as the estimation issues associated with these models are outlined in section 2. Thereafter, data sources, empirical results, and hypotheses tests are presented in section 3. Finally, conclusions that can be drawn from the study are presented in section 4.

2. Empirical Model

State space models deal with dynamic time series modeling that use unobserved variables. These types of models have long range of applications in econometrics since economic theory often involves unobservable variables. For example for ex-ante real rate of interest that are expected to prevail sometimes in future, expected future inflation, future wage rates, future returns on investments, future returns on stocks, and so on. Therefore, Engle and Watson (1981) used these models to find the behavior of wage rates, Antoncic (1986) employed these models for the behavior of ex-ante real interest rates, Stock and Watson (1990) used these models for observing coincident economic indicators, and Bidarkota and McCulloch (2004), and Kiani (2007) for stock excess returns forecasts.

Recent literature suggests the use of GARCH model in conjunction with Paretian innovations in financial modeling. This type of modeling is attractive for researchers because it allows for conditional skewness and leptokurtosis of financial time series without ruling out normality. The present contribution illustrates the usefulness of modeling Canada and USA inflation rates using models that incorporate GARCH in the volatility specification of these models in predicting future change in price level in these countries.

2.1. State Space Model for Predicting Inflation

An unobserved component or state space model that encompasses stable distribution and GARCH-like effects is employed in the present work. However, the most general state space models that encompass stable distributions, GARCH-like effects, and predictable components that was also employed by Bidarkota and McCulloch (2004), and Kiani (2007) failed to converge for all the series, therefore, the present research abstract discussing it further in the text. The Paretian stable models where errors are assumed to come from a more general stable distribution employed here (shown in the Equations $1a$ and $1b$) does not incorporate predictable component.

$$r_t = \mu + \varepsilon_t, \qquad \varepsilon_t \sim c_t z_t, \qquad z_t \sim iid\ S_\alpha(0,1) \tag{1a}$$

$$c_t^\alpha = \omega + \beta c_{t-1}^\alpha + \delta \,| r_{t-1} - \mu |^\alpha + \gamma d_{t-1} \,| r_{t-1} - \mu |^\alpha \tag{1b}$$

where,

$$d_{t-1} = \begin{cases} 1 \; if \; r_{t-1} - \mu < 0 \\ 0 \; otherwise \end{cases}$$

Model 2 which is a general model where errors come from normal family is obtained restricting $\alpha = 2$ in model 1, which is presented in Equations $2a \; and \; 2b$.

$$r_1 = \mu + \varepsilon_t, \qquad \varepsilon_t \sim \sqrt{2}c_t z_t, \quad z_t \sim iid\, N(0,1) \tag{2a}$$

$$c_t^2 = \omega + \beta c_{t-1}^2 + \delta \mid r_{t-1} - \mu \mid^2 + \gamma d_{t-1} \mid r_{t-1} - \mu \mid^2 \tag{2b}$$

Restricting $\beta = \delta = \gamma = 0$ in model 1 gives model 3, which is shown in Equation 3.

$$r_t = \mu + \varepsilon_t, \qquad \varepsilon_t \sim S_\alpha(0,c) \tag{3}$$

A random variable x will have stable distribution $S_\alpha(0,c)$ when its log characteristic function can be represented by the following Equation.

$$\ln E \exp(ixt) = i\delta t - \mid c_t \mid^\alpha \tag{4}$$

where the parameter $c > 0$ measures scale, the parameter $\delta(-\infty, \infty)$ measures location, and $\alpha \in (o, 2]$ which is the characteristic exponent governs the tail behavior. A small value of α indicates thicker tail where errors come from symmetric stable family but when $\alpha = 2$ the errors come from the normal family with a variance that equals to $2c^2$.

The restrictions $\omega > 0,\; \beta \geq 0,\; \delta \geq 0$, and $\gamma \geq 0$ are imposed on the process that is shown in Equation $1b$ to contemplate various hypotheses tests. The theoretical term involving dummy variable d_{t-1} in Equation $2b$ captures leverage effects that is transmitted from negative shock to increase in future volatility more than a positive shock of equal magnitude (Nelson 1991, and Hamilton Susmel 1994). Abstracting from the threshold term, when the errors are normal, the model of volatility persistence reduces to GARCH-normal process.

2.2. Discussions of Model

The Equations $1a \; through \; 1c$ encompass two main features of the model. These features are non-normality, and persistence in volatility in the series. These features are elaborated in the following paragraphs.

While a comparative survey of stable distribution in financial application is given in McCulloch (1996a), Mandelbrot (1963) initially proposed stable distributions that are natural extensions of Gaussian distributions, and Gaussian errors are also motivated by their central limit attributes. Likewise, the generalized central limit theorem suggested that the limiting distribution of such a process must belong to a more general class of stable distributions to which the Gaussian distribution is a member (Zolotarev 1986).

To detect possible existence of time varying volatility in all the series, a simple GARCH (1,1)-like model for conditional scales is specified that is shown in the Equation 1b. This is because the literature in this area reveals that GARCH (1,1) model has been the most popular specification for the stock returns volatility. Pagan and Schwert (1990), and French Schwert, and Stambough (1987) employed GARCH (1, 2) model, but they found weak evidence of the second moving average term. Further, the GARCH (1,1) model employed here is augmented with dummy variable d_{t-1} to account for the leverage effects. Therefore, the model for volatility specification takes into account any asymmetric response to stock volatility due to positive and negative shocks in all the series.

2.3. Estimation Issues

The non-Gaussianity of the state space model in Equation1 creates complication in estimation even without the presence of conditional heteroskedasticity. This happens because the Kalman filter is no longer optimal due to the non-Gaussian nature of the shocks. In such situations, the general recursive-filtering algorithm due to Sorenson and Alspach (1971) provides optimal filtering and predictive densities under any distribution for the errors and the formula for computing the log likelihood function. These formulae are shown in Appendix-A. The recursive equation that is employed to compute the filtering and predicting densities are given in the form of integrals whose close form analytical expressions are generally intractable, especially in very special cases. These integrals are numerically evaluated in the present work.

The stable distribution and density may be evaluated using Zolotrav's (1986) proper integral representation or by taking the inverse Fourier transformation of the characteristic function. However, McCulloch (1996b) developed fast numerical approximations to the stable distribution and density that has an expected relative density of the precision of 10^{-6} for $\alpha \in [0.84, 2]$. Therefore, α is restricted in this range for computational convenience.

The effect of the initial values in the GARCH volatility process on the properties of the parameter estimates in the GARCH(1,1), and IGARCH(1,1) models is asymptotically negligible (Lumsdaine 1996). Diebold and Lopez (1995) suggested setting the initial conditional variance (equal to $2c^2$, when it exists) equal to the sample variance at the first iteration and at the subsequent iteration equal to the sample variance from a simulated realization with the estimated parameters from the previous iteration. Initialization of GARCH process using the estimate of c_0 based on samples values was suggested by Engle and Bollerslev (1986). Accordingly, the value of c_0 is set equal to its unconditional value obtained from the volatility process that is shown in Equation $6c$.

3. Empirical Results

3.1. Data Sources

The quarterly gross domestic product (GDP) deflator, and consumer price index (CPI) series for Canada and USA are obtained from International Financial Statistic's website. GDP deflator is used to measure inflation both for Canada and USA for two reasons. One, as mentioned in the preceding section, Darin and Hetzel (1995) employed GDP deflator for forecasting inflation who claimed that their inflation forecasts were comparable to Data Recourses Inc. (DRI), and two Bidarkota and McCulloch (1998) reported that the long series of CPI data for USA were flawed. However, in addition to GDP deflator series, CPI series are also employed for forecasting inflation both for Canada and USA. The inflation series are constructed from the first difference of the logarithm of the GDP deflator and CPI series both for Canada and USA. All the data series span from 1957:Q1 to 2008:Q3 that allow to use 205 workable quarterly observations for each of the series employed. Table 1 shows additional information on data series for all the series and figure 1 shows plots for all the series employed.

Table 1.1. Data Description: Inflation using Signal plus Noise Models

	Data Type	Source	Frequency	Data Span	Number of Observations
Canada	CPI	IFS Website	Quarterly	1957:1- 2008:3	205
Canada	GDP Deflator	IFS Website	Quarterly	1957:1- 2008:3	206
USA	CPI	IFS Website	Quarterly	1957:1- 2008:3	205
USA	GDP Deflator	IFS Website	Quarterly	1957:1- 2008:3	205

Quarterly data on GDP deflator and consumer price index (CPI) series was obtained from the International Financial Statistics' Website.

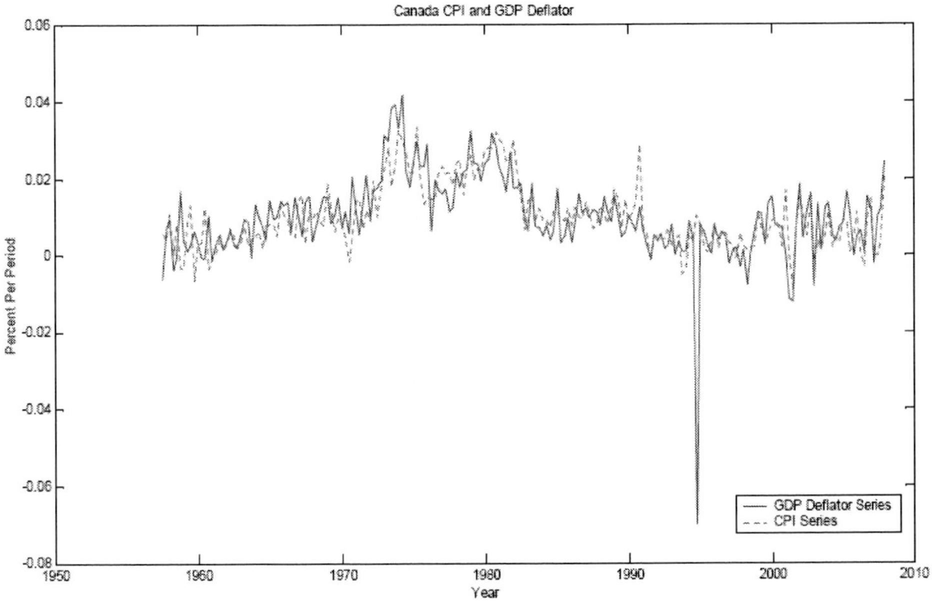

Figure 1. Continued on next page.

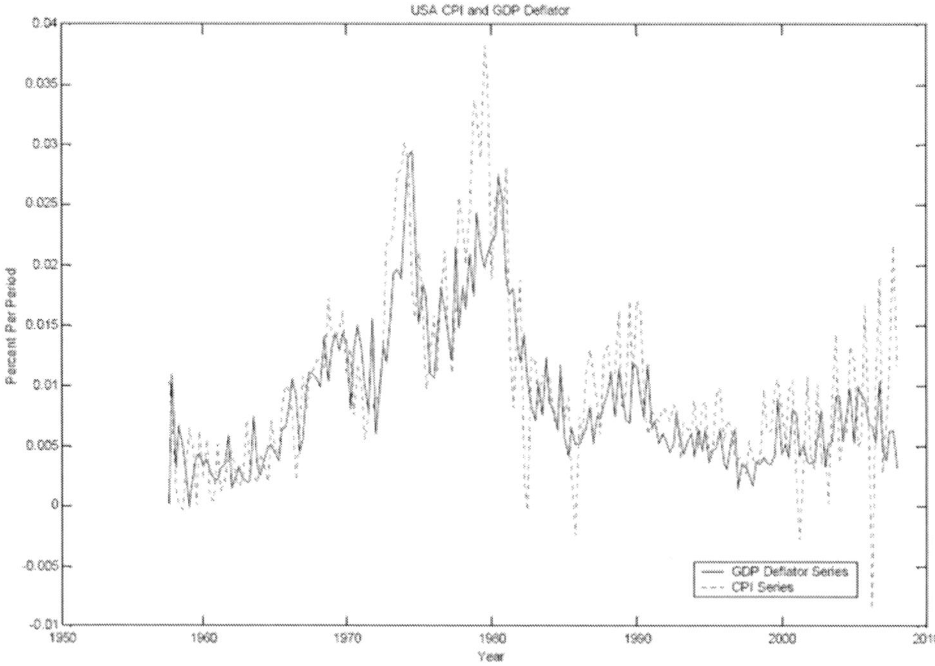

Figure 1. Inflation using Signal plus Noise Models.

3.2. Preliminary Data Analysis

Table 1.2 provides some useful statistics on the raw data and summarizes preliminary statistical inferences for some interesting hypotheses. The average growth in quarterly backward looking measure of inflation ranges from 0.009 for USA GDP deflator to 0.10 for Canada GDP deflator series. However, disparity between the future inflation measured by CPI ranges between 0.010 for Canada to 0.10 for USA. The quarterly standard deviation for inflation forecasts ranges from 0.006 for USA GDP deflator to 0.011 for Canada GDP deflator series. These preliminary data analysis show that the standard deviation generated by CPI for both the countries is relatively low.

Skewness measure ranges from -1.553 for Canada GDP deflator to 1.219 for USA GDP deflator series. Excess Kurtosis ranges from 0.108 for Canada CPI to 14.696 for Canada GDP deflator. The Jarque-Bera test rejects normality in both Canada and USA at all levels of significance. White Test fails to reject homoskedasticity in Canada CPI, although the null hypothesis is rejected against the alternative hypothesis of heteroskedasticity for all the remaining series included in the present study. The augmented Dickey Fuller Test shows unit roots at levels in all the series but rejects the null hypothesis of unit root at first difference in all the series. The LM test for ARCH shows significant evidence of conditional heteroskedasticity in all the series in exception of Canada CPI series. These preliminary results are subject to some qualification because the tests are based on the assumption that the inflation series are identically and independently (iid) distributed normal. As will be evident later, this assumption is not appropriate.

Table 1.2. Summary of Statistics

	Canada		USA	
	CPI	GDP Deflator	CPI	GDP Deflator
Nonzero Mean	0.010	0.010	0.100	0.009
Standard deviation	0.009	0.011	0.008	0.006
Skewness	0.708	-1.553	1.179	1.219
Excess Kurtosis	0.108	14.696	1.676	1.105
Normality	17.232 (0.000)	1927.099 (0.000)	71.820 (0.000)	61.234 (0.002)
Homoskedasticity				
F Statistics (White)	2.240 (0.109)	5.815 (0.004)	7.639 (0.001)	6.629 (0.002)
Chi Square (White)	4.448 (0.108)	11.158 (0.004)	14.415 (0.001)	12.329 (0.002)
ARCH Effects	0.072	3.713	18.143	545.225 (0.000)
F Statistics	3.740 (0.055)	-3.608 (0.006)	-2.478 (0.123)	-2.105 (0.243)
Chi Square	3.708 (0.542)	-13.395 (0.000)	-19.769 (0.000)	-7.787 (0.000)
ADF Test				
F Statistics	-2.065 (0.259)	-3.608 (0.006)	-2.477 (0.123)	-2.105 (0.243)
Chi Square	-15.199 (0.000)	-13.395 (0.000)	-19.769 (0.000)	-7.787 (0.000)

1. All statistics reported are for quarterly GDP deflator series that are converted from the yearly data.
2. *p*-values for statistics pertaining to Jarque-Bera, White and the LM test for ARCH are reported in parentheses below the test statistic.
3. Optimal lag order for the ADF tests (not reported for brevity) is chosen using the minimum SBC criterion. Asymptotic critical values at the 10% significance level for the model with constant, and with constant and time trend are -2.57 and -3.13, respectively.
4. Optimal lag order for the LM test is chosen using the minimum SBC criterion.

3.3. Estimation Results

Tables 2.1 and 3.1 show parameter estimates for characteristic exponent α, volatility persistence parameter β, ARCH parameter δ, and the leverage parameter that are estimated from models 1 through 3 for CPI series both for Canada and USA. Likewise, Tables 2.2 and 3.2 shows the estimates for such parameters respectively for GDP Deflator series both for Canada and USA. The hypotheses tests that are constructed from log likelihood estimates from these models are presented in the last two rows of these Tables.

Table 2.1. Canada Inflation Estimates using CPI Series

Parameters	Model 1	Model 2	Model 3
α	1.999 (0.002)	2 (restricted)	1.999 (0.000)
μ	0.007 (0.001)	0.007 (0.0001)	0.006 (0.0002)
ω	5.62e-06 (2.6e-06)	5.617e-6 (2.55e-6)	
β	0.349 (0.195)	0.349 (0.195)	
δ	0.242 (0.084)	0.242 (0.084)	
γ	2.60e-19 (0.000)	1.31e-8 (0.000)	
c			0.018 (0.008)
Log L	725.757	725.757	686.937
LR $(\alpha = 2)$	0.000		
LR $(\beta = \delta = \gamma = 0)$	77.640		

1. The following unobserved component or state space model with non-normality (stable model) is employed to estimate the results shown in the Table.

$$r_t = \mu + \varepsilon_t, \qquad \varepsilon_t \sim c_t z_t, \qquad z_t \sim iid\, S_\alpha(0,1) \tag{1a}$$

$$c_t^\alpha = \omega + \beta c_{t-1}^\alpha + \delta\,|\,r_{t-1} - \mu\,|^\alpha + \gamma d_{t-1}\,|\,r_{t-1} - \mu\,|^\alpha \tag{1b}$$

where,

$$d_{t-1} = \begin{cases} 1 \text{ if } r_{t-1} - \mu < 0 \\ 0 \text{ otherwise} \end{cases}$$

2. All estimates are rounded off to the third decimal place.
3. LR ($\alpha = 2$) gives the value of the likelihood ratio test statistic for the null hypothesis of normality.
4. The small-sample critical value at a significance level 0.01 for a sample size of 300 is reported to be 4.764 from simulations due to McCulloch (1997).
5. LR $(\beta = \delta = \gamma = 0)$ is the test for no volatility persistence that is evaluated using $p - values$ from χ_3^2 distribution.

Table 2.2. Canada Inflation Estimates using GDP Deflator Series

Parameters	Model 1	Model 2	Model 3
α	1.952 (0.145)	2 (restricted)	1.740 (0.113)
μ	0.008 (0.001)	0.009 (0.001)	0.006 (0.001)
ω	2.05e-5 (1.56e-5)	1.97e-5 (4.26e-6)	
β	9.57e-5 (2.98e-8)	1.96e-12 (1.17e-12)	
δ	0.292 (0.063)	0.356 (0.101)	

Table 2.2. Continued

Parameters	Model 1	Model 2	Model 3
γ	4.056 (0.000)	4.663 (0.000)	
c			0.009 (0.001)
Log L	693.003	655.678	667.667
LR $(\alpha = 2)$	74.650		
LR $(\beta = \delta = \gamma = 0)$	50.672		

See notes on Table 2.1.

Table 3.1. USA Inflation Estimates using CPI Series

Parameters	Model 1	Model 2	Model 3
α	1.378 (0.088)	2 (restricted)	1.538 (0.105)
μ	0.012 (0.000)	0.007 (0.000)	0.004 (0.000)
ω	5.329 (0.000)	1.27e-5 (7.25e-7)	
β	0.000 (0.000)	0.497 (0.092)	
δ	0.945 (0.179)	0.253 (0.622)	
γ	0.054 (0.225)	4.83e-12 (0.000)	
c			0.009 (0.000)
Log L	679.679	776.929	723.576
LR $(\alpha = 2)$	0.000		
LR $(\beta = \delta = \gamma = 0)$	106.706		

See notes on Table 2.1.

Table 3.2. USA Inflation Estimates using GDP Deflator Series

Parameters	Model 1	Model 2	Model 3
α	1.999 (0.006)	2 (restricted)	1.653 (0.134)
μ	0.006 (0.000)	0.006 (0.000)	0.003 (0.000)
ω	3.54e-7 (1.85e-7)	3.54e-5 (7.25e-7)	
β	0.594 (0.074)	0.594 (0.074)	
δ	0.087 (0.044)	0.087 (0.044)	

Table 3.2. Continued

Parameters	Model 1	Model 2	Model 3
γ	6.46e-7 (0.000)	7.33e-11 (0.000)	
c			0.008 (0.000)
Log L	843.640	843.640	764.894
LR $(\alpha = 2)$	0.000		
LR $(\beta = \delta = \gamma = 0)$	157.492		

See notes on Table 2.1.

3.4. Hypothesis Test

The present work contemplates hypotheses tests for normality, and no time varying volatility in all the series. All hypotheses tests that are based on likelihood ratio test statistics are elaborated in the following sub-sections.

3.4.1. Test for Normality

The likelihood ration (LR) test statistic for this test is calculated from log likelihood estimates of the most general model (model 1) and its version (model 2) that restricts non-normality ($\alpha = 2$). However, the LR test statistic for this test is non-standard because the null hypothesis lies on the boundary of the admissible values for α. The standard regularity conditions for this test are not satisfied, therefore, inferences are drawn using critical values due to McCulloch (1997).

The null hypothesis of normality can easily be rejected in GDP deflator sereis in canada only using critical values from McCulloch (1997). However, the null hypotheses of normality can not be rejected for Canada CPI, USA CPI, and USA GDP deflator series at conventional level of significance. The estimated value of the characteristic exponent α for Canada CPI and USA GDP deflator series are in the neighborhood of 2 showing normal behavior in these series. The results on normality tests for all the series are reported in the relevant Tables.

3.4.2. Test for Volatility Persistence

Homoskedasticity ($\beta = \delta = \gamma = 0$) is assumed in the most general model (model 1) to calculate likelihood ratio test statistics using log likelihood estimates from restricted and unrestricted versions of model 1. The statistical inferences for this test are drawn from the χ_3^2 distributions.

The LR test statistic for the null of no GARCH is used to test no time varying volatility ($\beta = \delta = \gamma = 0$) in all the series. The test statistic for this test is reported in the last row of the relevant Tables. Homoskedasticity can easily be rejected in all the series using critical values that are obtained from χ_3^2 distributions at conventional level of significance.

The study results on hypothesis tests reveal that quarterly GDP deflator as well as CPI series posses insignificant non-normality that is predictable even after accounting for conditional heteroskedasticity at all levels of significance in USA CPI and GDP deflator series. In addition, inflation in USA and Canada encompass volatility persistent even at 1 percent level of significance. Thus, the signal plus noise model (model 1) with such attributes is employed for forecasting Canada and USA inflation using CPI and GDP deflator series. The results do not show much disparity among the mean inflation forecasts that are obtained using CPI and GDP deflator for Canada which can be verified from Tables 2.1, and 2.2. The mean inflation forecast obtained from CPI is 0.007 whereas the forecast using GDP deflator is 0.008 which does not appears to be in conformance with the theory which states that compared to GDP deflator, CPI overstates the inflation forecasts. However, the results show substantial disparity among the mean inflation for USA that are predicted using CPI and GDP deflator series (Tables 3.1, and 3.2).

4. Conclusion

The present research employs non-Gaussian state space or unobserved component models for possible existence of volatility persistence, and non-normality, in growth in price levels in Canada and the USA. The methodology employed is fully parametric and the time series models employed fully account for non-normality and time varying volatility that may be present in Canada and USA CPI, and GDP deflator series.

The results show that Canada and USA series encompass significant leptokurtosis. Similarly, Canada and USA series show evidence of time varying volatility that can be characterized by GARCH-like behavior. There is insignificant leverage effect in all the series which shows that the negative shocks do not necessarily lead to a greater increase in the future volatility than the positive shocks of the equal magnitude in all the series. This shows that none of the series studied is unstable although all series have non-constant scales.

The efficiently estimated excess returns range between 0.007 percent per month (0.084 percent per annum) for Canada CPI to 0.009 percent per month (0.108 percent per annum) for Canada GDP deflator series. The characteristic exponent α ranges between 1.952 for Canada to 1.999 for all the remaining series included in the present empirical exercise. There appears no substantial disparity among the mean rates forecasted from CPI and GDP deflator series for Canada; although a substantial disparity does exist in the results among the inflation forecasts for USA that are obtained using CPI and GDP deflator series. This confirms the claim made by Bidarkota and McCulloch (1998) that the long CPI series for USA are flawed.

Appendix A: Sorenson-Alspach Filtering Equations

Let $y_t, t = 1, \ldots, T$, be an observed time series and x_t an unobserved state variable, stochastically determining y_t. Denote $Y_t = \{y_1, \ldots, y_t\}$. The recursive formulae for obtaining one-step-ahead prediction and filtering densities, due to Sorenson and Alspach (1971), are as follows:

$$p(x_t|Y_{t-1}) = \int_{-\infty}^{\infty} p(x_t|x_{t-1})p(x_{t-1}|Y_{t-1})dx_{t-1}\ , \tag{A1}$$

$$p(x_t|Y_t) = p(y_t|x_t)p(x_t|Y_{t-1}) / p(y_t|Y_{t-1})\ , \tag{A2}$$

$$p(y_t|Y_{t-1}) = \int_{-\infty}^{\infty} p(y_t|x_t)p(x_t|Y_{t-1})dx_t\ . \tag{A3}$$

Finally, the log-likelihood function is given by:

$$\log p(y_1,\ldots,y_T) = \sum_{t=1}^{T} \log p(y_t|Y_{t-1}). \tag{A4}$$

References

Antoncic, M. (1986). High and Volatile Real Interest Rates: Where Does The Fed Fit In?, *Journal of Money, Credit and Banking,* February 1986, 18, 18-27.

Baillie, R. T. Chung, C.F. and Tieslau, M.A. (1996). Analyzing Inflation by the Fractionally Integrated ARFIMA-GARCH Model, *Journal of Applied Econometrics*, **11**, 23-40

Balke, N. S. and Fomby, T.B. (1994). Large Shocks, Small Shocks and Economic Fluctuations: Outliers in Macroeconomic Time Series, *Journal of Applied Econometrics*, **9,** 181-200

Barsky, R. B. (1987). The Fisher Hypothesis and the Forecastability and Persistence of Inflation, *Journal of Monetary Economics*, **19**, 3-24

Batchelor, R. A. (1981). Aggregate Expectations Under the Stable Laws, *Journal of Econometrics*, **19**, 199-210

Bidarkota, P. V. and McCulloch, J. H. (1998). Optimal Univariate Inflation Forecasting with Symmetric Stable Shocks, *Journal of Applied Econometrics*, **13**, 659-670.

Bidarkota, P. V. and McCulloch, J. H. (2004). Testing for Persistence in Stock Returns with GARCH-stable Shocks, *Quantitative Finance*, **4**, 256- 265.

Blanchard, O. J. and Watson, M.W. (1986). Are Business Cycles All Alike? in R.J. Gordon (ed.). *The American Business Cycle: Continuity and Change*, University of Chicago Press, 123-156

Browne, F. and Manasse, P. (1989). Information Content of the Term Structure of the Interest Rates: Theory and Practice, *OECD Working Paper* No. **69**.

Buckle, D. J. (1995). Beyesian Inferences for Stable Distribution, *Journal American Statistical Association,* **90**, 605-13.

Burmeister, E. Wall, K.D. and Hamilton, J.D. (1986). Estimation of Unobserved Monthly Inflation Using Kalman Filtering, *Journal of Business and Economic Statistics*, **4**, 147-160

Carleton, W. T. and Cooper, I. (1976). Estimation and Uses of the Term Structure of Interest Rates, *Journal of Finance*, **31**, 1067-83.

Darin, R. and Hetzel, R. (1995) An Empirical Measure of the Real Rate of Interest. *Economic Quarterly of the Federal Reserve Bank of Richmond*, **81**, 17-47.

Davis, E. P. and Fagan, G. (1995). Are Financial Spreads Useful Indicators of Future Inflation and Output Growth, *Journal of Applied Econometrics,* **12**, 701-714.

Diebold, F. X. and Lopez, J. A. (1995). Modeling Volatility Dynamics Macroeconomics: Developments, Tensions and Projects Ed K Hoover (Boston, MA: Kulwer-Academics) pp. 427072.

Engle, R. F. and Bollerslev, T. (1986). Modeling the Persistence of Conditional Variances, *Econometric Reviews*, **5**, 1-50.

Engle, R.F. and Watson, M.W. (1981). A One-Factor Multivariate Time Series Model of Metropolitan Wage Rates. *Journal of the American Statistical Association*, **76**, 774-781.

Fama, E.F. (1975). Short Term Interest Rates as Predictors of Inflation, *American Economic Review*, **65**, 269-282

Fama, E. F. and Gibbons, M. R. (1982). Inflation, Real Returns and Capital Investment, *Journal of Monetary Economics*, **9,** 295-323

Fama, E. F. and Gibbons, M. R. (1984). A Comparison of Inflation Forecasts, *Journal of Monetary Economics*, **13**, 327-348

Fisher, I. (1928). *Money Illusion,* Adelphi Co.: New York.

Fisher, I. (1930). *The Theory of Interest.* Macmillan, New York.

French, K. R. Schwert, G. W. and Stambaugh, R. F. (1987). Expected Stock Returns and Volatility, *Journal of Financial Economics,* **19**, 3-29.

Friedman, M. and Schwartz, A. J. (1963). A Monetary History of the Unites States, 1867-1960. New York National Bureau of Economic Research, 583-84.

Hafer, R.W. and Hein, S. E. (1990). Forecasting Inflation Using Interest-Rate and Time-Series Models: Some International Evidence, *Journal of Business*, **63**, 1-17

Hamilton, J. D. (1985). Uncovering Financial Market Expectations of inflation, *Journal of Political Economy*, **93**, 1224-1241

Hamilton, J. D. (1985). Uncovering Financial Market Expectations of Inflation, *Journal of Political Economy*, **93**, 1224-1241

Hamilton J, Susmel R. (1994). Autoregressive Conditional Heteroskedasticity and Changes in Regime, *Journal of Econometrics,* **64**, 307–333

Harvey, A. C. (1989). Forecasting Structural Time Series Models and the Kalman Filter. Cambridge University Press.

Jorion, P. and Mishkin, F. (1991). A Multi-country Comparison of Term Structure Forecasts at Long Horizons, *Journal of Financial Economics*, **29**, 59-80

Kiani K (2007). Stock Returns Predictability in Transition Economies, *Transition Studies Review,* **14**, 93-104.

Lam, P. S. (1990). The Hamilton Model with a General Autoregressive Component: Estimation and Comparison with Other Models of Economic Time Series, *Journal of Monetary Economics*, **26**, 409-432

Laurent, R. D. (1988). An Interest-Based Indicator of Monetary Policy, *Economic Perspective*, Federal Reserve Bank of Chicago, 3-14

Lumsdaine, R., 1996. Consistency and Asymptotic Normality of the Quasi-Maximum Likelihood Estimator in IGARCH (1, 1), *Econometrica,* **64**, 575-96.

Mandelbrot, B. (1963). The Variation of Certain Speculative Prices, *Journal of Business,* **36**, 394-419

Mantegna, R. N. Stanley, H. E. (1995). Scaling Behavior in the Dynamics of an Economic Index, *Nature,* 376, 46-9.

McCulloch, J. H. (1996a). Financial Applications of Stable Distributions, in: G.S. Maddala and C.R. Rao (eds.), Handbook of Statistics, Vol.14 (Elsevier, Amsterdam) 393-425.

___________ (1996b). Numerical Approximation of the Symmetric Stable Distribution and Density, in R. Adler, R. Feldman, and M.S. Taqqu (eds.). *A Practical Guide to Heavy Tails: Statistical Techniques for Analyzing Heavy Tailed Distributions*, Birkhauser, Boston

___________ (1997) Measuring Tail Thickness in Order to Estimate the Stable Index: A Critique, *Journal of Business and Economic Statistics*, **15**, 74-81

Mehra, Y. P. (1988). The Forecast Performance of the Alternate Models of Inflation. Economic Review, Federal Reserve Bank of Richmond, September/October 1988, 10-18

Mishkin, F. (1981). The Real Rate of Inflation: An Empirical Investigation, *Carneige-Rochester Conference Series on Public Policy*, **15**, 151-200.

Mishkin, F. S. (1989). A multi-country study of the information in the term structure about future inflation. *NBER Working Paper* No **3I25**.

Mishkin, F. S. (1990a). The Information in the Longer Maturity Term Structure About Future Inflation. *Journal of International Money and Finance*, **5**, 77-95.

Mishkin, F. S. (1990b). What Does the Term Structure Tell Us About Future Inflation? *Journal of Monetary Economics*, **25**, 77-95.

Mishkin, F. S. (1991). A Multi-country Study of the Information in the Term Structure About Future Inflation, *Journal of International Money and Finance,* **10**, 2-22.

Nelson, C. R. (1972). The Prediction Performance of the FRB-MIT-PENN Model of the U.S. Economy, *The American Economic Review*, **LXII**, 902-17

Nelson, D. B. (1991). Conditional Heteroskedasticity in Asset Returns: A New Approach. *Econometrica,* 59**,** 347–70

Nelson, C. R. Schwert G. W. (1977). Short Term Interest Rates as Predators of Inflation: On Testing the Hypothesis That Real Rate of Interest is Constant. *American Economic Review* **67**, 478-86.

Oh, C. (1994). Estimation of Time-varying Term Premia of U.S. Treasury Securities: Using a STARCH Model with Stable Distributions. PhD dissertation, Ohio State University, Columbus, Ohio

Pagan, A. R. Schwert, G. W. (1990). Alternative Models for Conditional Stock Volatility, *Journal of Econometrics,* **45**, 267-90.

Robertson, D. (1992). Term Structure Forecast of Inflation, *The Economic Journal*, **102**, 1083-1093.

Sargent, T. J. (1973). Interest Rates and Prices in the Long Run, *Journal of Money Credit and Banking,* **5**, 385-449.

Schiller, R. J. and McCulloch, J. H. (1987). The Term Structure of Interest Rates. *NBER Working Paper* No. **234I.**

Sorenson, H. W. and Alspach, D. L. (1971). Recursive Bayesian Estimation using Gaussian Sums, *Automatica*, **7**, 465-79

Stock, J. H., and Watson, M. W. (1999). Forecasting Inflation, *Journal of Monetary Economics*, **44**, 293-335

Stock, J. H. and Watson, W. (1990). New Index of Coincident Leading Indicators, *NBER Working Paper* No. **R 1380**.

Stockton, D. J., and Glassman, J. (1987). An Evaluation of the Forecast Performance of Alternate Models of Inflation, *Review of Economics and Statistics*, 108-117.

Summers, L. H. (1983). The Non-Adjustment of Nominal Interest Rates: A Study of Fisher Effect. In Macroeconomic Prices and Quantities, J. Tobin ed. *The Brookings Institution*: Washington D.C.

Summers L. H. (1987). The non-adjustment of the Nominal Interest Rates, and Robert B Barky, Fisher Hypothesis and Forcastablity and Persistence of Inflation. *Journal of Monetary Economics,* **9**, 3-24.

Watson, M. (1986). Univariate Detrending Methods with Stochastic Trends, *Journal of Monetary Economics,* **18**, 49–75.

Zolotarev, M. (1986). *One Dimensional Stable Laws*. American Mathematical Society. (Translation of *Odnomernye Ustoichivye Raspredeleniia*, Nauka, Moscow, 1983.)

In: Inflation: Causes and Effects
Editor: Leon V. Schwartz, pp. 103-120
ISBN: 978-1-60741-823-8

Chapter 5

PRICE BEHAVIOR AT HIGH INFLATION: EVIDENCE FROM LATIN AMERICA

M. Ángeles Caraballo[1], Carlos Dabús[2] and Diego Caramuta[3]

[1] Universidad de Sevilla, Spain
[2] CONICET and Universidad Nacional del Sur, Argentina
[3] Universidad Nacional del Sur, Argentina

Abstract

This chapter presents evidence on a non linear "inflation-relative prices" relationship in three Latin American countries with very high inflation experiences: Argentina, Brazil and Peru. Our results show a non concave relation during the episodes of higher price instability, and particularly at hyperinflation. This non concavity is mainly explained by the component of unexpected inflation, which suggests that the volatility associated to episodes of extreme inflation can be particularly relevant to understand the non neutrality of inflation

1. Introduction

Without monetary rigidities money is neutral, and there is independence between nominal and real variables. Relative prices depend on real factors and the general price level is determined in the monetary sector; therefore, changes in the general price level do not affect real prices. Nevertheless, this is no supported by the empirical evidence; in fact, there is a vast literature showing a strong relationship between inflation and relative prices variability (RPV)[1]. But there is no consensus about the mechanisms underlying the positive correlation

---

[1] See Vining and Elwertowski (1976) for US, Parks (1978) for the Netherlands and US, Fischer (1981) for US, Fischer (1982) for Germany, Blejer and Leiderman (1982) and Palerm (1991) for Mexico, Quddus et al. (1988) for the Chinese hyperinflation, Tommasi (1993) and Dabús (2000) for Argentina, Fielding and Mizen (2000) for ten countries of European Union, Barnejee et al. (2007) for UK and US, Kucuk-Tuger and Tuger (2004) for Turkey, Caraballo and Usabiaga (2004) for the 17 regions of Spain, and Scharff (2007) for a cross country analysis. In turn, more recently Balderas and Nath (2008) for Mexico show that an external shock,

between inflation and RPV[2]. Moreover, theoretical approaches like "imperfect information" or "adjustment costs" have similar implications on such relationship.

The predictions of the main theoretical models can be summarized as follows. Firstly, signal-extraction model, based on the Lucas-type confusion between aggregate and relative shocks, emphasizes the positive effect of unexpected inflation on RPV: as inflation is not always correctly anticipated, it creates "misperceptions" of absolute and relative prices. Hence, increases in unexpected inflation will raise RPV. Likewise, Lucas' imperfect information model emphasizes the role of unexpected inflation in generating intermarket RPV and points out the positive impact of inflation volatility on RPV as well (Lucas (1973)). In both models the relevant concept is the dispersion of the individual products inflation rates around the aggregate rate of inflation, i.e. the intermarket RPV. However, the empirical evidence is mixed. On one hand, several studies for very different countries confirm that intermarket RPV increases mainly with unexpected inflation, but expected inflation has no effect on RPV –see, among others, Parks (1978) for USA, Blejer (1981) for Argentina in a period in which the annual rate of inflation was over 140%, Nautz and Scharff (2005) for Germany-. On the other hand, there is evidence showing that both expected and unexpected inflation affect RPV. For example, Fischer (1981, 1982) and Aarstol (1999) conclude for different periods in US that RPV increases with both expected inflation and positive unexpected inflation, but not with negative unexpected inflation. Tang and Wang (1993) show for the Chinese hyperinflation period (1946-1949) that RPV increases with both expected inflation and the absolute value of unexpected inflation. Moreover, Silver and Ioannidis (2001) find for nine European countries that coefficients for unexpected inflation are generally statistically significant and negative, while Nautz and Scharff (2006) find that expected inflation increases significantly RPV at very low and very high inflation (in European standards) in the euro area, but there is no effect at intermediate values of inflation rate. Finally, as far as inflation volatility is concerned, empirical evidence shows that it is positively correlated to inflation, both for low and high inflation countries, as it has been found by Chang and Cheng (2000) for US and Caraballo et al. (2006) for Spain and Argentina.

A second approach assumes that nominal price changes are subject to menu costs. In this case, the optimal policy is to set prices discontinuously according to an (S,s) price rule: the firm changes its nominal price when the real price hits a lower threshold, s, and the nominal price is changed so that the new real price equals a higher return point S. The distance between S and s increases with the expected value of inflation and, therefore, expected inflation affects RPV. Moreover, if menu costs are different among firms or firms experience specific shocks, staggered price setting will arise exacerbating the effect of higher inflation on RPV. Strictly speaking, these models are usually concerned with the price setting behavior of sellers of a single product, i.e. they compare the behavior of the price of a single product with the average inflation of that product. Therefore, they have direct implications for intramarket RPV. But generally such distinction is not found in the literature, and the common practice is

given by remittances, provokes a positive inflation-RPV relationship. On the contrary, Sainz and Manuelito (2006) find that recent low inflation experiences of several countries of Latin America have been accompanied by higher price dispersion.

2 It is useful to distinguish between intermarket RPV - the standard deviation of the individual rate of price change around the average inflation rate- and intramarket RPV -the standard deviation of relative price changes of a given product across stores around its average inflation rate-. In this chapter we use the intermarket RPV.

to interpret the positive relation between expected inflation and intermarket RPV as an implication of the menu costs model. An exception is the contribution of Lach and Tsiddon (1992) for Israel. These authors obtain the intramarket RPV for 26 food products. They conclude that the effect of expected inflation on intramarket RPV is stronger than the effect of unexpected inflation.

Finally, models based on costly consumer search lead to a positive relation between inflation and intramarket RPV. This type of models tries to explain why the same good has different prices in the market, therefore the relevant variable is the intramarket RPV. In this model, the information's obsolescence due to inflation reduces the optimal stock of price information that consumers wish to hold, and as the consumers are differentially informed, inflation leads to a higher RPV. In this sense, Domberger (1987) for the United Kingdom, Amano and Macklem (1997) for Canada, and Parsley (1996) for some cities of the US have found a positive relationship between inflation and intramarket RPV. However, the evidence suggests that when economies are experiencing very high inflation rates, intramarket RPV can even decrease when inflation increases, which imply a concave relation between RPV and inflation –see Dazinger (1987) and Van Hoomisen (1988) for Israel, and Tommasi (1993) for Argentina-.

In short, different theories posit alternative channels by which inflation affects RPV, while the empirical evidence does not support unambiguously a particular approach. This can be due to the fact that the inflation-RPV relationship is very sensitive to changes in disaggregation, periodicity of the data, price indexes and, specially, to inflation regimes. Concerning to the latter issue, Caglayan and Filiztekin (2003) for Turkey and Caraballo et. al (2006) for Spain and Argentina show that failures to control for structural changes in the inflation series will lead to biased results and misleading conclusions. Our chapter is focused on this issue and, more precisely, on the changes in the relation between inflation and RPV across different inflation regimes and the mechanisms underlying such changes. In particular, we study if such relation is non-linear, as well as which factors could explain a non-concave relation at higher inflation. As it was above mentioned, Dazinger(1987), Van Hoomisen (1988) and Tommasi (1993) suggest that in economies experiencing very high inflation rates, intramarket RPV can even decrease when inflation increases, which is implying some evidence of concavity due to the presence of some unifying forces in pricing at very high inflation. On the contrary, our hypothesis is that the effects of inflation on relative prices are even stronger when inflation is increasing and therefore inflation is far from being neutral. In other words, the relation between both variables should be non concave. In order to test our hypothesis, we have chosen three countries with a very rich inflationary history: Argentina, Brazil and Peru. Our results show a clear non-concave inflation-RPV relationship at high inflation, -in fact, RPV explodes in hyperinflation- while this relation is concave at lower inflation. In turn, unexpected inflation appears to be the main explanatory factor of the non-linearity in such relation.

In those three economies inflation has fluctuated from moderate levels to hyperinflation periods; monthly inflation rates surpassed 200% in Argentina and 400% in Peru. This sample allows us to carry out an exhaustive study to determine if there are similarities among the inflation processes in these economies, and then if it is possible to reach a greater consensus about the channels underlying the relationship between inflation and RPV. Moreover, this comparative analysis can shed some light on the price behaviour at different inflation regimes. In these cases an economy exhibits a higher level of "noise", induced by a more erratic and less predictable evolution of the inflation rate, and then a loss of information that induces adaptive changes in expectations. Thus, a higher level of inflation may imply modifications in the behaviour of prices, and then larger effects on the price system.

The chapter is organised as follows. Section 2 describes the data and variables. Section 3 reports the empirical findings on the relation between inflation and RPV, two alternative methodologies to obtain the inflation regimes and the changes in the inflation-RPV relationship when inflation regimes are introduced . Section 4 explains the results obtained in section 3 by means of decomposing inflation in its unexpected, expected and volatility components. Finally, section 5 concludes.

2. Price Data and Variables

The data set includes monthly time series of disaggregated prices. For Argentina price series have been extracted from the statistical bulletins of the Instituto Nacional de Estadísticas y Censos, from January 1960 to November 1993. Individual price data correspond to the items of the national Wholesale Price Index (WPI), at the level of WPI groups (i.e. three digits of the International Standard Industrial Classification). Since the structure of WPI in Argentina changed in July 1984, we use 87 price indexes for the January 1960-June 1984 and 64 for the July 1984-November 1993 periods.

In the case of Peru we use 168 individual prices from the Consumer Price Index (CPI) for the January 1980-April 1994 period, extracted from the Instituto Nacional de Estadísticas. Price data include changes of price weights in 1985, 1988 and 1989. Finally, for Brazil we use 52 individual prices of the WPI for the January 1974-August 1996 period, which were obtained from the Fundação Getulio Vargas.

2.1. Price Data

In general price data are collected in two ways. Some prices are sampled daily or several times a week, and from this information a monthly average is obtained. Other prices are sampled the same day each month. In Argentina, for example, the WPI price data are collected in those two ways. The prices of agricultural products are sampled as a monthly average from daily information, and the prices of industrial and imported products are sampled the same day (the 15th) of each month. In Brazil, agricultural prices are collected in the same way as in Argentina, and industrial prices are sampled once a month.

Finally, in Peru there are different ways and frequencies of price collection. The prices of goods sold in fruits and vegetables markets are sampled weekly (on Thursdays and Saturdays), and from this information a monthly average is obtained. Prices of products in commercial stores are sampled the same day each month, and rental and public utilities prices are collected once a month.

In sum, most of the prices are collected the same day each month, or result from a monthly average from daily (or nearly daily) information. Hence, these methodologies of price collection should not provoke spurious correlation between inflation and RPV[3]. A clear example is the notorious increase of RPV in both Argentine hyperinflations, during 1989 and 1990. This should be a real increment, because most of the prices used to calculate this variability are prices of the industrial and imported goods sectors, which are collected the same day of each month (data include 77 industrial and imported good prices from a total of 87 for the 1960-1984 period, and 55 of a total of 64 for the 1984-1993 period).

2.2. Variables

The variables used in this study are the monthly inflation rate (IN), a measure of inflation volatility, expected and unexpected inflation, and RPV[4]. The expected inflation (INE) is the inflation rate forecasted by economic agents for the current period and it is obtained from an ARMA model. Its specification was selected by applying the Schwartz and Akaike criteria. From the results of these criteria we use an ARMA (1,1) model for Argentina and Brazil, and an ARMA (1,2) for Peru. Unexpected inflation (INO) is the error of expected inflation, which results from the difference between the actual and the expected inflation (INO=IN-INE).

On the other hand, inflation volatility is measured by the variance of inflation rate (VAR) obtained from a GARCH (1,1) model. In this model we use the same specification of the expected inflation as the one used in the ARMA model to compute INE. In this way, VAR is obtained using the forecasted values from this GARCH model. Finally, as it is common in this kind of literature, RPV is measured as the standard deviation of the individual rate of price change around the average inflation rate. We introduce a slight variation because at high inflation the usual RPV can be spuriously correlated with the mean of the distribution -the average inflation rate-. In order to avoid this problem, we define RPV as:

$$RPV_t = \frac{\sum_i w_{it}(IN_{it} - IN_t)^2}{(1 + IN_t)^2}$$

where RPV denotes the relative price variability, w_{it} is the weight of price i in the price index, IN_{it} is the inflation rate of price i at month t and IN_t is the inflation rate at period t[5].

3 Otherwise this correlation could be "contaminated" by the methodology of price collection and by the inflation process itself. For example, if two prices are always equal and every month a price is sampled on the first day and the other one the last day, the actual variability of relative prices is zero. At lower (higher) inflation lower (higher) relative price variability should be detected, which would be only consequence of the periodicity of price collection.

4 In order to analyze the stationarity of the series, we have applied the ADF test to the monthly inflation rate and to RPV, which leads us to reject the unit root hypothesis even at the 1% level.

5 Except for Brazil, where we only estimate a non-weighted RPV due to the unavailability of the corresponding weights of individual prices.

3. Empirical Evidence

This section presents the empirical results. Given that the series show an important autocorrelation component, the conclusions about the significance of the regressors are based on the Newey-West consistent covariance estimator. In addition, to test the robustness of the results, we apply a nonlinear least squares estimation method, by assuming a first order autocorrelation component.

The results of the estimations appear in Table 1, where RPV is explained by a polynomial of the inflation rate. To test autocorrelation, we use the Ljung-Box test. In turn, figures 1, 2 and 3, obtained from these estimations, illustrate such results. Moreover, when the estimation presents a serious case of autocorrelation, the results of the nonlinear least squares estimation are also presented.

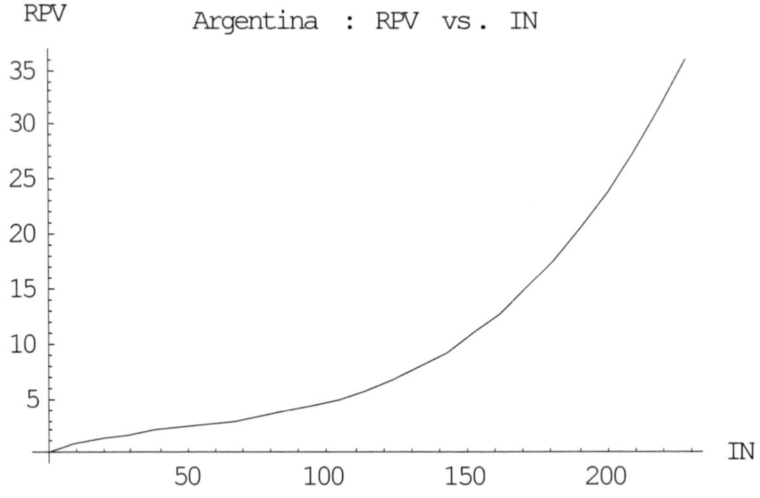

Figure 1. Argentina.

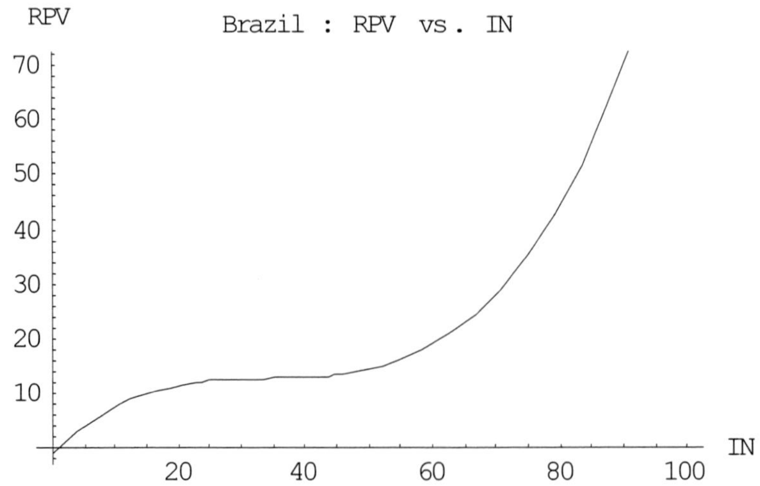

Figure 2. Brazil.

Table 1.

Dependent Variable: RPV								
	Argentina			**Brazil**		**Peru**		
	(I)*‡	**(II)*‡**	**(III)**†**	**(I)*‡**	**(II)*†**	**(I)*‡**	**(II)*‡**	**(III)**†**
IN	0.07038	0.06866	0.07644	1.14831	1.05836	1.13353	0.96401	1.14849
	(2.884)	(2.887)	(3.631)	(4.210)	(4.509)	(4.695)	(3.532)	(3.552)
IN^2	-0.00076	-0.00081	-0.00092	-0.0329	-0.0306	-0.0058	-0.0040	-0.00597
	(-2.129)	(-2.319)	(-3.036)	(-3.223)	(-3.469)	(-2.236)	(-1.516)	(-1.974)
IN^3	0.000005	0.000005	0.000005	0.00032	0.00029	0.00001	0.00001	0.00001
	(3.911)	(4.239)	(5.041)	(3.450)	(3.523)	(2.648)	(1.980)	(2.423)
VAR		0.00874			0.51631		0.06070	
		(1.765)			(1.833)		(5.669)	
Constant	0.18697	0.13817	0.16885	-0.7707	-2.4955	-1.2072	-0.8631	-1.31060
	(2.832)	(1.913)	(1.810)	(-1.013)	(-1.982)	(-0.967)	(-0.622)	(-0.764)
AR(1)			0.56439					0.15689
			(4.175)					(1.233)
Adjusted R^2	0.742	0.748	0.823	0.236	0.318	0.903	0.915	0.905
p-value Ljung-Box(L=1)	0.000	0.000		0.054	0.469	0.043	0.084	
p-value Ljung-Box(L=2)	0.000	0.000	0.387	0.025	0.492	0.008	0.047	0.013
Observations	407	407	406	270	270	171	171	171

The values in brackets are the t-statistics.
* Estimated by Ordinary Least Squares
** Estimated applying a Marquardt Non Linear Least Squares Algorithm
† White Heteroskedasticity-Consistent Standard Errors & Covariance
‡ Newey-West HAC Standard Errors & Covariance.

Table 1 shows a clear non-linear inflation-RPV relationship, which is particularly evident in the figures. This relationship is concave in lower inflation periods, but convex at high inflation, and particularly at hyperinflation. In lower inflation the quadratic term prevails over the cubic term, while in high inflation the cubic term begins to be more significant than the quadratic term. Therefore, in low inflation the negative sign associated to the quadratic term suggests a concave relationship, while the positive sign associated to the cubic term points out a convex relationship between those variables at high inflation.

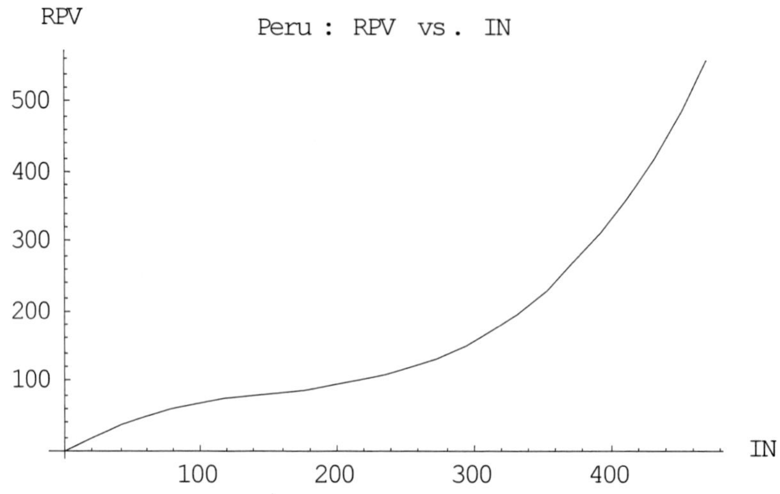

Figure 3. Peru.

In short, our results suggest that the inflation-RPV relationship changes at different inflation levels. This evidence deserves a more careful study in order to see if these conclusions hold when inflationary regimes are introduced as controls. Thus, in order to verify if the results are robust to alternative methods of classifying the total period in inflationary regimes, we apply two methodologies. On one hand, it can be considered that the thresholds of inflation that divide the regimes are determined exogenously, and on the other hand it can be assumed that regimes are generated endogenously. The first methodology follows a version of the criterion previously applied in Dabús (1993,2000) for Argentina. This method sets three thresholds of monthly inflation to distinguish such regimes, 1%, 10%, and 50%[1]. Therefore, we obtain four regimes: moderate (under 1%), high (1-10%), very high (10-50%) and hyperinflation (over 50%). After that, the different inflation periods of each country are classified in these regimes, which are presented in table 1 in the Appendix. The second methodology is based on a Markov switching regression model – see Hamilton (1989,1994)-. With this method, regimes are defined using a model that endogenously determines the probability of being in a regime. We assume that a particular period can be included in a specific regime when the probability of being in such regime is above 0.5[2]. Finally, the

[1] This methodology was developed by Dabús (1993). See Caraballo et al. (2006) for further details.

[2] We specified the Markov switching regression model as an autorregresive model of order 1 with three states. To estimate this model we used a reformulated version of the algorithm provided by James D. Hamilton in his web page. Since the algorithm does not converge to any result for each of the complete series, the hyperinflation months were removed from the estimation. Hence, we obtained four regimes, one of

inflation regimes obtained with both methodologies are represented by dummy variables, D1, D2, D3 and D4, which mean moderate, high, very high and hyperinflation, respectively.

Table 2 shows the results of estimations with Dabús' methodology and table 3 presents the results corresponding to the Markov switching model method. The cubic term of inflation was not included because the dummy variables combined with the inflation rate capture the linear relation between inflation and RPV, and a convex or concave relation when they are combined with the inflation quadratic term. For example, results obtained in table 1 show a convex relation under hyperinflation. This fact is also captured by the regime dummies, the inflation rate and the inflation quadratic term, therefore it can be concluded that the cubic term is relevant only when the regimes are removed from the regression.

Table 2.

Dependent Variable: RPV						
Estimated by Ordinary Least Squares						
	Argentina		**Brazil**		**Peru**	
	(I)‡	**(II)‡**	**(I)‡**	**(II)‡**	**(I)†**	**(II)‡**
D1	0.3019*		1.4034*			
D2	0.4909*		2.0668*		4.564735*	
D3	1.2448*		11.4095*		40.75923*	
D4	6.409*					
D1*IN		0.0969**		0.2201		
D1*IN²		0.0070		1.0353**		
D2*IN		0.1227*		0.4867*		0.8595*
D2*IN²		-0.0049*		0.0028		-0.0021
D3*IN		0.0313		0.5553*		0.7879*
D3*IN²		0.0014		-0.0024		0.0005
D4*IN		-0.0124				
D4*IN²		0.0006*				
Adjusted R^2	0.290	0.730	0.172	0.186	0.156	0.896
p-val Ljung-Box(L=1)	0.000	0.000	0.015	0.004	0.309	0.059
Observations	407	407	270	270	171	171

* (**) Coefficient different from cero at 1% (5%) significance level
† White Heteroskedasticity-Consistent Standard Errors & Covariance
‡ Newey-West HAC Standard Errors & Covariance
Estimations include dummies variables that were obtained by Dabús' methodology.

For both methodologies, the dummies were statistically significant and with the expected sign, which suggests the relevance of the different regimes to explain RPV. On the other hand, when the inflation rate is included, results are slightly different depending on the methods applied in order to obtain the inflation regimes. As far as for Dabús' method is concerned, Table 2 shows mixed evidence for the hypothesis of a non-linear relationship (a concave relationship in low levels of inflation and a convex relationship in high levels of

---

hyperinflation, which includes the hyperinflation periods that were excluded from the sample, while the other three regimes (moderate, high and very high inflation) were determined by the model.

inflation) in Argentina, but it doesn't hold for Brazil and Peru. Thus, in Argentina the concave relationship is significant for the high inflation regime and the convex relationship is significant for the hyperinflation one but the non-linear relationship is not significant in the moderate inflation regime. On the contrary, Brazil shows a convex relationship in the moderate inflation regime and a linear relationship in high and very high inflation contexts, while in Peru only the linear relationships are statistically different from zero.

Table 3.

Dependent Variable: RPV						
Estimated by Ordinary Least Squares						
	Argentina		Brazil		Peru	
	(I)‡	(II)‡	(I)‡	(II)†	(I)†	(II)‡
D1	0.4536*		5.5193*		6.2964*	
D2	0.9621*		8.6547*		45.61*	
D3	3.3885**		9.5048*		28.599*	
D4	6.7694*		37.5441*		180.40	
D1*IN		0.1129*		0.7512*		0.9621*
D1 *IN²		-0.0023		0.0034		-0.0083
D2 *IN		-0.0312		-0.0148		-0.6177
D2 *IN²		0.0034		0.0147		0.0802*
D3 *IN		0.0671		-0.0114		2.0845**
D3 *IN²		0.0003		0.0079**		-0.0328
D4 *IN		-0.0045		0.2060		0.3996*
D4 *IN²		0.0005*		0.0038		0.0013*
Adjusted R^2	0.329	0.726	0.091	0.288	0.434	0.957
p-val Ljung-Box(L=1)	0.000	0.000	0.000	0.220	0.284	0.002
Observations	407	407	270	270	171	171

* (**) Coefficient different from cero at 1% (5%) significance level
† White Heteroskedasticity-Consistent Standard Errors & Covariance
‡ Newey-West HAC Standard Errors & Covariance.
Estimations include dummies variables obtained by Markov switching regression model.

However, the results obtained with the Markov switching regression model –see table 3- support to a greater extent the non-linear relationship hypothesis: Although for the three countries we find a linear relationship in moderate inflation, results show a convex relationship for higher levels of inflation. Thereby, a convex relation is found in hyperinflation period for Argentina, in very high inflation regime in Brazil and in high inflation and hyperinflation regimes in Peru.

4. Inflation Expectations and Non-Linearities

In the previous section empirical results show a convex relationship between inflation and RPV in very high and hyperinflation regimes for the three countries under study. In this section we focus on the reasons for such non-linear relationship. In other words, we try to explain why the impact of inflation on RPV is increasing with the inflation level. In order to do that, we regress RPV on the components of the inflation rate: its volatility (VAR), and expected (INE) and unexpected inflation (INO). As it was explained in section 2.2, INE and INO were obtained from an ARMA model, and VAR from a GARCH model. In addition to this, and given that the results may depend on the specification of INE, an alternative way of constructing the expected inflation is introduced to test the robustness of the results. Thus, we define INE' as the expected inflation obtained assuming stationary expectations; i.e., the inflation in *t* is equal to the inflation in *t-1*. In turn, the alternative measure of unexpected inflation can be defined as: INO'= IN-INE'. Finally, in order to test a non-linear relationship between RPV and inflation expectations, once again we include the polynomial terms of INE, INO, INE' and INO'.

Table 4 shows the results of the regression of RPV on the expected inflation (INE and INE') and inflation volatility and table 5 presents the results of the regression of RPV on the unexpected inflation (INO and INO') and inflation volatility.

From table 4, it can be seen for Argentina and Brazil the INE-RPV relationship is non-convex, while the INE'-RPV one is non-convex just for Peru. On the other hand, table 5 shows that a convex relationship between unexpected inflation (both INO and INO') and RPV arises. Therefore, taken into account these results, it seems that the unexpected component of inflation has a clear convex effect on the RPV, while the results of expected inflation are sensitive to the specification of inflationary expectations. Finally, volatility is not significant in any case.

Table 6 presents the results of regressions including jointly both components (expected and unexpected inflation). As far as for Argentina is concerned, a concave (convex) relationship between expected inflation and RPV in low (high) values of expected inflation for both specifications (INE and INE', and INO and INO') can be observed. This result holds for Brazil for the INE' and INO' specifications, while the INE-RPV relationship is linear and the INO-RPV one is convex. Finally, for Peru results are ambiguous. There is a convex (linear) relationship between INE (INO) and RPV, while with the alternative specification a linear relationship between INE' and RPV is statistically significant. In short, except in Peru, the unexpected component presents a convex relationship with the RPV.

To sum up, the relationship between RPV and the unexpected component of the inflation appears to be convex in Argentina and Brazil but the expected inflation presents a more ambiguous relationship with the RPV. Hence, our results show that the unexpected inflation is crucial to explain the convex relationship between inflation and RPV, and this conclusion is more relevant considering high inflation contexts where the unexpected component is relatively more important than the expected component[3].

[3] In fact, in our specification of INE and INO we confirmed that unexpected inflation is relatively more important at higher inflation (this result was not included in the chapter but it is available from authors upon request).

Table 4.

Dependent Variable: RPV Estimated by Ordinary Least Squares												
	Argentina				Brazil				Peru			
	(I)*‡	(II)*‡	(III)*‡	(IV)**‡	(I)*†	(II)*†	(III)*†	(IV)*†	(I)*†	(II)*†	(III)*†	(IV)**†
INE	0.0825*	0.0896**			0.4597*	0.3566**			3.5761*	3.5293*		
INE^2	-0.0002	-0.0002			-0.0005	-0.0005			-0.054*	-0.0576*		
INE^3									0.0002**	0.0002*		
INE'			-0.0274	-0.0286			1.0953*	0.9954*			1.5548	1.5534**
INE'^2			0.0023**	0.0023**			-0.0313**	-0.0287*			-0.0032	-0.0032
INE'^3			-0.00001**	-0.00001**			0.0003**	0.0002*				
VAR		-0.006726		0.0036		0.4249		0.5147		0.055347		0.0013
Constant	0.07753	0.081557	0.4822*	0.4656*	1.1799	0.3561	-0.4248	-2.0430	-11.3838	-11.2625	-4.2614	-4.2618
Adjust edR2	0.310	0.311	0.518	0.517	0.214	0.261	0.206	0.285	0.193	0.196	0.269	0.265
p-val Ljung -Box(L=1)	0.008	0.011	0.000	0.000	0.212	0.344	0.892	0.819	0.719	0.410	0.206	0.205
Observations	407	407	407	407	270	270	270	270	171	171	171	171

* (**) Coefficient different from cero at 1% (5%) significance level
† White Heteroskedasticity-Consistent Standard Errors & Covariance
‡ Newey-West HAC Standard Errors & Covariance.

Table 5.

Dependent Variable: RPV Estimated by Ordinary Least Squares												
	Argentina				Brazil				Peru			
	(I)*‡	(II)*‡	(III)*‡	(IV)**‡	(I)*†	(II)*†	(III)*†	(IV)*†	(I)*†	(II)*†	(III)*†	(IV)**†
INO	0.01528	0.0179			0.2997	0.4987**			0.3966*	0.4958*		
INO^2	0.0013*	0.0012*			0.0413*	0.024**			0.0029*	0.0025*		
INO^3	0.000007*	0.000007*			0.0005	0.0002			-0.000003	-0.000002		
INO'			0.0259	0.0264			0.5805*	0.5389*			0.1599	0.2551**
INO'^2			0.0024*	0.0022*			0.0475*	0.0359*			0.0017*	0.0014*
INO'^3			0.00001*	0.00001*			0.0005*	0.0003*			0.000002*	0.000002*
VAR		0.004741		0.0099		0.5886*		0.6247**		0.1078*		0.1192
Constant	0.4735*	0.4423*	0.4448*	0.3779*	5.0811*	2.7575*	5.4550*	2.7055*	8.1807*	6.5296*	8.7508*	7.3752*
Adjusted R2	0.673	0.673	0.623	0.630	0.179	0.260	0.095	0.220	0.839	0.876	0.846	0.857
p-val Ljung-Box(L=1)	0.000	0.000	0.000	0.000	0.262	0.237	0.006	0.015	0.000	0.000	0.000	0.000
Observations	407	407	407	407	270	270	270	270	171	171	171	171

* (**) Coefficient different from cero at 1% (5%) significance level

† White Heteroskedasticity-Consistent Standard Errors & Covariance

‡ Newey-West HAC Standard Errors & Covariance.

Table 6.

Dependent Variable: RPV Estimated by Ordinary Least Squares												
	Argentina				Brazil				Peru			
	(I)*‡	(II)*‡	(III)*‡	(IV)**‡	(I)*†	(II)*†	(III)*†	(IV)*†	(I)*†	(II)*†	(III)*†	(IV)**†
INE	0.0677*	0.0665*			0.9298**	0.7037			1.7279*	1.3702*		
INE^2	-0.001**	- 0.0011**			-0.0275	-0.0197			-0.0203	- 0.016182		
INE^3	0.00001*	0.00001*			0.0003	0.0002			0.00007**	0.00008*		
INE'			0.0648*	0.0642*			1.1658*	1.0673*			0.9319*	0.9161*
INE'^2			-0.0012*	-0.0012*			-0.0373*	-0.0341*			-0.0018	-0.0018
INE'^3			0.00001*	0.00001*			0.0003*	0.0003*			0.00001	0.00001
INO	0.0169	0.017466			0.1641	0.3346			0.3974	0.6013**		
INO^2	0.0002	0.000121			0.0276**	0.0189**			0.0009	-0.0012		
INO^3	0.00001*	0.00001*			0.0004**	0.0003			0.000001	0.00001		
INO'			0.0149	0.0143			0.5199*	0.5068*			0.5431	0.5537
INO'^2			0.0007*	0.0007*			0.029*	0.0233*			-0.0003	-0.0004
INO'^3			0.00001*	0.00001*			0.0003*	0.0003**			0.000004	0.000005
VAR		0.002398		0.0034		0.3929		0.4828		0.066*		0.0185
Constant	0.1844*	0.1787*	0.2039*	0.1871*	-0.5610	-0.8646	-0.8993	-2.3864	-3.6219	-2.3820	-0.4540	-0.4911
Adjusted R 2	0.744	0.743	0.752	0.752	0.283	0.313	0.262	0.331	0.906	0.916	0.916	0.916
p-val Ljung-Box(L=1)	0.000	0.000	0.000	0.000	0.968	0.933	0.414	0.656	0.169	0.107	0.215	0.235
Observations	407	407	407	407	270	270	270	270	171	171	171	171

* (**) Coefficient different from cero at 1% (5%) significance level

† White Heteroskedasticity-Consistent Standard Errors & Covariance

‡ Newey-West HAC Standard Errors & Covariance.

5. Conclusion

This chapter is focused basically on two issues concerning the RPV-inflation relationship. On one hand, previous literature has shown that such relationship is very sensitive to changes in the average inflation rate, finding evidence of concavity at very high inflation. This result leads us to analyse such relation in high inflation countries, with sundry inflation regimes: Argentina, Brazil and Peru. On the other hand, as there are different theoretical models that can explain the RPV-inflation relationship, we have tried to identify which explanation could fit better the evidence found for the aforementioned countries.

Our results differ from previous literature. Firstly, we find that changes in inflation regimes affect strongly the RPV-inflation relationship, and this result is robust to the two methodologies applied in this chapter in order to obtain the inflation regimes. In all cases our evidence shows a convex relationship between inflation and RPV. Furthermore, this evidence is even stronger at higher inflation when Markov switching regression model is applied to determine different inflation regimes.

On the other hand, such convexity is mainly explained by unexpected inflation, which is not compatible with the menu costs model, since expected inflation has a key role to explain RPV in this approach. Moreover, our evidence shows that the uncertainty associated to very high inflation periods can be particularly relevant to understand the non neutrality of inflation in extreme price instability, while the expected component is sensitive to the expectations mechanism used. This is suggesting that in an environment of very changing and high inflation, the price decisions of economic agents is quite complex because there are not appropriate mechanisms to avoid the impact of inflation on relative prices, like a satisfactory model to form expectations on current inflation.

In short, the inflation-RPV relationship seems to depend crucially of the inflationary experience of the countries under study. Meanwhile previous findings show that such relation is concave, our results point out that it becomes convex in extreme inflation.

Appendix

Table 1. Inflation Regimes. Dabús' Methodology

Country\ Regime	Argentina	Brazil	Peru
Moderate Inflation	January 1960-April 1970 April 1991-November 1993	March 1986-November 1986 August 1994-August 1996	
High Inflation	May 1970-January 1975 May 1976-June 1982 July 1985-June 1987 September 1988-March 1989 August 1989-November 1989 April 1990-March 1991	February 1974-December 1982	January 1980-February 1988 February 1991-April 1994
Very High Inflation	February 1975-April 1976 July 1982-June 1985 July 1987-August 1988	January 1983-February 1986 December 1986-July 1994	March 1988-January 1991
Hyper-inflation	April 1989-July 1989 December 1989-March 1990	*	*

* Although both countries experienced months of hyperinflation, a hyperinflation regime doesn't arise with this method because periods of hyperinflation lasted less than 3 months.

Table 2. Inflation Regimes. Markov's Methodology

Country\ Regime	Argentina	Brazil	Peru
Moderate Inflation	January 1960-May 1975 August 1975-December 1975 May 1976-May 1981 August 1981-June 1982 August 1982 October 1982-January 1983 March 1983-July 1983 July 1985-September 1987 November 1987-February 1988 September 1988-February 1989 August 1989-November 1989 April 1990-July 1990 October 1990-January 1991 March 1991-November 1993	March 1974-November 1988 February 1989-May 1989 April 1990-September 1991 August 1994-August 1996	February 1980-December 1980 February 1981-February 1988 April 1988-June 1988 April 1989-March 1990 May 1990 September 1990-November 1990 February 1991-April 1994
High Inflation	July 1975 January 1976-February 1976 April 1976 June 1981-July 1981 July 1982, September 1982 February 1983 August 1983-May 1985 October 1987 March 1988-August 1988 March 1989 August 1990-September 1990	June 1989 October 1991-April 1992 July 1994	January 1981 March 1988 August 1988 November 1988 March 1989 April 1990 December 1990-January 1991
Very High Inflation	June 1975, June 1985 December 1989, February 1991	December 1988-January 1989 July 1989-December 1989 May 1992-June 1994	July 1988, October 1988 December 1988-February 1989 June 1990
Hyper-inflation	March 1976 April 1989-July 1989 January 1990-March 1990	January 1990-March 1990	September 1988 July 1990-August 1990

References

Aarstol, M. (1999). Inflation, Inflation Uncertainty, and Relative Price Variability. *Southern Economic Journal*, **66 (2)**, 414-423.

Amano, R.A. & Macklem, R. (1997). Menu Costs, Relative Prices, and Inflation: Evidence for Canada, *Bank of Canada*, Working Paper 97-14.

Balderas, J. & Nath, H. (2008). Inflation and Relative Price Variability in Mexico: The Role of Remittances. *Applied Economic Letters,* **15 (1-3)**, 151-85.

Blejer M. (1981). The Dispersion of Relative Commodity Prices under very Rapid Inflation. *Journal of Development Economics,* **9 (3)**, 347-356.

Blejer, M. & Leiderman, L. (1982). Inflation and Relative Price Variability in the Open Economy. *European Economic Review*, **18 (2)**, 387-402.

Banerjee, A., Mizen, P. & Russell, B. (2007). Inflation, Relative Price Variability and the Markup: Evidence from the United States and the United Kingdom. *Economic Modelling,* **24 (1)**, 82-100.

Caglayan, M. & Filiztekin, A. (2003). Nonlinear Impact of Inflation on Relative Price Variability. *Economics Letters,* **79 (2)**, 213-218.

Caraballo, M.A. & Usabiaga, C. (2004). Análisis de la Estructura de la Inflación de las Regiones Españolas: La Metodología de Ball y Mankiw. *Investigaciones Regionales,* **5**, 63-86.

Caraballo, M.A., Dabús, C. & Usabiaga, C. (2006). Relative Prices and Inflation: New Evidence from Different Inflationary Contexts. *Applied Economics,* **38**, 1931-1944.

Chang, E.C. & Cheng, J.W. (2000). Further Evidence on the Variability of Inflation and Relative Price Variability. *Economics Letters,* **66 (1)**, 71-77.

Dabús, C. (1993). *Inflación y Precios Relativos: Estudio del Caso Argentino*. Doctoral Dissertation, Universidad Nacional del Sur (Argentina).

Dabús, C. (2000). Inflationary Regimes and Relative Price Variability: Evidence from Argentina. *Journal of Development Economics,* **62 (2)**, 535-547.

Dazinger, L. (1987). Inflation, Fixed Cost of Price Adjustment, and the Measurement of Relative Price Variability: Theory and Evidence. *American Economic Review,* **77 (4)**, 704-713.

Domberger, S. (1987). Relative Price Variability and Inflation: a Disaggregated Analysis. *Journal of Political Economy*, **95 (3)**, 547-566.

Fielding, D. & Mizen, P. (2000). Relative Price Variability and Inflation in Europe. *Economica*, **67 (265)**, 57-78.

Fischer, S. (1981). Relative Shocks, Relative Price Variability, and Inflation. *Brookings Papers on Economic Activity,* **2**, 381-431.

Fischer, S. (1982). Relative Price Variability and Inflation in the United States and Germany. *European Economic Review,* **18 (1)**, 171-196.

Hamilton J. (1989). A New Approach to the Economic Analysis of Nonstationary Time Series and the Business Cycle. *Econometrica,* **57 (2)**, 357-384.

Hamilton J. (1994). *Time Series Analysis*, Princeton: Princeton University Press.

Kucuk-Tuger, H. & Tuger, B. (2004). Relative Price Variability: The Case of Turkey 1994-2002. *Turkey Central Bank Review Issues,* **4**, 1-40.

Lach, S. & Tsiddon, D. (1992). The Behavior of Prices and Inflation: An Empirical Analysis of Disaggregated Price Data. *Journal of Political Economy,* **100 (2)**, 349-389.

Lucas, R.E. (1973). Some International Evidence on Output-Inflation Tradeoffs. *American Economic Review*, **63 (2)**, 326-344.

Nautz, D. & Scharff, J. (2005). Inflation and Relative Price Variability in a Low Inflation Country: Empirical Evidence for Germany, *German Economic Review,* **6(4)**, 507-523.

Nautz, D. & Scharff, J. (2006). Inflation and Relative Price Variability in the Euro Area: Evidence from a Panel Threshold Model. *Deutsche Bundesbank,* Discussion Papers No. 14/2006.

Palerm, A. (1991). Market Structure and Price Flexibility. *Journal of Development Economics*, **36 (1)**, 37-54.

Parks, R.W. (1978). Inflation and Relative Price Variability. *Journal of Political Economy,* **86 (1)**, 79-95.

Parsley, D.C. (1996). Inflation and Relative Price Variability in the Short and Long Run: New Evidence from the United States. *Journal of Money, Credit and Banking,* **28 (3)**, 323-342.

Quddus, M.; Butler, J.S. & Liu, J.T. (1988). Variability of Inflation and the Dispersion of Relative Prices: Evidence from the Chinese Hyperinflation of 1946-1949. *Economic Letters,* **27(3)**, 239-249.

Sainz, P. & Manuelito, S. (2006). Relative Prices in Latin America in Periods of Low Inflation and Structural Change. *CEPAL Review,* **89**, 95-122.

Scharff, J. (2007). Inflation and the Divergence of Relative Prices: Evidence from a Cointegration Analysis. *Advanced in Statistical Analysis,* **91**, 141-58.

Silver, M. & Ioannidis, C. (2001). Intercountry Differences in the Relationship between Relative Price Variability and Average Prices. *Journal of Political Economy,* **109 (2)**, 355-374.

Tang, D. & Wang, P. (1993). On Relative Price Variability and Hyperinflation. *Economics Letters*, **42 (2-3)**, 209-214.

Tommasi, M. (1993). Inflation and Relative Prices: Evidence from Argentina. In E. Sheshinski & Y. Weiss (1993) (Eds.), *Optimal Pricing, Inflation and Cost of Price Adjustment*, (pp. 487-513). Cambridge (Mass.): MIT Press.

Van Hoomissen, T. (1988). Price Dispersion and Inflation: Evidence from Israel. *Journal of Political Economy,* **96 (6)**, 1303-1314.

Vining, D.R. & Elwertowski, T.C. (1976). The Relationship between Relative Prices and General Price Level. *American Economic Review,* **66 (4)**, 699-708.

In: Inflation: Causes and Effects
Editor: Leon V. Schwartz, pp. 121-136

ISBN: 978-1-60741-823-8

Chapter 6

WAGE INFLATION AND LABOR MARKET PRESSURE: A PRINCIPAL COMPONENTS APPROACH

Takashi Senda*

Graduate School of Social Sciences Hiroshima University, 1-2-1 Kagamiyama, Higashihiroshima, Hiroshima, 739-8525, Japan

Abstract

In this paper, we investigate what is the best measure of labor market pressure for predicting wage inflation in Japan. Principal components analysis is used to select a subset of independent variables from 11 labor market variables. The first component is interpreted as the active opening rate and the second component is interpreted as total hours worked. We estimate a standard Phillips curve for wage inflation that incorporates the active opening rate and total hours worked as regressors. We find that (hourly) real wage growth is positively related to the active opening rate and negatively related to total hours worked. The second component (representing total hours worked) may help explain why wage inflation has not risen substantially despite Japan experiencing high active opening rates in the mid-2000s, when both total hours worked and active opening rates increased. Although higher active opening rates put upward pressure on real wage growth, this upward pressure is offset by longer working hours, which tend to reduce (hourly) real wage growth.

1. Introduction

Wage inflation is one of many economic indicators that are closely monitored by policymakers to predict inflation. Most economists believe that the Japanese GDP gap has turned from approximately zero to be positive in 2006, and that this positive GDP gap will soon pull up wages and prices. In fact, the active opening rate, which reached a low of 0.48 in 1999, rose steadily thereafter, increasing from 0.83 in 2004 to 1.06 in 2006. The active opening rate in 2006 was at its highest level since the early 1990s. Despite this tight labor market, the inflation rate failed to rise.[1]

* E-mail address: tsenda@hiroshima-u.ac.jp. Tel.: +81-82-424-7261; fax: +81-82-424-7212.

[1] For a discussion of the inflation forecast in 2006-2007, see Nishimura (2007) and Ueda (2007).

On the other hand, other indicators, such as unemployment, suggest that the labor market was weaker than the active opening rate suggests. The unemployment rate, which hit a peak of 5.38 percent in 2002, did not decline substantially; it was still as high as 4.14 percent in 2006.

The purpose of this paper is to build a measure of labor market pressure that explains wage inflation in Japan. In particular, this study focuses on the principal components of wage inflation and unemployment as a measure of labor market pressure.

Section 2 compares the evolution of the key labor market variables with the evolution of the first principal component. Section 3 estimates a wage Phillips curve with Japanese data. In the process, many issues in the specification of the wage equation are discussed. Section 4 uses more than one principal component to estimate the wage Phillips curve. Section 5 considers time-varying natural rate models. Section 6 concludes.

2. Labor Market Series and a Principal Components Approach

The unemployment rate and the active opening rate have been the leading indicators for measuring labor market pressure in Japan.[2] Both indicators are closely watched by policymakers. At times, however, the unemployment rate and the active opening rate have sent somewhat different signals. In 2006, for example, the active opening rate was quite high, suggesting a tight labor market in Japan. On the other hand, the unemployment rate remained high, by historical standards, although the rate had been declining since 2003.

This study follows the recent literature and estimates the common movement in a large set of correlated labor market variables using a principal components approach.[3] Principal components analysis is a statistical technique that linearly transforms an original set of variables into a substantially smaller set of uncorrelated variables. Its goal is to reduce the dimensionality of the original data set. Principal components analysis can be used in regression analysis. If the independent variables are highly correlated, then they can be transformed to principal components and the principal components can be used as the independent variables. This study uses 11 labor market variables to compute principal components. The first principal component accounts for 49 percent of the variance of the 11 labor market variables.

Figure 1 compares the active opening rate and the reciprocal of the unemployment rate with the first principal component.[4] The figure shows that the active opening rate closely tracks the first principal component. Both series indicate tight labor markets in the periods 1988–1992 and after 2005, and loose ones in the periods 1975–1987 and 1993–2003. In contrast, the reciprocal of the unemployment rate tracks the principal component poorly.

---

[2] The active opening rate is the ratio of active job openings to the number of active applicants. That is, the active opening rate is the ratio of the number of job offers (new jobs plus those carried forward from the previous month) to the number of job seekers registered at public employment security offices ("Hello Work") throughout the country. The active opening rate indicates the number of job offers per job seeker and is published monthly by the Ministry of Health, Labor and Welfare.

[3] See, for example, Stock and Watson (2002a, 2002b), Bernanke and Boivin (2003), Bernanke, Boivin, and Eliasz (2005), and Barnes, Chahrour, Olivei, and Tang (2007).

[4] Figure 1 plots the values of the first principal component. To make the labor market indexes comparable with the principal component series, we rescale the labor market indexes to have the same mean and standard deviation as the principal component over the sample period.

Hence, the figure suggests that the active opening rate captures labor market pressure better than the unemployment rate in Japan.

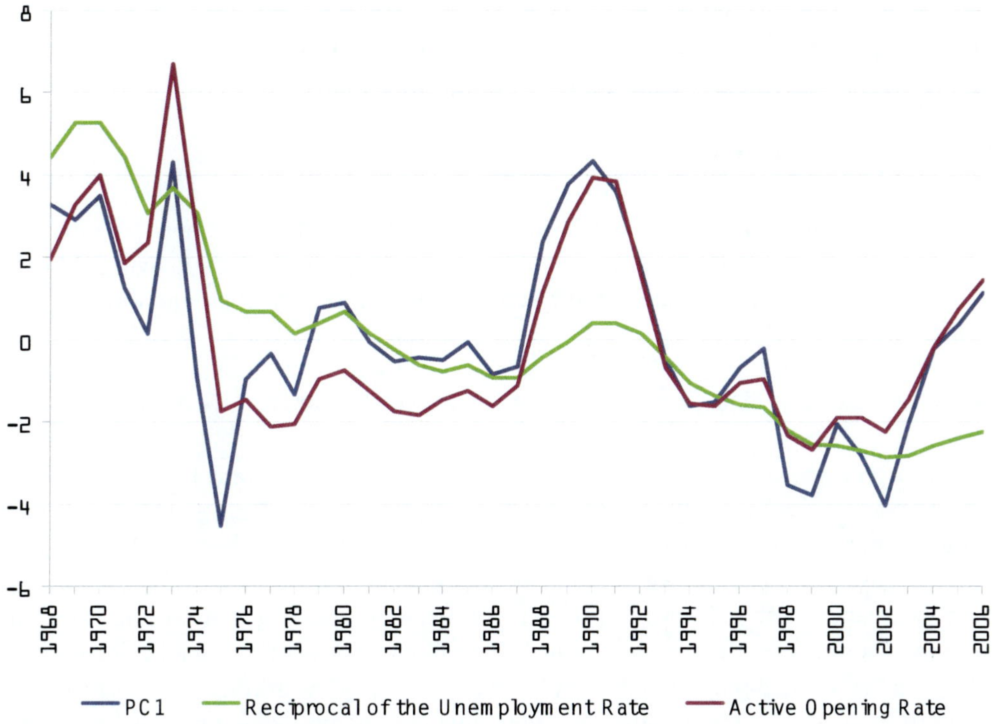

Figure 1. Reciprocal of the Unemployment Rate, Active Opening Rate and First Principal Component (PC1) (1968-2006).

3. Estimates of the Wage Phillips Curve

This section estimates a wage Phillips curve and examines the relationship between wage inflation and labor market indexes. The Phillips curve specification follows Blanchard and Katz (1997), Katz and Krueger (1999), and Ball and Moffitt (2001).[5]

In the wage Phillips curve specification, we assume that the difference between expected real-wage growth and labor-productivity growth depends on excess demand, as follows:

$$\left(\omega - \pi^{e}\right) - \theta = D, \tag{1}$$

where ω is nominal-wage growth, π^{e} is expected inflation, θ is labor-productivity growth, and D is excess demand. This equation implies that expected real wages tend to grow faster than productivity when labor market variables indicate tight employment conditions.

[5] On the dynamic path of inflation and unemployment in response to monetary policy shocks, see Mankiw (2001).

The data are annual. The wage-inflation rate ω is the change in the log of employee compensation per hour. Productivity growth θ is the change in the log of output per hour.[6] All these series are taken from the *System of National Accounts* produced by the Cabinet Office.

Before estimating the effects of labor market pressure on wage inflation, we need to discuss several issues in the specification of the wage equation.

Indexes of Excess Demand

The gross domestic product gap, the unemployment rate, the active opening rate, and the rate of capacity utilization are commonly used as measures of excess demand. This study focuses on the unemployment rate and the active opening rate, which are more relevant to the labor market.

Univariate Analysis: The Unemployment Rate and the Active Opening Rate

The unemployment rate gap is one of the most widely used indexes measuring labor market pressure. A recent study by Barnes, Chahrour, Olivei, and Tang (2007) shows that the unemployment rate gap is a good summary statistic for the current state of the labor market.

In the case of Japan, however, the unemployment rate is not a good indicator for predicting inflation. Labor hoarding prevents the unemployment rate from fluctuating much over the business cycle. Because of the lack of responsiveness of the unemployment rate to the business cycle, unemployment is found to be statistically insignificant in most regressions of the Phillips curve.[7] It is only after the 1990s that the unemployment rate in Japan starts to fluctuate over the business cycle.

Because the unemployment rate in Japan was very low and stable in the 1970s and the 1980s, an alternative variable, i.e., the active opening rate, is often used to estimate the Phillips curve. In this paper, we use both the unemployment rate and the active opening rate. The correlation between the two series is –0.54.

Multivariate Analysis: A Principal Components Approach

As we have seen, a single variable such as the unemployment rate is often used to capture labor market conditions. In this case, one has to select one variable as the best measure of labor market activity. An alternative is to use multivariate procedures that transform a set of variables into a smaller set of variables. The procedure that we focus on in this paper is principal components analysis.

The 11 series are taken from the 'Labor and Wages' section of the *Financial and Economic Statistics Monthly* published by the Bank of Japan. Seven of the 11 series are

---

6 Output per hour may be an imperfect measure of labor productivity because labor input varies when work effort changes. Basu and Kimball's (1997) method is used to estimate the relation between labor productivity and the business cycle. The result shows that the coefficient on the changes in hours is wrong signed. Hence, we do not adjust our measure of labor productivity to cyclical movements in effort.

7 A number of studies have considered the development of more accurate measures of labor market pressure in Japan. For example, Fujiki, Nakada, and Tachibanaki (2001) calculate the discouraged workers adjusted-base

originally produced by the Ministry of Health, Labor and Welfare: new job openings; new job openings to applicants ratio; active opening rate; total hours worked; nonscheduled working hours; regular employees: all enterprises; and regular employees: manufacturing. The remaining four series are maintained by the Ministry of Internal Affairs and Communications: labor force: employed; labor force: unemployed; ratio of unemployed in labor force; and employees.[8]

The principal components are extracted from the 11 labor market series over the period 1968 to 2006. The first principal component explains 49 percent of the variability in the original data. The correlation between the first principal component and the unemployment rate is –0.59, whereas the correlation between the first principal component and the active opening rate is higher at 0.85.

The Shape of the Phillips Curve

Two functional forms of the excess demand function are considered. One is a linear model $D = \alpha + \gamma U$, where U is either the unemployment rate, the active opening rate, or the first principal component. The other is a nonlinear model, where U is the reciprocal of the unemployment rate. The nonlinear model implies that the wage Phillips curve is vertical at high levels of wage inflation and it becomes flat at low levels of wage inflation.

Expected Inflation

Expected inflation π^e is equal to a weighted average of past inflation, and past inflation is measured by either wages (a wage–wage specification) or prices (a wage–price specification).[9] The wage–wage Phillips curve reflects the institutional framework in which workers compare their wages with wages paid to the same worker in the past and with wages paid to other workers of the same type.

The wage–price Phillips curve captures the fact that some labor contracts have indexation clauses and include catch-up provisions related to past inflation. For the wage–price specification, we need to select a price index that feeds back to wage setting. In theory, the price affecting labor supply is a consumer price index (CPI) while the variables affecting labor demand are the producer price index (PPI) and the wholesale price index (WPI). These price index series are from the *International Financial Statistics* of the International Monetary Fund.

Hence, the three variables—wage inflation, the consumer price index, and the producer (wholesale) price index—are considered as a measure of price feedback.

---

unemployment rate. They find that the fall and rise in the discouraged workers adjusted-base unemployment rate is faster compared with the official rate.

[8] Additional details are given in the Appendix.

[9] Expected inflation could be modeled as a forward-looking function. Thus, we apply the method proposed by Carlson and Parkin (1975) and estimate the expected inflation rate from qualitative survey data. However, so far, we have not found a way to make good use of these estimates of the expected inflation rate for predicting wage inflation.

Lag Length on Prices (or Wages)

Choosing the length of the distributed lag on prices or wages is a critical issue in that it determines the degree of inertia in the system. The wage regressions are compared with lags of one to four years.

The sum of the distributed lag on the change in prices or wages is constrained to unity while no specific distribution is assumed for the shape of the lag. That is, $\pi^e = \sum_{i=1}^{n} \beta_i \pi_{-i}$ ($n = 1,2,3, and 4$), where π is the change in nominal wages, the CPI, or the PPI (WPI). The restriction on the distributed lag $\sum_i \beta_i = 1$ implies that the long-run Phillips curve is vertical and there is no long-run trade-off between unemployment and inflation.

Estimates of the Wage Phillips Curve

We now estimate a wage Phillips curve of the form:

$$\omega - \theta = \alpha + \gamma U + \sum_i \beta_i \pi_{-i} + \delta z, \qquad \sum_i \beta_i = 1 .$$

This is the wage Phillips curve, equation (1), with the addition of a supply shock term. The supply shock is measured by a change in import prices.

Tables 1-1 to 1-3 present salient statistics for comparison of wage equations. Table 1-1 reports the results for the wage–wage specification, where π is the change in nominal wages. Tables 1-2 and 1-3 present the results for the wage–price specifications, where π is the change in the consumer price index or the producer (wholesale) price index.

We begin with a discussion on the choice of a wage–wage or wage–price model. For the wage–wage specification, the results in Table 1-1 show that the coefficient on the unemployment rate is positive, and the coefficients on the reciprocal of the unemployment rate, the active opening rate, and the first principal component are negative. These coefficients have the wrong sign, suggesting that the wage–wage models are not appropriate for explaining wage movements in Japan. For the wage–price specification, Tables 1-2 and 1-3 report the results for two measures of price feedback. In contrast to the wage–wage models, the coefficient on the unemployment rate is negative and the coefficients on the reciprocal of the unemployment rate, the active opening rate, and the first principal component are positive, as predicted by theory. All the coefficients on U are statistically significant at least at the 5 percent level.

The difference between Tables 1-2 and 1-3 is the choice of the price variable. Because the regressions using the consumer price index produce a larger adjusted R^2 than those using the producer (wholesale) price index, the consumer price index seems more appropriate for a price variable in the wage–price models.

Table 1-1. Wage Phillips Curves, 1968 to 2006
Wage–Wage Phillips Curves (Compensation of employees as regressor)

Unemployment rate as the measure of labor market pressure				
Wage lag (yr)	**1**	**2**	**3**	**4**
Constant	–7.439***	–7.452***	–7.506***	–7.511***
Unemployment	1.233***	1.224***	1.188***	1.203***
Import Prices	0.080**	0.084**	0.079**	0.078**
$\bar{R}^2$	0.72	0.72	0.76	0.77
Reciprocal of the unemployment rate as the measure of labor market pressure				
Wage lag (yr)	**1**	**2**	**3**	**4**
Constant	–0.262	–0.307	–0.643	–0.433
$(\text{Unemployment})^{-1}$	–8.594***	–8.523***	–8.096***	–8.421***
Import prices	0.090***	0.092***	0.086***	0.086***
$\bar{R}^2$	0.75	0.74	0.79	0.79
Active opening rate as the measure of labor market pressure				
Wage lag (yr)	**1**	**2**	**3**	**4**
Constant	–2.848*	–3.041*	–3.692**	–3.547**
Active opening rate	–1.361	–1.170	–0.594	–0.734
Import prices	0.074*	0.076*	0.068*	0.069*
$\bar{R}^2$	0.65	0.65	0.70	0.69
PC1 as the measure of labor market pressure				
Wage lag (yr)	**1**	**2**	**3**	**4**
Constant	–4.000***	–4.043***	–4.206***	–4.189***
PC1	–0.048	–0.046	–0.067	–0.074
Import prices	0.066*	0.071*	0.067*	0.067*
$\bar{R}^2$	0.65	0.64	0.70	0.69

Note: ***, **, * indicates statistical significance at 1%, 5%, and 10%, respectively.

Table 1-2. Wage Phillips Curves, 1968 to 2006
Wage–Price Phillips Curves (CPI as regressor)

Unemployment rate as the measure of labor market pressure				
Price lag (yr)	**1**	**2**	**3**	**4**
Constant	2.079	2.078	2.073	2.036
Unemployment	–0.909**	–0.908**	–0.922**	–0.901**
Import prices	0.109***	0.109***	0.107***	0.106***
$\bar{R}^2$	0.69	0.68	0.70	0.69
Reciprocal of unemployment rate as the measure of labor market pressure				
Price lag (yr)	**1**	**2**	**3**	**4**
Constant	–3.639***	–3.656***	–3.754***	–3.686***
$(\text{Unemployment})^{-1}$	7.314***	7.344***	7.467***	7.343***
Import prices	0.099***	0.099***	0.098***	0.097***
$\bar{R}^2$	0.72	0.72	0.73	0.72
Active opening rate as the measure of labor market pressure				
Price lag (yr)	**1**	**2**	**3**	**4**
Constant	–5.709***	–5.761***	–5.948***	–5.889***
Active Opening Rate	6.215***	6.266***	6.430***	6.373***
Import prices	0.080**	0.082**	0.079**	0.079**
$\bar{R}^2$	0.77	0.77	0.79	0.78

Table 1-2.Continued

PC1 as the measure of labor market pressure				
Price lag (yr)	**1**	**2**	**3**	**4**
Constant	–0.427	–0.406	–0.439	–0.416
PC1	0.603***	0.620***	0.585**	0.579**
Import prices	0.104***	0.100***	0.101***	0.099***
$\overline{R}^2$	0.71	0.71	0.71	0.70

Note: ***, **, * indicates statistical significance at 1%, 5%, and 10%, respectively.

Table 1-3. Wage Phillips Curves, 1968 to 2006
Wage–Price Phillips Curves (PPI (WPI) as regressor)

Unemployment rate as the measure of labor market pressure				
Price lag (yr)	**1**	**2**	**3**	**4**
Constant	5.951***	5.880***	5.852***	5.866***
Unemployment	–1.594***	–1.591***	–1.593***	–1.610***
Import prices	0.031	0.059	0.075*	0.089**
$\overline{R}^2$	0.46	0.51	0.58	0.59
Reciprocal of the unemployment rate as the measure of labor market pressure				
Price lag (yr)	**1**	**2**	**3**	**4**
Constant	–3.594**	–3.739**	–3.798***	–3.918***
$(\text{Unemployment})^{-1}$	11.723***	11.904***	11.959***	12.151***
Import prices	0.015	0.045	0.061	0.076*
$\overline{R}^2$	0.52	0.57	0.65	0.66
Active opening rate as the measure of labor market pressure				
Price lag (yr)	**1**	**2**	**3**	**4**
Constant	–4.916*	–5.528***	–5.735***	–5.959***
Active opening rate	7.599***	8.230***	8.433***	8.649***
Import prices	0.001	0.032	0.048	0.064*
$\overline{R}^2$	0.52	0.60	0.68	0.70
PC1 as the measure of labor market pressure				
Price lag (yr)	**1**	**2**	**3**	**4**
Constant	1.548**	1.485**	1.451**	1.421**
PC1	0.856***	0.849***	0.753***	0.750***
Import prices	0.028	0.055	0.072	0.084*
$\overline{R}^2$	0.46	0.50	0.55	0.55

Note: ***, **, * indicates statistical significance at 1%, 5%, and 10%, respectively.

As for the measure of labor market pressure, the regressions using the active opening rate yield the largest adjusted R^2 in Table 1-2, and thus fit the data better than those using the unemployment rate, the reciprocal of the unemployment rate, and the first principal component.

Regarding the best-fitting lag length, Table 1-2 compares regressions with lags of one to four years. The fit improves moving from lags of two to three years and then edges down from lags of three to four years.

These results lead to the conclusion that the best-fitting wage equation is a wage–price model that uses the active opening rate to represent U and the consumer price index to represent π, with π lags of three years. The best-fitting regression implies that the "natural" active opening rate is 0.925, and a one-point increase in the active opening rate raises real-wage growth by 6.4 percent.[10]

4. A Set of Principal Components

Up to now, we have focused on the *first* principal component. To further test the model, we now use more than one principal component as the measure of labor market pressure. We begin by using Kaiser's (1960) criterion to decide how many principal components to retain. Kaiser recommends discarding principal components with eigenvalues less than one. We then use the retained components as the independent variables in the regression analysis, and discard the components whose estimated regression parameters are statistically insignificant.

Table 2 presents a principal components analysis of the correlation matrix of the 11 labor market variables. Kaiser's criterion leads to the retention of the first two components.

The first principal component is highly correlated with eight variables (new job openings to applicants ratio, active opening rate, labor force: employed, labor force: unemployed, ratio of unemployed in labor force, regular employees: all enterprises, regular employees: manufacturing, and employees) and the correlations are of about the same magnitude. Therefore, the first component is interpreted as an equally weighted average of the eight standardized variables. Similarly, the second principal component can be interpreted as an equally weighted average of the remaining three standardized variables (new job openings, total hours worked, and nonscheduled working hours). The first two components account for 77 percent of the total variation.

Table 3 presents wage Phillips curve estimates with the first and second principal components. In regression 3.2, the second principal component as well as the first component is statistically significant. The adjusted R^2 for the regression with the second principal component is larger than that for the regression without the second component: the adjusted R^2 for regression 3.2 is 0.78, compared with 0.71 for regression 3.1. The results suggest that the second principal component is an important indicator for predicting wage inflation.

---

[10] Using the data for the entire sample period, 1968 to 2006, and for two subperiods, 1968 to 1987 and 1988 to 2006, we obtain three estimated regressions for each specification. Table A in the appendix presents the regressions for the data ending in 1987 and the data beginning in 1988. A Chow test fails to reject the null hypothesis that the coefficient vectors are the same in the two subperiods. Thus, a conventional statistical test suggests that the wage equation describes a stable relation between wage inflation and its determinants.

Table 2. Eigenvectors and Eigenvalues of the Correlation Matrix of Labor Market Variables (N = 39)

	Eigenvector										
Variable	**PC1**	**PC2**	**PC3**	**PC4**	**PC5**	**PC6**	**PC7**	**PC8**	**PC9**	**PC10**	**PC11**
New job openings	0.151	–0.469	–0.346	–0.021	–0.227	–0.324	0.411	–0.153	0.054	0.530	0.061
New job openings to applicants ratio	0.372	0.109	–0.451	0.123	–0.024	–0.062	–0.132	0.151	0.265	–0.303	0.651
Active opening rate	0.373	0.138	–0.424	–0.035	–0.147	–0.064	–0.192	–0.075	0.205	–0.175	–0.721
Labor force: employed	0.325	–0.203	0.181	0.474	0.416	0.430	0.314	–0.149	0.329	–0.004	–0.096
Labor force: unemployed	–0.292	0.279	0.183	0.503	–0.409	–0.367	0.222	–0.259	0.297	–0.207	–0.011
Ratio of unemployed in labor force	–0.331	–0.235	–0.111	–0.306	–0.433	0.549	0.179	0.117	0.397	–0.193	0.004
Total hours worked	–0.078	–0.511	0.240	0.182	–0.035	–0.206	–0.639	0.198	0.371	0.111	–0.035
Nonscheduled working hours	0.044	–0.554	0.015	0.049	–0.019	–0.169	0.138	–0.074	–0.408	–0.682	–0.055
Regular employees: all enterprises	0.356	0.080	0.433	–0.277	–0.063	–0.286	0.360	0.576	0.207	–0.086	–0.080
Regular employees: manufacturing	0.361	–0.004	0.380	–0.426	–0.160	0.003	–0.155	–0.665	0.139	–0.048	0.177
Employees	0.366	0.018	0.171	0.344	–0.606	0.336	–0.129	0.164	–0.406	0.168	0.030
Eigenvalue	5.434	3.057	0.902	0.600	0.332	0.283	0.172	0.087	0.070	0.057	0.007
Cumulative percent variance explained	49.40	77.19	85.38	90.83	93.85	96.42	97.99	98.78	99.41	99.93	100

Table 3. Wage Phillips Curves, 1968 to 2006
Wage–Price Phillips Curves (CPI as regressor, Price lag = three years)

	3.1	3.2
Constant	–0.439	–0.524
PC1	0.585**	0.501**
PC2		1.106***
Import prices	0.101***	0.100***
$\overline{R}^2$	0.71	0.78

Note: ***, **, * indicates statistical significance at 1%, 5%, and 10%, respectively. Regression 3.1 is originally reported in Table 1-2.

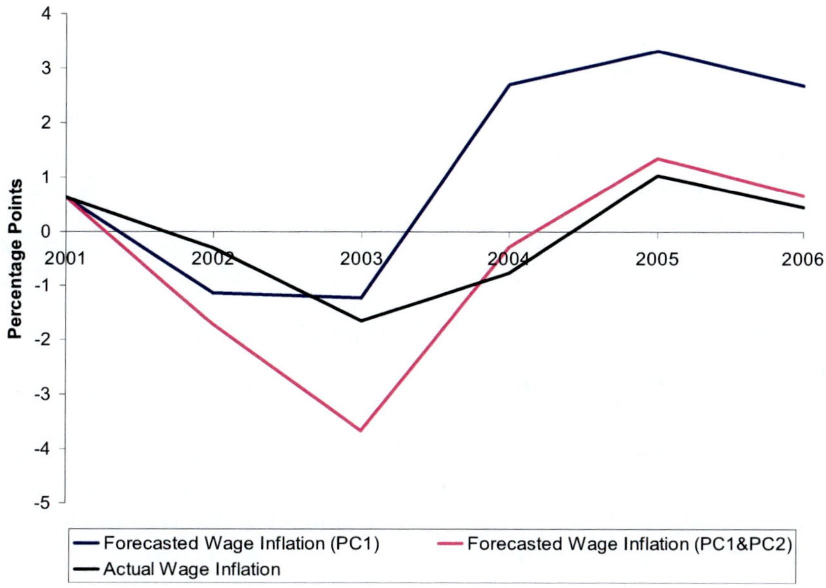

Figure 2. Wage Inflation Forecasts.

What do the first and second principal components suggest about the recent state of the labor market? Figure 2 shows actual wage inflation and predicted wage inflation from the wage Phillips curves with and without the second principal component. We estimate the wage Phillips curves for 1968 to 2001, and using these estimates, we compute forecasts of wage inflation over the period 2002 to 2006. This figure shows that the wage equation without the second principal component overpredicts wage inflation in 2006. For the period 2002 to 2006, the equation without the second principal component overpredicts wage inflation by a total of 7.6 percentage points, while the equation with the second principal component underpredicts wage growth by a total of 2.4 percent.

The equation including the second principal component suggests less labor market pressure in 2006 than the one excluding the second component. This finding may be because of the change in the score on the second principal component, which can be interpreted as the change in total hours worked.[11] Low wage inflation in recent years can be explained by a

[11] Total hours worked is the sum of scheduled working hours and nonscheduled working hours. Scheduled working hours are the actual hours worked between the starting and finishing hours of employment according to the

combination of upward pressure on wages because of tight employment conditions (the first principal component) and downward pressure on hourly wages because of the increase in total hours worked (the second principal component). In other words, upward pressure on wages caused by the tight labor market is canceled out by downward pressure on wages caused by the decrease in labor hoarding.

When we regress wage inflation on the changes in the active opening rate and the log of total hours worked, we find that:

$$\underset{}{\omega-\theta} = \underset{(1.152)}{-5.575} + \sum_i \beta_i \pi_{-i} + \underset{(1.382)}{4.975AOR} - \underset{(0.502)}{1.324THW} + \underset{(0.027)}{0.080IMPORT}, \quad \overline{R}^2 = 0.82.$$

Numbers in parentheses are standard errors. The active opening rate (AOR) and the change in total hours worked (THW) are statistically significant at least at the 5 percent level. The regression implies that high growth rates of total hours worked reduce wage inflation.

As a matter of course, there will be an upper limit to which firms can increase total hours worked during an economic upturn. Once total hours worked reach this limit, a further increase in labor demand will surely raise wage inflation.

5. Time-varying Natural Rate of Unemployment (NRU) and Natural Active Opening Rate (NAOR)

Thus far, this paper has estimated constant-NRU and constant-NAOR models. However, the NRU and NAOR may change over time because of demographic and other factors.[12] This study uses the Hodrick–Prescott filter to extract a trend in the labor market series, which represents our estimates of the time-varying natural rate.[13] We reestimate the wage Phillips curve with time-varying NRUs and time-varying NAORs. Table 4 presents the results. The unemployment rate, the reciprocal of the unemployment rate, and the active opening rate in regressions 4.2, 4.4, and 4.6 are expressed as the deviation from the Hodrick-Prescott trend. For regression 4.8, three new series are produced by detrending in new job openings, the active opening rate, and the ratio of unemployed in the labor force. Then the principal components are reextracted from the 11 series, i.e., three new series plus the eight original series.

work regulations of the establishment. Nonscheduled working hours are those worked when reporting to work early in the morning, working overtime, being on call, or working when on leave. Information on hours worked is published monthly by the Ministry of Health, Labor and Welfare.

12 For a discussion of why the NRU changes over time, see Ball and Mankiw (2002).

13 The filter has smoothing parameter 10^3.

Table 4. Wage Phillips Curves, 1968 to 2006
Wage–Price Phillips Curves (CPI as regressor, Price lag = three years)

	4.1	**4.2**	**4.3**	**4.4**	**4.5**	**4.6**	**4.7**	**4.8**
	Constant	**Time-varying**	**Constant**	**Time-varying**	**Constant**	**Time-varying**	**Constant**	**Time-varying**
Constant	2.073	–0.426	–3.754***	–0.459	–5.948***	–0.552	–0.439	–0.443
Unemployment	–0.922**	–2.399**						
$(\text{Unemployment})^{-1}$			7.467***	23.696***				
Active opening rate					6.430***	7.065***		
PC1							0.585**	0.553**
Import prices	0.107***	0.106***	0.098***	0.100***	0.079**	0.082***	0.101***	0.101***
$\overline{R}^2$	0.70	0.69	0.73	0.77	0.79	0.78	0.71	0.71

Note: ***, **, * indicates statistical significance at 1%, 5%, and 10%, respectively. Regressions 4.1, 4.3, 4.5, and 4.7 are originally reported in Table 1-2.

Table 4 presents the results for constant and time-varying natural rate models. The coefficients on the labor market variables and the adjusted R^2 s for time-varying natural rate models are similar to those for constant natural rate models. Therefore, we conclude that our results do not depend crucially on the assumption of constant natural rates.

6. Conclusion

In this paper, we investigated what is the best measure of labor market pressure for predicting wage inflation in Japan. Principal components analysis was used to select a subset of independent variables from 11 labor market variables. The first component is interpreted as the active opening rate and the second component is interpreted as total hours worked.

We estimated a standard Phillips curve for wage inflation that incorporates the active opening rate and total hours worked as regressors. We found that (hourly) real wage growth is positively related to the active opening rate and negatively related to total hours worked.

The second component (representing total hours worked) may help explain why wage inflation has not risen substantially despite Japan experiencing high active opening rates in the mid-2000s. Although higher active opening rates put upward pressure on real wage growth, this upward pressure is offset by longer working hours, which tends to reduce (hourly) real wage growth.

However, there will be an upper limit to which firms can increase total hours worked during an economic upturn. Once total hours worked reach this limit, a further increase in labor demand will raise wage inflation.

Appendix

Data Description

New job openings	First difference of logarithms
New job openings to applicants ratio	No transformation
Active opening rate	No transformation
Labor force: employed	First difference of logarithms
Labor force: unemployed	First difference of logarithms
Ratio of unemployed in labor force	No transformation
Total hours worked (2005 = 100)	First difference of logarithms
Nonscheduled working hours (2005 = 100)	First difference of logarithms
Regular employees: all enterprises (2005 = 100)	First difference of logarithms
Regular employees: manufacturing (2005 = 100)	First difference of logarithms
Employees	First difference of logarithms

Note: "Labor force: employed" and "Labor force: unemployed" are both adjusted for labor-force growth. The survey population for "Total hours worked," "Nonscheduled working hours," "Regular employees: all enterprises," and "Regular employees: manufacturing" is establishments with 30 employees or more through 1990 and establishments with five employees or more from 1991.

Table A. Sensitivity to Sample Splits of Wage Equations
Wage–Price Phillips Curves (CPI as regressor, Price lag = three years)

Sample period	1968–1987	1988–2006	1968–1987	1988–2006	1968–1987	1988–2006	1968–1987	1988–2006
Constant	5.788	2.232***	–6.305*	–3.715***	–7.875***	–3.444***	–0.375	–0.649**
Unemployment	–3.023	–0.829***						
$(\text{Unemployment})^{-1}$			10.867*	9.544***				
Active opening rate					8.899***	3.202***		
PC1							1.201**	0.335***
Import prices	0.096	0.028	0.103*	0.035	0.080*	–0.030	0.105**	–0.029
$\overline{R}^2$	0.51	0.82	0.55	0.82	0.71	0.75	0.57	0.75

Note: ***, **, * indicates statistical significance at 1%, 5%, and 10%, respectively.

References

Ball, L., & Mankiw, N. G. (2002). The NAIRU in Theory and Practice. *Journal of Economic Perspectives*, **16**, 115-136.

Ball, L., & Moffitt, R. (2001). Productivity Growth and the Phillips Curve. In A. B. Krueger, & R. Solow (Eds.), *The Roaring Nineties: Can Full Employment Be Sustained?* (pp. 61-90). New York: The Russell Sage Foundation and The Century Foundation Press.

Barnes, M., Chahrour, R., Olivei, G., & Tang, G. (2007). A Principal Components Approach to Estimating Labor Market Pressure and Its Implications for Inflation. Public Policy Briefs no. 07-2. Federal Reserve Bank of Boston.

Basu, S., & Kimball, M. S. (1997). Cyclical Productivity with Unobserved Input Variation. NBER working paper no. 5915. Cambridge, Mass.: National Bureau of Economic Research.

Bernanke, B. S., & Boivin, J. (2003). Monetary Policy in a Data-Rich Environment. *Journal of Monetary Economics*, **50**, 525-46.

Bernanke, B. S., Boivin, J. & Eliasz, P. (2005). Measuring the Effects of Monetary Policy: A Factor-Augmented Vector Autoregressive (FAVAR) Approach. *Quarterly Journal of Economics*, **120**, 387-422.

Blanchard, O., & Katz, L. F. (1997). What We Know and Do Not Know about the Natural Rate of Unemployment. *Journal of Economic Perspectives*, **11**, 51-72.

Carlson, J. A., & Parkin, J. M. (1975). Inflation Expectations. *Economica*, **42**, 123-38.

Fujiki, H., Nakada, S. K., & Tachibanaki, T. (2001). Structural Issues in the Japanese Labor Market: An Era of Variety, Equity and Efficiency or an Era of Bipolarization? *Monetary and Economic Studies*, **19**, 177-208.

Kaiser, H. F. (1960). The Application of Electronic Computers to Factor Analysis. *Educational and Psychological Measurement*, **20**, 141-151.

Katz, L. F. & Krueger, A. B. (1999). The High-Pressure U.S. Labor Market of the 1990s. *Brookings Papers on Economic Activity* (**1**), 1-65.

Mankiw, N. G. (2001). The Inexorable and Mysterious Tradeoff Between Inflation and Unemployment. *The Economic Journal*, **111**, C45-C61.

Nishimura, K. G. (2007). Increased Diversity and Deepened Uncertainty: Policy Challenges in a Zero-Inflation Economy. *International Finance*, **10**, 281-300.

Stock, J., & Watson, M. (2002a). Macroeconomic Forecasting Using Diffusion Indexes. *Journal of Business Economics and Statistics*, **20**, 147-162.

Stock, J., & Watson, M. (2002b). Forecasting Using Principal Components from a Large Number of Predictors. *Journal of the American Statistical Association*, **97**, 1167-79.

Ueda, K. (2007). Trying to Make Sense of the Bank of Japan's Monetary Policy since the Exit from Quantitative Easing. *International Finance*, **10**, 301-316.

In: Inflation: Causes and Effects
Editor: Leon V. Schwartz, pp. 137-143
ISBN: 978-1-60741-823-8

Chapter 7

MACROECONOMIC POLICIES AND INFLATION

***Magda Kandil*[1] *and Ida A. Mirzaie*[2]**
International Monetary Fund, 700 Nineteenth St., Washington D.C., USA
Department of Economics, The Ohio State University, Ohio, USA

JEL Classification Numbers: F41, F43, E31

Keywords: Price inflation, anticipated and unanticipated exchange rate movements

Introduction

There has been an ongoing debate on the causes of inflation in developing countries. The debate focuses on the degree of fluctuations in the exchange rate in the face of internal and external shocks in order to curb inflation. As exchange rate policies are mostly geared toward containing inflation in developing countries, it is necessary to evaluate the effects of exchange rate fluctuations on price inflation. Demand and supply channels determine these effects.

A depreciation (or devaluation) of the domestic currency may stimulate economic activity through the initial increase in the price of foreign goods relative to home goods. By increasing the international competitiveness of domestic industries, exchange rate depreciation diverts spending from foreign goods to domestic goods. As illustrated in Guittian (1976) and Dornbusch (1988), the success of currency depreciation in promoting trade balance largely depends on switching demand in proper direction and amount, as well as on the capacity of the home economy to meet the additional demand by supplying more goods[3].

---

[1] E-mail address: mkandil@imf.org. International Monetary Fund, 700 Nineteenth St., Washington D.C. 2043.
[2] E-mail address: Mirzaie.1@osu.edu. Department of Economics, The Ohio State University, 410 Arps Hall, 1945 N. High Street, Columbus, Ohio 43210.
The views in the paper are those of the authors and should not be interpreted as those of the International Monetary Fund.

[3] Empirical support of this proposition for Group 7 countries over the 1960-89 period is provided in Mendoza (1992).

While the traditional view indicates that currency depreciation is expansionary, new structuralism school stresses some contractionary effects. Meade (1951) discusses this theoretical possibility. If the Marshall-Lerner condition is not satisfied, currency depreciation could produce contraction.[4] Hirschman (1949) points out that currency depreciation from an initial trade deficit reduces real national income and may lead to a fall in aggregate demand. Currency depreciation gives with one hand, by lowering export prices, while taking away with the other hand, by raising import prices. If trade is in balance and terms of trade are not changed these price changes offset each other. But if imports exceed exports, the net result is a reduction in real income within the country. Cooper (1971) confirms this point in a general equilibrium model.

Diaz-Alejandro (1963) introduced another argument for contraction following devaluation. Depreciation may raise the windfall profits in export and import-competing industries. If money wages lag the price increase and if the marginal propensity to save from profits is higher than from wages, national savings will go up and real output will decrease. Krugman and Taylor (1978) and Barbone and Rivera-Batiz (1987) have formalized the same views.

Supply-side channels further complicate the effects of currency depreciation on economic performance. Bruno (1979) and Wijnbergen (1989) postulate that in a typical semi-industrialized country where inputs for manufacturing are largely imported and cannot be easily produced domestically, firms' input cost will increase following devaluation. As a result, the negative impact from the higher cost of imported inputs may dominate the production stimulus from lower relative prices for domestically traded goods. Gylfason and Schmid (1983) provide evidence that the final effect depends on the magnitude by which demand and supply curves shift because of devaluation.[5]

To summarize, currency depreciation increases net exports and increases the cost of production. Similarly, currency appreciation decreases net exports and the cost of production. The combined effects of demand and supply channels determine the net results of exchange rate fluctuations on price.[6]

Price Fluctuations

This paper revisits the relationship between exchange rate fluctuations and inflation in developing countries. Anticipated movement in the exchange rate is assumed to vary with agents' observations of macro-economic fundamentals, which determine changes in the exchange rate over time. Deviation in the realized exchange rate from its anticipated value captures the unanticipated component of the exchange rate.

---

[4] The Marshall-Lerner condition states that devaluation will improve the trade balance if the devaluing nation's demand elasticity for imports plus the foreign demand elasticity for the nation's exports exceed 1.

[5] Hanson (1983) provides theoretical evidence that the effect of currency depreciation on output depends on the assumptions regarding the labor market. Solimano (1986) studies the effect of devaluation by focusing on the structure of the trade sector. Agenor (1991) introduces a theoretical model for a small open economy and distinguishes between anticipated and unanticipated movement in the exchange rate. Examples of empirical investigations include Edwards (1986), Gylfason and Radetzki (1991), Roger and Wang (1995), Hoffmaister and Vegh (1996), Bahmani (1998), Kamin and Rogers (2000), and Kandil and Mirzaie (2002, and 2003).

[6] For an analytical overview, see Lizondo and Montiel (1989).

In this context, the output supplied varies with unanticipated price movements and the cost of the output produced. Anticipated exchange rate movements determine the cost of the output produced. In contrast, unanticipated exchange rate movements determine economic conditions in three directions: net exports, money demand, and the output supplied. Positive shocks to the exchange rate indicate an unanticipated increase in the price of domestic currency in foreign currency, i.e., unanticipated currency appreciation. Similarly, negative shocks indicate unanticipated depreciation of the exchange rate.

In the real world, stochastic uncertainty may arise on the demand or supply sides of the economy. Economic agents are assumed to be rational. Accordingly, rational expectations of demand and supply shifts enter the theoretical model. Economic fluctuations are then determined by unexpected demand and supply shocks impinging on the economic system. The complexity of demand and supply channels may determine the results of exchange rate fluctuations as follows:

1. In the goods market, a positive shock to the exchange rate of the domestic currency (an unexpected appreciation) will make exports more expensive and imports less expensive. As a result, the competition from foreign markets will decrease the demand for domestic products, decreasing domestic output and price.
2. In the money market, a positive shock to the domestic currency (an unexpected temporary appreciation), prompts agents to hold less domestic currency and decreases the interest rate. This channel moderates the contraction of aggregate demand and, therefore, the reduction in output and price in the face of a positive exchange rate shock.
3. On the supply side, a positive shock to the exchange rate (an unanticipated appreciation) decreases the cost of imported intermediate goods, increasing domestic output and decreasing the cost of production and, hence, the aggregate price level.[7]

Theory predicts that an increase in the energy price, both anticipated and unanticipated, increases the cost of the output produced. Hence, the output supplied decreases and price inflation increases. In oil-producing countries, however, an increase in the energy price is likely to cause an expansion in the output supplied and a reduction in price inflation. Anticipated changes in the energy price are generally insignificant on price in various countries. Unanticipated change in the energy price is consistent with significant price inflation in Algeria, Bolivia and Malaysia.

Theory predicts that agents adjust wages and prices in the face of anticipated monetary shifts, neutralizing their effects on output. Consistent with theory's predictions, the inflationary effect of anticipated monetary shifts is significant on price in Bolivia, Brazil, Jordan, and Peru.

Unanticipated monetary shifts are distributed between real output growth and price inflation with a coefficient that is dependent on the slope of the short-run supply curve. There

[7] Other supply-side channels may reinforce the negative effect of currency appreciation on the output supplied. Recent crises in developing countries have illustrated the mismatch effect of currency depreciation on balance sheets. Many developing countries rely on foreign sources of financing. Currency depreciation increases the cost of borrowing by raising the burden of foreign currency denominated liabilities. A higher cost of borrowing has an adverse effect on the supply side of the economy, further reinforcing the negative effect on output growth and the positive effect on price inflation in the theoretical model.

is evidence of an increase in price inflation in the face of unanticipated monetary growth in Bolivia, Brazil, Egypt, Pakistan, and Peru.

Except for Turkey, anticipated government spending does not accelerate price inflation significantly.[8] There is evidence, however, of a significant reduction of price inflation in the face of anticipated government spending in Bangladesh.[9] The inflationary effect of unanticipated government spending is evident and significant in Algeria, Brazil, Ghana, Mexico, Paraguay, and Turkey.[10] There is evidence, however, of a significant reduction in price inflation in the face of unanticipated government spending in Iran.

The exchange rate is measured by the real price of domestic currency in U.S. dollar. Accordingly, a rise in the exchange rate indicates real appreciation of the domestic currency.[11] Theory predicts that anticipated appreciation in the value of the domestic currency decreases the cost of imported goods and decreases price inflation. There is no evidence of significant price deflation in any country. Hence, the supply-side channel is not significant to transmit the effects of anticipated exchange rate shifts.

Unanticipated fluctuations of the domestic currency affect the demand and supply sides of the economy. A positive shock to the exchange rate (an unanticipated appreciation) increases the output supplied and decreases money demand and net exports. Price inflation is likely to decrease with the increase in the output supplied and the reduction in net exports. Price inflation is likely to accelerate with the decrease in money demand. Price inflation increases significantly in the face of unanticipated currency appreciation in Bangladesh, Bolivia, Libya, and Qatar. Price inflation decreases significantly in the face of unanticipated currency appreciation in Indonesia and Philippines. Hence, the results are mixed concerning the inflationary effect of unanticipated currency appreciation.

Price inflation is evident and significant in the face of unanticipated energy price increase in Egypt, Libya, Malaysia, and Turkey. Hence, the evidence remains robust concerning the limited effects of fluctuations in the energy price on price inflation in the sample of developing countries under investigation.

Anticipated aggregate demand shifts increase price inflation significantly in Algeria, Bangladesh, Bolivia, Brazil, Ghana, Jordan, Malaysia, Mexico, Paraguay, Peru, and Turkey. Evidence of significant price inflation appears also pervasive in the face of unanticipated aggregate demand shifts, as evident by the positive and significant response in Algeria, Bangladesh, Bolivia, Brazil, Egypt, Ghana, Indonesia, Iran, Mexico, Pakistan, Paraguay, Peru, and Philippines and Turkey.

Overall, the significant effects of aggregate demand shifts appear more pervasive compared to specific policy shifts. Hence, constraints on the demand side of the economy limit the transmission mechanism of specific policy shifts, namely fiscal and monetary, to price inflation in many developing countries. Further, sources of spending do not appear to be closely tied to monetary or fiscal policies in many developing countries.

---

[8] This evidence indicates slow adjustment of price inflation towards its full-equilibrium value, as implied by anticipated government spending.

[9] This evidence indicates significant crowding out effect of government spending.

[10] Price inflation appears more flexible in the short-run, relative to output growth in the face of unanticipated increase in government spending.

[11] Throughout the paper, appreciation will describe increase in the foreign price of domestic currency attributed to either market forces or managed policy within a year. The estimation technique accounts for the endogeneity of the exchange rate with respect to domestic economic conditions. Exogenous shocks are attributed to domestic and/or external shocks.

Anticipated appreciation of the exchange rate is not consistent with significant price deflation. Hence, the evidence remains robust concerning the limited effect of the supply-side channel in transmitting anticipated exchange rate shifts to the product market of the developing countries under investigation.

Consistent with theory's predictions, the effects of unanticipated exchange rate fluctuations may be positive or negative on price inflation. Consistent with reduction in money demand, price inflation increases significantly in the face of unanticipated currency appreciation in Jordan, Libya, and Qatar. Consistent with the increase in output supplied and the reduction in net exports, price inflation decreases significantly in the face of unanticipated currency appreciation in Bangladesh, Brazil, Indonesia, Mexico, and Turkey. The mixed significant evidence provides further support for the complexity of demand and supply channels in determining the effects of exchange rate fluctuations on price inflation in many developing countries.

Summary and Conclusion

The analysis has focused on the effects of macroeconomic policies in a sample of 18 developing countries. To that end, the paper presents a theoretical rational expectation model that decomposes movements in the exchange rate into anticipated and unanticipated components. Anticipated changes in the exchange rate enter the production function through the cost of imported goods. Unanticipated currency fluctuations determine aggregate demand through exports, imports, and the demand for domestic currency, and determine aggregate supply through the cost of imported intermediate goods.

In general, developing countries are characterized by a high degree of price flexibility in the face of aggregate demand shifts, both anticipated and unanticipated. Nonetheless, the inflationary effects of specific policy shocks, fiscal and monetary, appear limited on price. Hence, demand-side constraints block the transmission mechanism of domestic policies to the product market in many of the developing countries under investigation. Further, aggregate spending does not appear to be closely tied to monetary and fiscal policies in many developing countries.

The limited effects of anticipated exchange rate appreciation on price inflation indicate that rational forecast of exchange rate movement is rather limited to gauge the strategy of agents in developing countries. Hence, producers do not adjust the supply side to react to a lower (higher) cost of imported goods in response to anticipated exchange rate appreciation (depreciation). In contrast, unanticipated fluctuations of the exchange rate appear more significant in determining fluctuations in price in many developing countries.

Consistent with theory's predictions, price adjustments in the face of exchange rate shocks vary across countries. Consistent with the effects of unanticipated currency appreciation (depreciation) in decreasing (increasing) net exports and increasing (decreasing) the output supplied, price inflation decreases (increases) significantly in six countries. Consistent with the effects of unanticipated currency appreciation (depreciation) in decreasing (increasing) money demand, price inflation increases (decreases) significantly in seven countries.

Given the mixed results, high variability of exchange rate fluctuations around its anticipated value may generate adverse effects in the form of higher price inflation in many developing countries. To minimize the adverse effects of currency fluctuations, policy makers should aim at minimizing the dependency of the economy on foreign imports towards reducing fluctuations in the output supplied. While stimulating net exports through currency depreciation is desirable, it is crucial to ensure a concurrent increase in productive capacity to cope with the increased demand without accelerating price inflation. Finally, monetary policy should aim at minimizing extensive fluctuations in the exchange rate that may induce speculative attacks and undermine the stability of the money demand function. Towards this objective, exchange rate policy should aim at striking the right balance between necessary flexibility to ensure competitiveness and desirable stability to increase confidence in domestic currency and underlying fundamentals that provide support to the currency value over time.

References

Agenor, Pierre-Richard, 1991, "Output, Devaluation and the Real Exchange Rate in Developing Countries," *Weltwirtschaftliches Archive*, Band 127.

Bahmani, Mohsen, 1991, "Are Devaluation Contractionary in LDCs?" *Journal of Economic Development*, (June).

Barbone, Luca, and Francisco Rivera-Batiz, 1987, "Foreign Capital and the Contractionary Impact of Currency Devaluation, with an Application to Jamaica," *Journal of Development Economics,* Vol. 26, (June), pp. 1–15.

Bruno, M., 1979, "Stabilization and Stagflation in a Semi-Industrialized Economy," in R. Dornbusch and J. Frankel, eds. *International Economic Policy,* Johns Hopkins University Press, Baltimore, MD.

Buiter, William H., 1990, *International Macroeconomics*, Oxford University Press.

Cooper, Richard N., 1971, "Currency Devaluation in Developing Countries," *Essays in International Finance*, No. 86, International Finance Section, Princeton University.

Diaz-Alejandro, Carlos F., 1963, " Note on the Impact of Devaluation and Redistributive Effect," *Journal of Political Economy,* Vol. 71, (August), pp. 577–80.

Dornbusch, Rudiger, *Open Economy Macroeconomics*, 2nd edition, New York, 1988.

Edwards, S., 1986, "Are Devaluation Contractionary?," *The Review of Economics and Statistics*, August.

Engle, R. R., 1982, "A General Approach to Lagrange Multiplier Model Diagnostics," *Journal of Econometrics*, Vol. 20, pp. 83–104.

Gylfason, Thorvaldur, and Schmid, Michael, ``Does Devaluation Cause Stagflation?" *Canadian Journal of Economics*, Vol. XV1, November 1983.

Gylfason, T. and Radetzki, 1991, "Does Devaluation Make Sense in Least Developed Countries?" *Economic Development and Cultural Change*, (October).

Guittian, Manuel, 1976, "The Effects of Changes in the Exchange Rate on Output, Prices, and the Balance of Payments," *Journal of International Economics*, Vol. 6, pp. 65–74.

Hanson, James A., 1983, "Contractionary Devaluation, Substitution in Production and Consumption, and the Role of the Labor Market," *Journal of International Economics*, Vol. 14, pp. 179–89.

Hirschman, Albert O., 1949, "Devaluation and the Trade Balance: A Note," *Review of Economics and Statistics*, Vol. 31, pp. 50–53.

Hoffmaister and Vegh, 1996, "Disinflation and the Recession Now Versus Recession Later Hypothesis: Evidence from Uruguay," *IMF Staff Papers,* Vol. 43.

Kandil, Magda, 1996, "Sticky Wage or Sticky Price? Analysis of the Cyclical Behavior of the Real Wage," *Southern Economic Journal*, (October), pp.440-99.

Kandil, Magda, and Ida Mirzaie, 2002, "Exchange Rate Fluctuations and Disaggregated Economic Activity in the U.S.: Theory and Evidence," *Journal of International Money and Finance*, No. **1**, (February), pp. 1–31.

Kandil, Magda, and Ida Mirzaie, 2003, "The Effects of Dollar Appreciation on Sectoral Labor Market Adjustments: Theory and Evidence," *Quarterly Review of Economics and Finance*, Vol. 43, No. 1, pp. 89–117.

Kandil, Magda, and Jeffrey Woods, 1997, "Cyclical Comovements in Industrial Labor and Product Markets: Theory and Evidence," *Economic Inquiry*, Vol. XXXV, pp. 725–44.

Kamin, and Rogers, 2000, "Output and the Real Exchange Rate in Developing Countries: An Application to Mexico," *Journal of Development Economics*, No. **61**.

Krugman and Taylor, 1987, "Contractionary Effects of Devaluation," *Journal of International Economics*, No. **8**, pp. 445–56.

Kwiatkowski, Denis, Peter C. B. Phillips, Peter Schmidt, and Yongcheol Shin, 1992, "Testing the Null Hypothesis of Stationarity Against the Alternative of a Unit Root: How Sure Are We That Economic Time Series Have a Unit Root?" *Journal of Econometrics*, No. **54**, pp. 159–78.

Lizondo, J. Saul, and Peter J. Montiel, 1989, "Contractionary Devaluation in Developing Countries: An Analytical Overview," *IMF Staff Papers*, **36** (1), (March), pp. 182–227.

Meade, James E., 1951, *The Theory of International Economic Policy, I: The Balance of Payment*, Oxford University Press, Oxford.

Mendoza, E. G., 1992, "The Effect of Macroeconomic Shocks in a Basic Equilibrium Framework," *IMF Staff Papers*, **39**, 4, pp. 855–89.

Pagan, Adrian, 1984, "Econometric Issues in the Analysis of Regressions with Generated Regressors," *International Economic Review*, No. **25**, pp. 221–47.

Pagan, Adrian, 1986, "Two Stage and Related Estimators and Their Applications," *Review of Economic Studies*, No. **53**, pp. 517–38.

Rogers, and Wang, 1995, "Output, Inflation, and Stabilization in a Small Open Economy: Evidence from Mexico," *Journal of Development Economics*, No. **46**.

Shone, Ronald, 1989, "Open Economy Macroeconomics," Harvester Wheatsheaf.

Solimano, Andres, 1986, "Contractionary Devaluation in the Southern Cone-The Case of Chile," *Journal of Development Economics*, No. **23**, pp. 135–51.

Wijnbergen, Sweder Van, 1989, "Exchange Rate Management and Stabilization Policies in Developing Countries," *Journal of Development Economics*, No. **23**, pp. 227–47.

In: Inflation: Causes and Effects...
Editor: Leon V. Schwartz, pp. 145-164
ISBN 978-1-60741-823-8

Chapter 8

INFLATION PERSISTENCE AND MONETARY POLICY IN AN OPEN ECONOMY SETTING

Séverine Menguy
EconomiX, University of Paris X, Nanterre, France

Abstract

In the context of a new Keynesian macroeconomic model, this paper studies the optimal monetary policy in an open economy setting. This policy depends on the preferences of the central bank, but also on the inflation persistence. Indeed, the inflation rate is the higher and the monetary policy should be all the more contractionary as the inflation inertia is high after positive fiscal, demand or foreign inflationary shocks. Then, in the event of a negative supply shock, the monetary policy is all the more expansionary as the monetary authority aims at sustaining the economic activity and as the inflation persistence is low. Finally, the monetary policy is only more expansionary if the inflation persistence increases after a positive shock on the foreign interest rate.

1. Introduction

In the most recent economic literature, the New-Keynesian models are the favored framework in which to study optimal monetary policy. These models are all characterized by nominal price rigidities and rational expectations. They thus have the advantage of combining optimal behavior with rigidities avoiding the Lucas critique. Nevertheless, most of these models only concern *monetary* policy, ignoring the presence of fiscal policies, and often relate to a closed economy setting. However, Fornero *et al.* (2007) show that in an open economy setting, the management of monetary policy is complicated further, the exchange rate becoming an important channel of transmission of monetary policy. Furthermore, policy-makers are also concerned about instrument smoothing: they prefer lower and more gradual adjustment of policy instruments, which is often neglected by policy modelling. So, the current chapter aims at explaining the determinants of monetary policy in an open economy setting for the stabilization of various shocks. In particular, it underlines the importance of the preferences of the monetary authority, but also the role of inflation inertia in the definition of optimal monetary policy. In this framework, we show that the inflation risks are higher, and therefore the monetary policy is all the more contractionary, as the inflation persistence increases, in case of domestic or foreign, positive demand or negative supply shocks. To the contrary, in case of a positive shock on the foreign interest rate, monetary policy is all the more expansionary as inflation persistence increases.

The second section describes our model. The third section underlines the importance of the parameter representing the inflation persistence, whereas the fourth section defines the levels of inflation and economic activity. The fifth, the sixth, the seventh and the eighth section respectively study the demand, supply, foreign inflationary and foreign interest rate shocks. Finally, the ninth section concludes the chapter.

2. Description of the Model

We use a New Keynesian Dynamic Model in an open economy. However, we do not develop the underlying micro-economic structure of the model, and we use a set of plausible values for the parameters. The variables (except the interest rate) are expressed in logarithms and refer to deviations from the steady state values. Our modelling is very standard, and quite similar to Garretsen *et al.* (2007) or Fornero *et al.* (2007), for example.

The aggregate demand -(IS) curve- is the following:

$$y_t = a_1 y_{t-1} + (1\text{-}a_1)E_t(y_{t+1}) - a_2[i_t\text{-}E_t(\pi_{t+1})\text{-}\overline{r}] + a_3 g_t + a_4 y_t^* + a_5(e_t\text{+}p_t^*\text{-}p_t) + d_t \quad (1)$$

With, in period (t): (y_t): output; (i_t): short term nominal interest rate; (p_t): price level; π_t=p_t-p_{t-1}: inflation rate; (g_t): fiscal balance (there is a deficit if $g_t>0$); (e_t): nominal exchange rate, number of domestic currencies necessary to obtain one unit of foreign currency (the euro depreciates if $e_t>0$); ($\overline{r}$): equilibrium real interest rate; (d_t): positive demand shock (white noise). The foreign variables are denoted by an asterisk.

Traditionally, aggregate demand is driven by the optimizing behavior of households, which maximize an intertemporal utility function. Moreover, output depends on past output, because of "habit formation" in consumption decisions. But it also depends on expected future output, because rational agents can maximize their decisions intertemporally and smooth their consumption. Besides, in empirical estimations, authors generally find that the values of the forward and backward parameters (a_1+a_2) approximately sum to one. Furthermore, aggregate demand also depends on the real interest rate, because of the intertemporal substitution of consumption. Nevertheless, in the economic literature, this interest rate channel seems controversial (a_2 is low), perhaps because monetary policy operates through other channels (asset prices, exchange rate, credit, wealth effect). Finally, aggregate demand also depends on net government spending, on a demand shock, and on the net exports, the latter being a increasing function of the foreign economic activity and price competitiveness of the country.

The supply function takes the form of a "new Keynesian Phillips curve":

$$\pi_t = b_1\pi_{t-1} + (1 - b_1)E_t(\pi_{t+1}) + b_2 y_t + b_3(\pi_t^* + \Delta e_t) + s_t \quad (2)$$

With (s_t): inflationary supply shock (white noise).

Indeed, in the new Keynesian models, aggregate supply results from the behavior of firms that set prices for their products so as to maximize profits in a monopolistic competition setting. Lagged inflation has been motivated in the literature by the presence of partial price indexation or of rule-of-thumb price-setters. So, inflation depends on past inflation, expressing the inertia in price adjustment or adaptive expectations, but it also depends on expectations about future prices, because of learning effects. Besides, the output gap expresses the demand-pull factor and the tensions on the utilization of the productive capacities, whereas imported prices (the so-called "pass through") express the cost-push factor affecting inflation: namely the foreign inflation and the depreciation of the domestic currency. Finally, (s_t) captures an inflationary shock unrelated to excess demand or to cost-push factors (mark-up, etc.).

Let us also mention that (b_2) is related to the degree of price stickiness in the economy: more stickiness or price rigidity in the labor market implies a lower value of (b_2). However, the traditional New Keynesian Phillips Curves introduce generally real marginal costs as demand-pull indicator. Theoretically, this variable can be replaced by measures of cyclical pressures (output gaps) only if the labor markets are frictionless, if there is no capital stock, or if consumption and work hours are proportional. More concretely, Domenech *et al.* (2001) find that a measure of the output gap performs better in econometrical estimations than real marginal costs. Nevertheless, in most studies, the empirical estimations of the coefficient (b_2) are often insignificant, or even negative... In fact, Jondeau and Le Bihan (2005) find that the real Unit Labor Cost specification with a single lag and lead combined with a large forward looking component is relevant in the US and the UK. Conversely, the output gap specification with three lags and leads and a low degree of forward lookingness would provide a better fit for continental Europe. In any case, the choice of the forcing variable does not seem to affect the degree of inflation persistence (b_1).

Finally, in an open economy, we can consider that exchange rates adjust according to the Uncovered Interest Rate Parity condition:

$$E_t(e_{t+1}) = e_t + i_t - i_t^* \tag{3}$$

Indeed, in open economies, there isn't only an interest rate channel, but also an exchange rate channel of monetary policy. Even in a monetary union, whereas internal exchange rates are fixed, external exchange rates adjustments may be a shock absorber.

Finally, here is, according to some econometrical studies, the calibration that we can retain for the parameters of our model.

3. Inflation Persistence

Inflation persistence is defined by the Inflation Persistence Network (IPN) as the delay by which inflation converges towards its long run value following a shock which has led inflation away from it. More precisely, the IPN defines three kinds of persistence. First, 'intrinsic persistence' corresponds to our parameter (b_1) as it relates to nominal rigidities and to the way wages and prices are set. Secondly, 'expectations-based persistence' (1-b_1) is related to the perception and the credibility for the public of the inflation target of the monetary authority. Finally, 'extrinsic persistence' (b_2) is inherited from persistent fluctuations in the economic environment and in the inflation-driving real variables (see Altissimo *et al.* (2006)). In general, 'hybrid' monetary policy models, taking into account both backward and forward inflation determinants, are more consistent with empirical data as well as

Table 1. Calibration of our parameters

	a_1	a_2	a_3	a_4	a_5	b_1	b_2	b_3
Coenen-Wieland(2002) 1980:1−1998:4		0.08			0.02		0.02	
Djoudad-Gauthier(2003) 1983−2000	0.52	0.03				0.62	0.17	
Domenech *et al.*(2001) 1986:1−2000:4	0.57	0.10				0.46	0.06	
Faruqee (2006) 1990−2002								0.15
Fornero *et al.* (2007) 1980:1−2005:4	0.61	0.23	0.6	0.25	0.20	0.46	0.08	0.05
Gagnon-Ihrig (2001) 1981:1−2003:4								0.05
Leith-Malley (2002) 1970:1−1998:2	0.22	0.06				0.3	0.02	
Sahuc (2002) 1970:1−2002:4	0.49	0.06				0.54	0.06	
Smets (2003) 1974−1998	0.44	0.06				0.48	0.18	
Smets-Wouters (2002) 1980:2−1999:4	0.57	0.3				0.33		
our calibration	0.6	0.1	0.6	0.25	0.1	0.4	0.1	0.1

with the concrete gradual response of inflation to shocks than the traditional forward looking models. In fact, Smets and Wouters (2002) or Leith and Malley (2002) show that there is more inertia in the price-setting behavior in Europe than in the US. Nevertheless, even in Europe, a forward looking behavior seems dominant: the coefficient on expected future inflation substantially exceeds the coefficient on lagged inflation ($b_1<0.5$). Besides, other econometrical studies show that additional inflation lags would be insignificant.

In various countries, the labor markets (real wage rigidities) have an important role in generating various levels of inflation persistence. Nevertheless, studies disagree on the levels of inflation persistence and even on the ranking of the countries! For example, in the current monetary policy regime, Altissimo *et al.* (2006) find that inflation persistence is only moderate in the Euro Area, and may even have fallen over the last decade. Indeed, today, inflation expectations are largely anchored by the price objective of the European Central Bank (ECB). Therefore, the importance of past inflation is less essential to form these expectations, and actual inflation developments are less persistent. However, Cecchetti and Debelle (2005) show that the change in the inflation process at least since the 1990s is essentially due to a decrease in its mean, the decline in the persistence of the process being of lesser importance. Indeed, in Europe, monetary policy has been gradually more focused on achieving low inflation, which has increased the credibility of the central bank, and which in turn anchored inflation expectations. Nevertheless, inflation persistence seems to remain quite high in certain categories of goods: food, housing and transportation, whereas it would be low for alcohol, tobacco, furniture and health, and even negative for communication, recreation, clothing, restaurants and education (Altissimo *et al.*, 2006).

In this framework, the estimations of the degree of inflation persistence (b_1) are very heterogeneous, in the economic literature. Generally, Rumler (2005) finds that price rigidity and persistence are lower in open economies, indicating than when firms face more variable input costs, they tend to adjust their prices more frequently. But the estimations and even the classification of the countries according to this criterion differ widely. Here are some of these results:

Table 2. Inflation persistence (b_1) in Europe

	Rumler (2005) 1970-2003:2	Cecchetti Debelle (2005) 1990-2003	Benigno Lopez -Salido (2002) 1970:1-1997:1	Jondeau -Le Bihan (2005) 1970:1-1994:4
Austria	0.38	-0.05		
Belgium	0.21	-0.27		
Finland	0.42	0.26		
France	0.45	0.09	0.30	0.45
Germany	0.46	-0.20	0.09	0.19
Greece	0.43			
Italy	0.41	0.44	0.52	0.52
Luxembourg		-0.33		
Netherlands	0.33	0.06	0.37	
Portugal		0.65		
Spain	0.20	0.21	0.50	
Sweden		0.24		
U. Kingdom		0.59		0.27
EU	0.40	0.30		0.37

4. Levels of Inflation and Economic Activity

Regarding the preferences of the economic authorities, Muscatelli *et al.* (2003) directly estimate monetary and fiscal policy rules, without deriving them from loss functions. Domenech *et al.* (2001) or Djoudad and Gauthier (2003) also estimate Taylor types interest rate rules, whereas Garretsen *et al.* (2007) or Fornero *et al.* (2007) estimate fiscal rules. Nevertheless, in the current chapter, we want to derive the monetary rule and the interest rate from the loss function of the central bank. Therefore, we consider that this loss function takes the following form:

$$L^M = \frac{1}{2}[c^M y_t^2 + \pi_t^2 + v^M(\Delta i_t)^2] \tag{4}$$

In this loss function, the output target is given by the potential output level; so the central bank aims at a zero output gap (excluding the possibility of a systematic inflation bias). The target for the inflation rate is also zero. Furthermore, we take into account the fact that central banks aim at limiting the variations in their instrument (the interest rate), which is often observed in their empirical behavior. As price stability remains generally the main objective of the central banks (in particular for the ECB), we take the following calibration for our parameters: $c^M = v^M = 0.5$.

Furthermore, we consider the equilibrium in the case of 'time consistent' discretion: the monetary policy is the one that the central bank has an interest in conducting, if the agents' expectations are rational (taken as given) and if it can't surprise these agents in an unexpected way. Indeed, empirically, no central bank appears to make any commitment about the course of its future monetary policy [1].

Now, let us suppose that the inflation rate is the following:

$$\pi_t = b\pi_{t-1} + b_p(\pi_t^* + \Delta e_t) + b_i(i_t - i_{t-1}) + b_{i2}(i_t - i_t^*) + b_s s_t \qquad \text{with } 0<b<1 \quad (5)$$

If the expectations are rational, we have: $E_t(\pi^*_{t+1})=0$, $E_t(i^*_{t+1}) = E_t(i_{t+1}) = i_t$.

Thus, (3) implies: $E_t(\pi_{t+1}) = b\pi_t + b_p(i_t - i_t^*)$ (6)

So, (b) measures the speed of convergence to the inflation target under the optimal policy. Nevertheless, in comparison with Clarida *et al.* (1999) for example, the specificity of our model is that the future anticipated inflation also depends on the differential between the domestic and foreign interest rates. Indeed, a higher domestic interest rate increases the anticipations of a depreciation of the national currency, which would be inflationary.

Then, the optimal monetary policy rule, which verifies $dL^M/di_t = 0$, is (with Appendix A):

$$\begin{aligned} c^M[(1-b+bb_1)a_2 - (a_2 - a_5 + a_5 b_1)b_p]y_t + [a_2 b_2 - (1 - b_1 + a_2 b_2)b_p]\pi_t \\ -v^M[1 + b_2 a_5 - b(1 - b_1 + a_2 b_2)](i_t - i_{t-1}) &= 0 \quad (7) \end{aligned}$$

In this framework, as mentioned by Clarida *et al.* (1999), the values of the parameters in equation (5) depend on the basic parameters of our model. More precisely, we can't solve our model analytically, except for specific values of our basic parameters (see Appendix B). Nevertheless, the parameters in (5) are only a function of the supply Phillips curve (2) and of the parameters (a_2) and (a_5) of the demand function (1). Regarding the speed of convergence towards the inflation target, we have the following stable roots for (b), that is to say the unique stable solutions comprised between 0 and 1 (see Appendix B):

►If $b_1=0$, $b=0$; if $b_1=1$, $b=\dfrac{c^M}{(c^M + b_2^2)}$.

Thus, (b) is an increasing function of (b_1): as endogenous inflation persistence increases, the serial correlation of inflation increases, due to the greater degree of backward-lookingness in the New-Keynesian Phillips curve.

►If $c^M=0$, $b=\dfrac{b_1 a_2 b_2}{(1 - b_1 + a_2 b_2)b_3}$; if $c^M \to \infty$, $b=\dfrac{b_1}{(1-b_1)}$ with $b_1<\dfrac{1}{2}$.

[1]For the study of the equilibrium in the case of commitment, see e.g. Clarida *et al.* (1999). In particular, the authors show that credibility problems emerge whenever private sector behavior depends on beliefs about the future, even without the desire of the central bank to raise output beyond its potential level. They also show that commitment could enable the policy-makers to smooth the stabilization costs over time.

Thus, (b) is an increasing function of (c^M): when the central bank gives more weight to price stability, (c^M) is smaller and (b) is also smaller, as there is a quicker convergence of inflation towards the target and less inflation inertia.

Furthermore, (5) implies the following inflation rate (see Appendix B):

$$\pi_t = b\pi_{t-1} + \frac{bb_3}{b_1}(\pi_t^* + \Delta e_t) + bb_2b_hb_k(i_t - i_{t-1}) + \frac{b^2(1-b_1)b_3}{b_1^2}(i_t - i_t^*) + \frac{b}{b_1}s_t \quad (8)$$

$$b_k = \frac{[a_2b_2b_1 - (1-b_1+a_2b_2)bb_3]}{b_z} \quad b_h = \frac{v^M[1+b_2a_5 - b(1-b_1+a_2b_2)]}{[b_1a_2b_2 - (1-b_1+a_2b_2)bb_3]}$$

$$b_z = c^M[(1-b+bb_1)a_2b_1 - (a_2 - a_5 + a_5b_1)bb_3] \quad (9)$$

So, inflation is an increasing function of the lagged inflation, of the imported inflation (pass through), and of an exogenous inflationary shock. Furthermore, the differential between the domestic and foreign interest rates increases the anticipations of a depreciation of the exchange rate, and then the "expectations-based" inflation persistence. In the same way, in our model, as the central bank cares about variations in its interest rate ($v^M>0$), monetary policy doesn't fully compensate for the "extrinsic" inflationary consequences of the demand-pull shocks ($b_2>0$). That is why the variation in interest rates (i_t-i_{t-1}) remains more limited than necessary to stabilize these shocks, which affects both the inflation and the economic activity.

Putting equation (8) into (7), we also have the following economic activity:

$$\begin{aligned} y_t &= -bb_k\pi_{t-1} - \frac{bb_3b_k}{b_1}(\pi_t^* + \Delta e_t) + b_kb_h(b_1 - bb_2b_k)(i_t - i_{t-1}) \\ &\quad -\frac{b^2(1-b_1)b_3b_k}{b_1^2}(i_t - i_t^*) - \frac{bb_k}{b_1}s_t \end{aligned} \quad (10)$$

And thus: $E_t(y_{t+1}) = -b_kE_t(\pi_{t+1}) = -bb_k\pi_t - \frac{bb_3b_k}{b_1}(i_t - i_t^*)$ (11)

So, the consequences on the level of economic activity and on the inflation of the demand shocks (d_t) and of the shocks on the real interest rate ($\overline{r}$) or on the foreign economic activity (y_t^*) could fully be compensated by the monetary and budgetary authorities [a_2i_t-a_3g_t=$a_2\overline{r}$+$a_4y_t^*$+d_t] if the variations in interest rates were without cost (v^M=0 implies b_h=0). On the contrary, the imported inflation (π_t^*), the supply shocks (s_t) or the current (Δe_t) or anticipated (i_t-i_t^*) depreciation of the exchange rate modify the price level, and therefore also the long run price competitiveness and the current economic activity of the country. The inflationary consequences of these shocks can only be avoided if b=0, that is to say if the inflation targeting policy of the monetary authority is perfectly credible. In the same way, their consequences on the level of economic activity can only be avoided if b=0 or c^M=0 (which implies b_k=0).

Then, by combining equations (1), (7), (8) and (10), we can find the optimal interest rate, and the levels of inflation and economic activity (see Appendix C).

5. The Demand or Fiscal Shocks

In case of a positive domestic (d_t) or external (y_t^*) demand shock, or of a fiscal policy shock (g_t), the monetary policy must be contractionary, in order to reduce both the inflationary and expansionary consequences of the shock. However, in a purely forward-looking model ($b_1 \rightarrow 0$), we have:

$$i_t = \frac{a_2 c^M}{[a_2^2 c^M + v^M(1 + b_2 a_5)]} d_t \qquad y_t = \frac{v^M(1 + b_2 a_5)}{[a_2^2 c^M + v^M(1 + b_2 a_5)]} d_t \tag{12}$$

So, the contractionary monetary policy is credible for the anticipations, and the future and current inflation levels are thus stabilized (π_t=0). Nevertheless, there remains a large increase in economic activity. With our numerical calibration of the parameters, we have: i_t=0.1d_t and y_t=d_t. However, these variables essentially depend on the preferences of the central bank. Indeed, if the central bank cares for interest rate volatility (v^M>0), it isn't optimal to fully offset these demand or fiscal shocks in the current period, because it would imply too much interest rate volatility, whereas the shocks are only temporary. Nevertheless, monetary policy is all the more contractionary and the increase in economic activity is all the more reduced as the preference of the central bank for limiting the variations in its instrument (v^M) is weak, as its preference for stabilizing the economic activity (c^M) is high, and as monetary policy is efficient in influencing the demand (a_2 is high). Furthermore, in the purely backward-looking model and with extreme inflation inertia ($b_1 \rightarrow 1$), everything depends on the values of our parameters. However, the main difference with the preceding results is that the current increase in economic activity is always inflationary. Indeed, we have: π_t =0.1d_t with our numerical calibration, and this inflation is all the more accentuated as the demand-pull inflation (b_2) is high.

Furthermore, we can see that the monetary authority doesn't react at all to demand or fiscal shocks, in case of a policy of strict inflation targeting ($c^M \rightarrow 0$). Indeed, even if the monetary policy of strict inflation targeting isn't perfectly credible (b >0), the current increase in activity (y_t=d_t) is only moderately inflationary and therefore, it doesn't necessitate a large variation in interest rates. More precisely, we have:

$$\begin{aligned} \pi_t &= \frac{a_2 b_2^2 b_3(1 - b_1 + a_2 b_2)}{[b_3^2(1 - b_1 + a_2 b_2)^2 + a_2 b_2^2 a_5 b_3(1 - b_1 + a_2 b_2) - a_2^3 b_2^3 b_1]} d_t \\ y_t &= \frac{b_3^2(1 - b_1 + a_2 b_2)^2}{[b_3^2(1 - b_1 + a_2 b_2)^2 + a_2 b_2^2 a_5 b_3(1 - b_1 + a_2 b_2) - a_2^3 b_2^3 b_1]} d_t \end{aligned} \tag{13}$$

That corresponds to π_t=0.02d_t with our calibration of the parameters. More precisely, the inflation rate is a decreasing function of the pass through (b_3), but an increasing function of the importance of the demand-pull inflationary factors (b_2) and of the efficiency of the monetary policy (a_2) in influencing the demand, two factors that seem empirically quite small.

On the contrary, if the monetary authority aims at stabilizing the economic activity ($c^M \rightarrow \infty$), this can perfectly be achieved (y_t=0) but with a very contractionary monetary policy, and even then, the inflation appears as non negligible. Indeed, we have:

$$i_t = \frac{(1 - b_1)^2}{[a_2(1\text{-}b_1)^2 + a_5 b_3(1\text{-}b_1)\text{-}a_2 b_3]} d_t \qquad \pi_t = \frac{(1 - b_1) b_3}{[a_2(1\text{-}b_1)^2 + a_5 b_3(1\text{-}b_1)\text{-}a_2 b_3]} d_t \tag{14}$$

Thus, we obtain: i_t=11.25d_t and π_t =1.88d_t with the numerical calibration of our parameters. However, the monetary policy can be less contractionary and the inflation rate is smaller if the monetary policy is more efficient in influencing the economic activity (a_2 is high) and if the price-competitiveness is important in influencing the exports (a_5 is high). Furthermore, the interest and inflation rates are then an increasing function of the inflation persistence (b_1)[2]. Indeed, when the inflation inertia increases, the consequences of a positive and inflationary demand or fiscal shock are, naturally, more difficult to stabilize for the central bank.

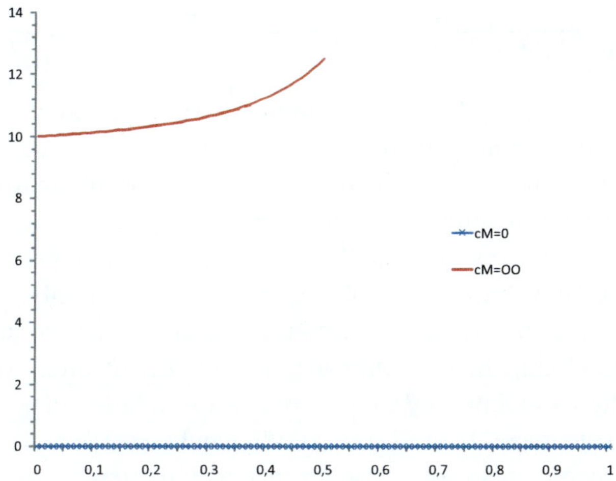

Figure 1. Interest rate according to (b_1)

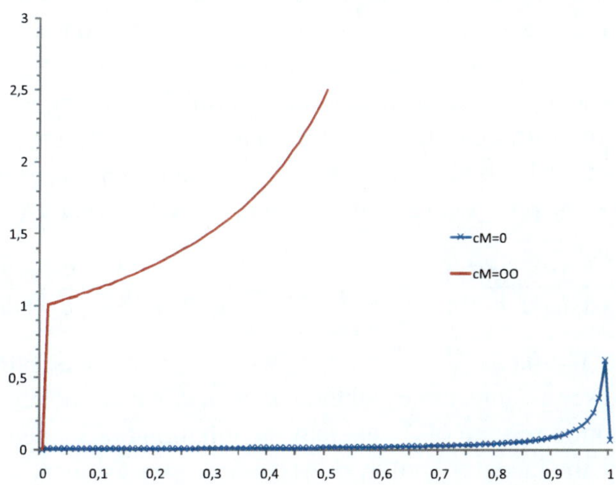

Figure 2. Inflation rate according to (b_1).

[2]All the figures are made supposing the following calibration: $a_2 = a_5 = b_2 = b_3 = 0.1$.

6. The Supply Shocks

If there is no inflation inertia ($b_1 \to 0$), that is to say if the monetary policy of inflation targeting is perfectly credible, inflation and economic activity are perfectly stabilized and no variation in interest rates is necessary. Nevertheless, if the monetary policy of inflation targeting is not perfectly credible ($c^M \to 0$ and b>0), then, inflation can't be avoided. Indeed, we have:

$$\pi_t = \frac{a_2 b_2 b_3 (1 - b_1 + a_2 b_2)}{[b_3^2 (1 - b_1 + a_2 b_2)^2 + a_2 b_2^2 a_5 b_3 (1 - b_1 + a_2 b_2) - a_2^3 b_2^3 b_1]} s_t \qquad (15)$$

This corresponds to: π_t=0.16s_t with our numerical calibration of the parameters. However, this inflation is an increasing function of the inflation persistence (b_1), of the efficiency of the monetary policy in influencing the demand (a_2), of the demand-pull inflationary factors (b_2), but a decreasing function of the pass through (b_3)[3].

Besides, in a backward-looking model with extreme inflation persistence ($b_1 \to 1$), everything depends on the values of our parameters. After a supply shock, the variations in interest rates remain generally quite negligible, as the monetary authority then faces a dilemma between stabilizing the economic activity and the inflation. Thus, the variation in economic activity often remains quite weak, whereas the inflation rate is nearly proportional to the shock. Indeed, we have: i_t=0.01s_t, π_t=0.99s_t and y_t=-0.08s_t with our numerical calibration. However, there is naturally a bigger increase in interest rates, a smaller inflation rate but a higher slowdown in economic activity if the monetary authority has a smaller preference for sustaining the economic activity (c^M is weak), or if the demand-pull inflationary factors (b_2) are high. Furthermore, the increase in interest rates is accentuated if the monetary policy is more efficient in influencing the economic activity (a_2 is high) whereas in these circumstances, the inflation rate is higher, and the recession is reduced; the decrease in the real interest rates can even sometimes create an economic growth. The same results are obtained if the demand function is strongly backward-looking (a_1 is high), or if the price-competitiveness has a small importance in influencing the economic activity (a_5 is weak), even if the importance of these factors is much more marginal.

Finally, if the central bank aims at stabilizing the economic activity ($c^M \to \infty$ and y_t=0), then, the monetary policy is very expansionary. Indeed, we have:

$$i_t = \frac{-[a_5 - b_1(a_2 + a_5)]}{[a_2(1\text{-}b_1)^2 + a_5 b_3(1\text{-}b_1)\text{-}a_2 b_3]} s_t \qquad \pi_t = \frac{a_2(1 - b_1 - b_3)}{[a_2(1\text{-}b_1)^2 + a_5 b_3(1\text{-}b_1)\text{-}a_2 b_3]} s_t \qquad (16)$$

Thus, we obtain: i_t=-0.63s_t and π_t=1.56s_t with our numerical calibration. However, there can be an increase in interest rates all the wider as monetary policy is more efficient in influencing the economic activity (a_2), whereas the inflation rate is then a little bit accentuated. On the contrary, the monetary policy must be more expansionary and the inflation rate is more limited if the pass through (b_3) is high, if the price-competitiveness is important in influencing the exports of a county (a_5 is high), or if the inflation persistence (b_1) is weak.

So, as mentioned by Clarida *et al.* (1999), in case of a supply shock, there is a trade-off between fighting against inflation and sustaining the economic activity. Thus, if the

[3]In this last case, $y_t = \frac{-a_2 b_2 [a_5 b_3 (1 - b_1 + a_2 b_2) - a_2^2 b_2 b_1]}{[b_3^2 (1 - b_1 + a_2 b_2)^2 + a_2 b_2^2 a_5 b_3 (1 - b_1 + a_2 b_2) - a_2^3 b_2^3 b_1]} s_t$ remains negligible.

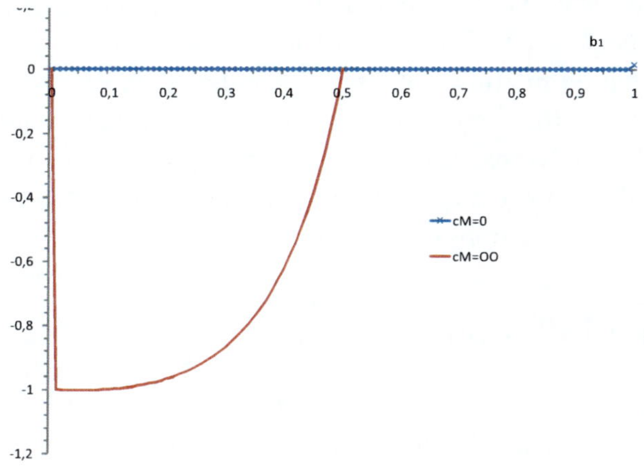

Figure 3. Interest rate according to (b_1).

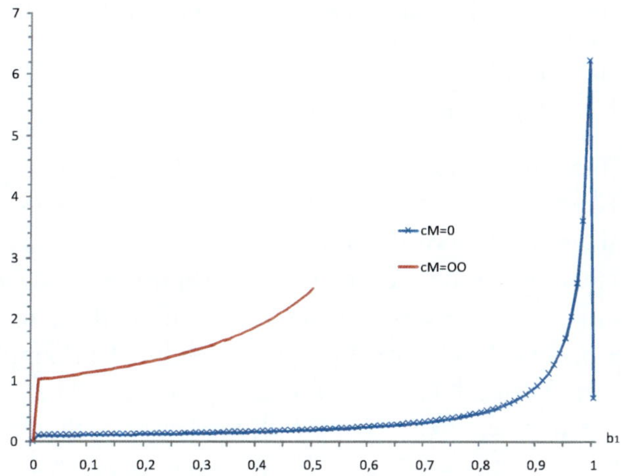

Figure 4. Inflation rate according to (b_1).

weight given to inflation is high ($c^M \rightarrow 0$), the inflation is more limited, but at the cost of a higher variation in economic activity. On the contrary, the more the central bank cares about stabilizing the economic activity, the higher the inflation. Furthermore, as mentioned by Bofinger *et al.* (2005), monetary policy can be quite destabilizing in case of a negative supply shock. Indeed, such a shock has initially inflationary consequences which lower the real interest rate, and which reduce then automatically the recessive consequences of the shock. On the contrary, a contractionary monetary policy and an increase in interest rates would risk accentuating the recessive consequences of the shock. That is why following a supply shock, the monetary policy is generally quite passive.

Finally, our model also shows that the inflationary risks are accentuated if the endogenous inflation persistence (b_1) is high; indeed, inflation returns then more slowly to equilibrium. So, as mentioned by Clarida *et al.* (1999), if endogenous inflation persistence is higher, the monetary policy must react more strongly to supply shocks, since any disturbance not eliminated today will continue and will imply more output contractions in the future. The monetary policy is thus more contractionary (or less expansionary), since a potentially higher inflation inertia would imply that the effect of cost-push shocks persists for longer, possibly requiring greater output contractions in the future. In the same way, Altissimo *et al.* (2006) show that in the case of a cost-push shock, a smaller degree of inflation persistence reduces the contractionary policy necessary to respond to this shock, as the agents reduce their expectations of future inflation.

7. The Foreign Inflationary Shocks

A foreign inflationary shock has two kinds of expansionary consequences: it increases the price competitiveness and the exports of the domestic country, and it increases also the imported inflation. Monetary policy should then be contractionary, in order to reduce the expansionary and inflationary consequences of the shock. However, without inflation inertia ($b_1 \rightarrow 0$), the rise in interest rates can be limited in order to stabilize the inflation rate (π_t=0), even if there remains an increase in economic activity. Indeed, we have:

$$i_t = \frac{a_2 a_5 c^M}{[a_2^2 c^M + v^M(1 + b_2 a_5)]} \pi_t^* \qquad y_t = \frac{a_5 v^M(1 + b_2 a_5)}{[a_2^2 c^M + v^M(1 + b_2 a_5)]} \pi_t^* \tag{17}$$

Therefore, with the numerical calibration of our parameters, we obtain: i_t=0.01 (π_t^*+Δe_t) and y_t=0.10(π_t^*+Δe_t). More precisely, the increase in interest rates is an increasing function of the efficiency of the transmission of the monetary policy (a_2). But it essentially depends on the preferences of the monetary authority. Indeed, it can be proportional to the foreign inflation if the weight given to sustaining the economic activity (c^M) is particularly high or if the central bank doesn't care about stabilizing the fluctuations of its instrument ($v^M \rightarrow 0$). Furthermore, the monetary policy must be all the more contractionary and the increase in economic activity is all the larger as the price competitiveness of a country increases its exports (a_5 is high). The main consequence of the inflation inertia ($b_1 \rightarrow 1$) seems then to increase the inflation rate. Indeed, we have: π_t=0.11(π_t^*+Δe_t) with our numerical calibration. Furthermore, this inflation is an increasing function of the demand pull (b_2) or imported (b_3) inflationary factors.

Besides, in case of a policy of inflation targeting ($c^M \rightarrow 0$), the monetary authority doesn't react at all to foreign inflationary shocks (i_t=0). However, as this policy isn't perfectly credible ($b>0$), with the increase in economic activity, there is also a moderate inflation. Indeed, π_t=0.02(π_t^*+Δe_t) and y_t=0.10(π_t^*+Δe_t) with our numerical calibration, but these variables are an increasing function of the parameters (a_2) (a_5) and (b_1). More precisely, the growth rate is mainly an increasing function of the sensibility of the exports to the price competitiveness (a_5), whereas inflation is mainly an increasing function of the inflation inertia (b_1)[4].

Finally, if the most important aim of the monetary authority is to stabilize the economic activity ($c^M \rightarrow \infty$ and y_t=0), then the monetary policy is much more contractionary,

[4]If c^M=0, $\pi_t = \frac{a_2 b_2 b_3(b_3 + b_2 a_5)(1 - b_1 + a_2 b_2)}{[b_3^2(1 - b_1 + a_2 b_2)^2 + a_2 b_2^2 a_5 b_3(1 - b_1 + a_2 b_2) - a_2^3 b_2^3 b_1]} \pi_t^*$

and $y_t = \frac{b_3[a_5 b_3(1 - b_1)(1 - b_1 + a_2 b_2) + a_2^3 b_2^2 b_1]}{[b_3^2(1 - b_1 + a_2 b_2)^2 + a_2 b_2^2 a_5 b_3(1 - b_1 + a_2 b_2) - a_2^3 b_2^3 b_1]} \pi_t^*$.

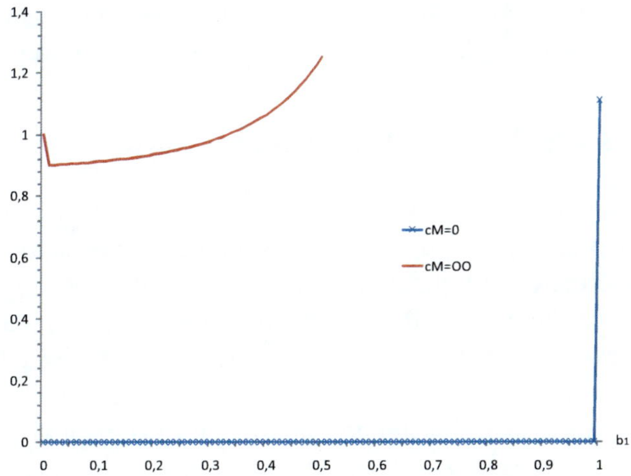

Figure 5. Interest rate according to (b_1).

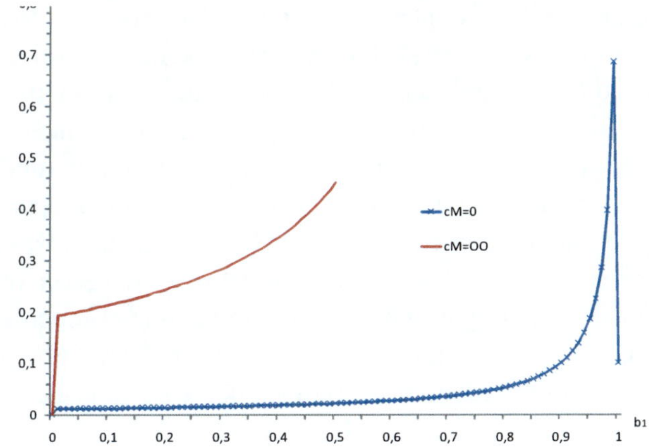

Figure 6. Inflation rate according to (b_1).

whereas the inflation rate remains non negligible. Indeed, we have:

$$i_t = \frac{[a_5(1\text{-}b_1)(1\text{-}b_1\text{-}b_3) + b_1 b_3 a_2]}{[a_2(1\text{-}b_1)^2 + a_5 b_3(1\text{-}b_1)\text{-}a_2 b_3]}\pi_t^* \qquad \pi_t = \frac{b_3[a_2(1\text{-}b_1\text{-}b_3) + a_5(1\text{-}b_1)]}{[a_2(1\text{-}b_1)^2 + a_5 b_3(1\text{-}b_1)\text{-}a_2 b_3]}\pi_t^* \tag{18}$$

Thus, $i_t = 1.06(\pi_t^* + \Delta e_t)$ and $\pi_t = 0.34(\pi_t^* + \Delta e_t)$ with our numerical calibration. However, the necessary increase in interest rates and the inflation rate are both a decreasing function of the efficiency of monetary policy in affecting the demand (a_2), but an increasing function of the influence of the price competitiveness of a country on the level of its exports (a_5). Moreover, both variables are all the higher as the inflation inertia (b_1) as well as the pass-through (b_3) are high, accentuating the inflationary risks. So, in the current framework of an increase in the petroleum prices, for example, our model can thus contribute to justify the current behavior of the ECB. Indeed, even if it aims at sustaining the economic activity, the monetary authority shouldn't decrease its interest rates in order to compensate for the decrease in the purchasing power of the consumers, as the most important is then to maintain the price competitiveness of the Euro-zone and to limit the risks of imported inflation.

8. The Shocks on the Foreign Interest Rate

In our model, after an increase in the foreign interest rates, the rational agents anticipate a future appreciation of the domestic currency, which should be deflationary. Nevertheless, there are then many situations. Without inflation inertia, if the monetary policy of inflation targeting is perfectly credible ($b_1 \rightarrow 0$), then the future anticipated inflation is null, and no variation in interest rates is therefore necessary in order to perfectly stabilize the levels of inflation and economic activity. In the same way, the consequences of the variations in the foreign interest rate remain negligible for any values of the parameters of our model, if there are only rule of thumb price setters and with extreme inflation inertia ($b_1 \rightarrow 1$).

Nevertheless, if the monetary policy of inflation targeting is not perfectly credible ($c^M \rightarrow 0$ and $b>0$), then there is a small deflationary and recessive effect of an increase in the foreign interest rate[5]. However, both remain negligible with plausible values of our parameters. Indeed, these effects depend on anticipations: so, they don't depend much on the degree of inflation persistence (b_1), but they are essentially an increasing function of the parameters (a_2) and (b_2), empirically very small in the econometrical estimations. Our model could thus contribute to justify the possibility of big discrepancies between the world interest rates. Indeed, our results show that the ECB, for example, doesn't have to follow the American monetary policy and the variations in American interest rates.

In fact, the reaction of the monetary authority to foreign interest rates shocks is only wide if it gives a non negligible weight to the stabilization of the economic activity. Indeed, if ($c^M \rightarrow \infty$), the monetary policy is expansionary, in order to compensate for the recessive effect of the future appreciation of the exchange rate. The economic activity can then be perfectly stabilized ($y_t=0$) whereas there remains a decrease in prices. More precisely, we have:

$$i_t = \frac{-b_3[a_2 - a_5(1\text{-}b_1)]}{[a_2(1\text{-}b_1)^2\text{+}a_5b_3(1\text{-}b_1)\text{-}a_2b_3]} i_t^* \qquad \pi_t = \frac{-b_3a_2(1 - b_1)}{[a_2(1\text{-}b_1)^2\text{+}a_5b_3(1\text{-}b_1)\text{-}a_2b_3]} i_t^* \tag{19}$$

So the monetary policy is all the more expansionary and the deflation all the more accentuated as the pass through (b_3) is high. With our numerical calibration and if (b_3=0.1), we only have: i_t=-0.13i_t^* and π_t=-0.19i_t^*; but the decrease in the domestic interest rate could be very large for extreme values of (b_3). Furthermore, for specific values of our parameters [a_2=a_5(1-b_1)], no variation in interest rates is necessary, as the deflation implies an increase in the real interest rate whose recessive effect on the domestic economic activity is exactly compensated by the increase in the price-competitiveness and in the exports of the country. Otherwise, the monetary policy is all the more expansionary and the deflation all the more accentuated as the sensibility of the demand to the real interest rate (a_2) is high, whereas the sensibility of the exports to the price competitiveness of the country (a_5) is weak. Finally,

[5]If c^M=0, $\pi_t = \frac{-a_2^2b_2^2b_3(1 - b_1 + a_2b_2)}{[b_3^2(1 - b_1 + a_2b_2)^2 + a_2b_2^2a_5b_3(1 - b_1 + a_2b_2) - a_2^3b_2^3b_1]} i_t^*$
and $y_t = \frac{-a_2^2b_2\{b_3(1 - b_1 + a_2b_2)[b_3(1 - b_1 + a_2b_2) - b_2a_5(1 - b_1)] + a_2^2b_2^2b_1(1 - b_1)\}}{(1 - b_1 + a_2b_2)[b_3^2(1 - b_1 + a_2b_2)^2 + a_2b_2^2a_5b_3(1 - b_1 + a_2b_2) - a_2^3b_2^3b_1]} i_t^*$.

regarding the inflation inertia, the monetary policy is more expansionary and the deflation is more accentuated if the degree of inflation persistence (b_1) increases.

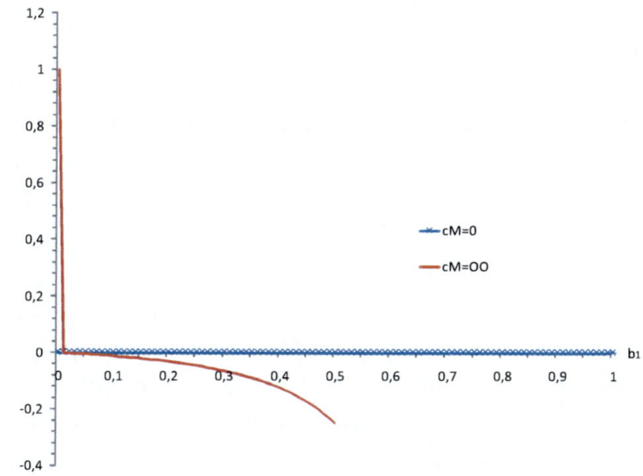

Figure 7. Interest rate according to (b_1).

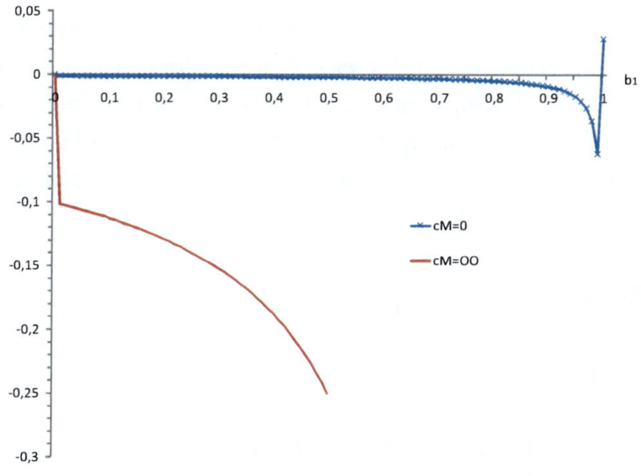

Figure 8. Inflation rate according to (b_1).

9. Conclusion

A New Keynesian Model in open economy allows underlining some important results, regarding optimal monetary policy in an open economy framework. First, the monetary policy depends, naturally, on the preferences of the central bank, on the respective weights given to the inflation and economic activity targets and to the limitation of the variations in its instrument. However, the structural parameters of our model have also a non negligible weight. More precisely, the degree of inflation inertia is a parameter which is quite difficult to estimate in econometrical studies, and which seems to diverge between countries, even between the members of the Economic and Monetary Union (EMU). Nevertheless, evaluating this inflation persistence would be quite useful, in the framework of our model, as it largely contributes defining the optimal monetary policy. In particular, the question of inflation persistence differentials in the Euro area is very important today. Indeed, if there are huge differences, the countries which have a higher inflation inertia would have to struggle harder to reduce inflation to its long run value. Therefore, in the context of the current oil shock for example, the consequences of a common monetary policy on the economic situation of the various countries would be very heterogeneous.

In our model, the inflation rate is the higher and the monetary policy must be all the more contractionary as the inflation inertia is high, after positive fiscal, demand or foreign inflationary shocks. Besides, in case of an inflationary negative supply shock, the monetary policy faces a dilemma between stabilizing the inflation rate and sustaining the economic activity: monetary policy remains thus quite passive. However, monetary policy becomes more expansionary as the weight given to stabilizing the economic activity increases; but it is then less expansionary if the inflation persistence increases, because of the higher inflationary risks. In fact, monetary policy is only more expansionary if the inflation persistence increases after a positive shock on the foreign interest rate, because of the higher deflationary risks due to the anticipations of a depreciation of the domestic currency. Therefore, our model underlines important results concerning the consequences of the degree of inflation persistence on the determination of the optimal monetary policy in an open economy framework, for stabilizing different kinds of shocks. Nevertheless, a continuation of the current chapter would be to study the implication, for the optimal common monetary policy, of the heterogeneity between the inflation inertia in the various member countries of a monetary union. This would be particularly useful to shed light on the policy of the ECB in the framework of the EMU, for example.

Appendix A: Inflation and Activity

By combining (1) and (2), we obtain:

$$\begin{aligned}(1+b_2a_5)\pi_t &= a_1b_2y_{t-1} - b_3e_{t-1} + b_2a_5(p^*_{t-1} - p_{t-1}) + b_1\pi_{t-1} \\ &\quad +(b_3+b_2a_5)(e_t+\pi^*_t) - b_2a_2(i_t - \overline{r}) + b_2a_3g_t + b_2a_4y^*_t + b_2d_t + s_t \\ &\quad +b_2(1-a_1)E_t(y_{t+1}) + (1-b_1+a_2b_2)E_t(\pi_{t+1})\end{aligned}$$

Moreover, (6) implies:

$$(1-b_1+a_2b_2)E_t(\pi_{t+1}) = b(1-b_1+a_2b_2)\pi_t + b_p(1-b_1+a_2b_2)(i_t - i^*_t)$$

Therefore, we have:

$$\begin{aligned}[1\text{+}b_2a_5\text{-}b(1\text{-}b_1\text{+}a_2b_2)]\pi_t &= a_1b_2y_{t-1} - b_3e_{t-1} + b_2a_5(p^*_{t-1} - p_{t-1}) + b_1\pi_{t-1} \\ &\quad +(b_3+b_2a_5)(e_t+\pi^*_t) + b_2a_2\overline{r} + b_2a_3g_t + b_2a_4y^*_t + b_2d_t \\ &\quad +s_t + [(1-b_1+a_2b_2)b_p - b_2a_2]i_t - (1-b_1+a_2b_2)b_pi^*_t\end{aligned}$$

$$
\begin{aligned}
& +b_2(1-a_1)E_t(y_{t+1}) \\
[1+b_2a_5\text{-}b(1\text{-}b_1+a_2b_2)]y_t \quad = \quad & (1\text{-}b+bb_1)[a_1y_{t\text{-}1}+a_5(p^*_{t\text{-}1}\text{-}p_{t\text{-}1})]+(a_5\text{-}ba_2)(b_3e_{t\text{-}1}-b_1\pi_{t\text{-}1}) \\
& +[a_5(1-b_3)-ba_5(1-b_1)+bb_3a_2](e_t+\pi^*_t) \\
& +(1-b+bb_1)(a_2\overline{r}+a_3g_t+a_4y^*_t+d_t)-(a_5-ba_2)s_t \\
& +[(a_2\text{-}a_5\text{+}a_5b_1)b_p-a_2(1\text{-}b\text{+}bb_1)]i_t-(a_2\text{-}a_5\text{+}a_5b_1)b_pi^*_t \\
& +(1-a_1)(1-b+bb_1)E_t(y_{t+1})
\end{aligned}
$$

Appendix B: Determination and Study of the Parameter (b)

If we put (7) in (2), if we use (6), and then, if we replace (π_t) by its value in (5), we have:

$$
\begin{aligned}
& \{(1\text{-}b\text{+}bb_1)c^M[(1\text{-}b\text{+}bb_1)a_2-(a_2\text{-}a_5\text{+}a_5b_1)b_p]-b_2[(1\text{-}b_1\text{+}a_2b_2)b_p-a_2b_2]\} \\
& \qquad [b\pi_{t-1}+b_p(\pi^*_t+\Delta e_t)+b_i(i_t-i_{t-1})+b_{i2}(i_t-i^*_t)+b_ss_t] \\
= \; & c^M[(1\text{-}b\text{+}bb_1)a_2-(a_2\text{-}a_5\text{+}a_5b_1)b_p][b_1\pi_{t-1}+b_3(\pi^*_t\text{+}\Delta e_t)+(1\text{-}b_1)b_p(i_t\text{-}i^*_t)+s_t] \\
& \qquad +b_2v^M[1+b_2a_5-b(1-b_1+a_2b_2)](i_t-i_{t-1})
\end{aligned}
$$

Then, by identification, we have:

$b_p=\dfrac{bb_3}{b_1}$ $\qquad b_i=\dfrac{bb_2v^M[1+b_2a_5-b(1-b_1+a_2b_2)]}{c^M[(1-b+bb_1)a_2b_1-(a_2-a_5+a_5b_1)bb_3]}$

$b_{i2}=\dfrac{b^2(1-b_1)b_3}{b_1^2}$ $\qquad b_s=\dfrac{b}{b_1}$

$$
\begin{aligned}
& c^M(1-b_1)[(a_2-a_5+a_5b_1)b_3+a_2b_1(1-b_1)]b^3 \\
& -[c^M(a_2-a_5+a_5b_1)b_3+2c^Ma_2b_1(1-b_1)+(1-b_1+a_2b_2)b_2b_3]b^2 \\
& +b_1[c^M(a_2-a_5+a_5b_1)b_3+c^Ma_2b_1(1-b_1)+c^Ma_2+a_2b_2^2]b-c^Mb_1^2a_2=0.
\end{aligned}
$$

We can't solve this equation, which is a cubic, to find (b), except for specific values of the parameters.

►<u>If $b_1=0$</u>: $c^M(a_2-a_5)b_3b^3-b_3[c^M(a_2-a_5)+(1+a_2b_2)b_2]b^2=0$

b=0 as $b'=\dfrac{[c^M(a_2-a_5)+(1+a_2b_2)b_2]}{c^M(a_2-a_5)}>1$ if $b_2>0$.

►<u>If $b_1=1$</u>: $a_2b_3(c^M+b_2^2)b^2-a_2(c^Mb_3+c^M+b_2^2)b+c^Ma_2=0$

$b=\dfrac{c^M}{(c^M+b_2^2)}$ as $b'=\dfrac{1}{b_3}>1$

►<u>If $c^M=0$</u>: $bb_2[(1-b_1+a_2b_2)b_3b+b_1a_2b_2]=0$

$b=\dfrac{b_1a_2b_2}{(1-b_1+a_2b_2)b_3}$ as b'=0

►<u>If $c^M\rightarrow\infty$</u>: $[(1-b+bb_1)b-b_1][(1-b+bb_1)a_2b_1-(a_2-a_5+a_5b_1)bb_3]=0$

The second member implies: $b''=\dfrac{a_2b_1}{[(1-b_1)a_2b_1+(a_2-a_5+a_5b_1)b_3]}$

but b''>1 as soon as $a_2(b_1^2-b_3)+a_5(1-b_1)b_3>0$ (empirically likely).

The first member implies: $b=\dfrac{b_1}{(1-b_1)}$ with $b_1\prec\dfrac{1}{2}$ as b'=1.

Appendix C: Interest Rate, Inflation and Economic Activity

If we put (7) in (1), and if we use (10), we have the implied optimal interest rate rule (i_t). Then, equation (8) gives:

$$\begin{aligned} D_i i_t &= b\{b_z[ba_2\text{-}a_5\text{-}(1\text{-}a_1)bb_k] + a_2b_2b_1 - (1\text{-}b_1\text{+}a_2b_2)bb_3\}(\pi_{t-1} - b_2b_hb_k i_{t-1} + \frac{1}{b_1}s_t) \\ &\quad + b_z[b_1b_hb_k i_{t-1} + a_1y_{t-1} + a_2\overline{r} + a_3g_t + a_4y_t^* + a_5(e_{t-1} + p_{t-1}^* - p_{t-1}) + d_t] \\ &\quad + \{\frac{bb_3b_z}{b_1}[ba_2\text{-}a_5\text{-}(1\text{-}a_1)bb_k] + bb_3a_2b_2 - \frac{b^2b_3^2}{b_1}(1\text{-}b_1\text{+}a_2b_2) + b_za_5\}(\pi_t^* + \Delta e_t) \\ &\quad - \frac{b^2(1\text{-}b_1)b_3}{b_1^2}\{b_z[ba_2\text{-}a_5\text{-}(1\text{-}a_1)bb_k]\text{+}a_2b_2b_1\text{-}(1\text{-}b_1\text{+}a_2b_2)bb_3\}i_t^* + \frac{bb_3b_z}{b_1}[(1\text{-}a_1)b_k\text{-}a_2]i \end{aligned}$$

$$\begin{aligned} D_i &= b_za_2 + \frac{bb_3b_z}{b_1}[(1-a_1)b_k - a_2] + b_1b_hb_kb_z \\ &\quad - b_2\{b_z[ba_2\text{-}a_5\text{-}(1\text{-}a_1)bb_k] + a_2b_2b_1 - (1\text{-}b_1\text{+}a_2b_2)bb_3\}[\frac{(1\text{-}b_1)b_3}{b_1^2} + bb_hb_k] \end{aligned}$$

Then, putting (i_t) in equations (8) and (10), we have:

$$\begin{aligned} D_i\pi_t &= bb_z\{a_2 + \frac{bb_3}{b_1}[(1-a_1)b_k - a_2] + b_1b_hb_k\}(\pi_{t-1} - b_2b_hb_k i_{t-1} + \frac{1}{b_1}s_t) \\ &\quad + bb_z[b_2b_hb_k\text{+}\frac{b(1\text{-}b_1)b_3}{b_1^2}][b_1b_hb_k i_{t\text{-}1}\text{+}a_1y_{t\text{-}1}\text{+}a_2\overline{r}\text{+}a_3g_t\text{+}a_4y_t^*\text{+}a_5(e_{t\text{-}1}\text{+}p_{t\text{-}1}^*\text{-}p_{t\text{-}1})\text{+}d_t] \\ &\quad + bb_z\{a_5[b_2b_hb_k + \frac{b(1\text{-}b_1)b_3}{b_1^2}] + \frac{a_2b_3}{b_1} + \frac{bb_3^2}{b_1^2}[(1\text{-}a_1)b_k\text{-}a_2] + b_3b_hb_k\}(\pi_t^* + \Delta e_t) \\ &\quad + \frac{b^2b_3b_z}{b_1}\{[(1-a_1)b_k - a_2]b_2b_hb_k - \frac{a_2(1-b_1)}{b_1} - (1-b_1)b_hb_k\}i_t^* \end{aligned}$$

$$\begin{aligned} D_iy_t &= -bb_kb_z\{a_2 + \frac{bb_3}{b_1}[(1-a_1)b_k - a_2] - b_1b_h[ba_2 - a_5 - (1-a_1)bb_k]\}(\pi_{t-1} + \frac{1}{b_1}s_t) \\ &\quad + b_kb_zb_h\{\frac{b^2(1\text{-}b_1)b_3}{b_1}[ba_2\text{-}a_5\text{-}(1\text{-}a_1)bb_k] - (1\text{-}\frac{bb_2b_k}{b_1})[(b_1\text{-}bb_3)a_2 + bb_3b_k(1\text{-}a_1)]\}i_{t-1} \\ &\quad + b_kb_z[b_1b_h\text{-}bb_2b_kb_h\text{-}\frac{b^2(1\text{-}b_1)b_3}{b_1^2}][a_1y_{t\text{-}1} + a_2\overline{r} + a_3g_t + a_4y_t^* + a_5(e_{t\text{-}1}\text{+}p_{t\text{-}1}^*\text{-}p_{t\text{-}1}) + \\ &\quad - b_zb_k\{b^2b_3(\frac{b_3}{b_1^2}\text{+}b_h)[(1\text{-}a_1)b_k\text{-}a_2]\text{+}\frac{a_5b^2b_3(1\text{-}b_1)}{b_1^2}\text{+}a_5b_h(bb_3\text{+}bb_2b_k\text{-}b_1)\text{+}\frac{a_2bb_3}{b_1}\}(\pi_t^*\text{+}\Delta \\ &\quad + b_zb_kbb_3\{\frac{b(1\text{-}b_1)a_2}{b_1^2} + b_h(1\text{-}\frac{bb_2b_k}{b_1})[(1\text{-}a_1)b_k\text{-}a_2] - \frac{b(1\text{-}b_1)b_h}{b_1}[ba_2\text{-}a_5\text{-}(1\text{-}a_1)bb_k]\}i_t^* \end{aligned}$$

References

[1] Altissimo, F., Ehrmann, M., & Smets, F. (2006). Inflation Persistence and Price-Setting Behaviour in the Euro-Area: A Summary of the Inflation Persistence Network Evidence. *Working Paper Research,* National Bank of Belgium, n°95, October.

[2] Benigno, P., & Lopez-Salido, D. (2002). Inflation Persistence and Optimal Monetary Policy in the Euro Area. *ECB Working Paper,* n°**178**.

[3] Bofinger, P., Mayer, E., & Wollmershäuser, T. (2005). Teaching New Keynesian Open Economy Macroeconomics at the Intermediate Level. August 9, available at SSRN: http://ssrn.com/abstract=870468.

[4] Cecchetti, S., & Debelle, G. (2005). Has the Inflation Process changed?. *Bis Working Paper*, n°**185**.

[5] Clarida, R., Gali, J., & Gertler, M. (1999). The Science of Monetary Policy: A New Keynesian Perspective. *Journal of Economic Literature*, vol.37, pp. 1661-1707.

[6] Coenen, G., & Wieland, V. (2002). Inflation Dynamics and International Linkages: A Model of the United States, the Euro Area and Japan. Board of Governors of the Federal Reserve System, *International Finance Discussion Papers*, n°**745**, July.

[7] Djoudad, R., & Gauthier, C. (2003). A Small Dynamic Hybrid Model for the Euro Area. *Bank of Canada Working Paper*, 2003-19, July.

[8] Domenech, R., Ledo, M., & Taguas, D. (2001). A Small Forward-Looking Macroeconomic Model for EMU. *BBVA Working Papers,* n°**102**, July.

[9] Faruqee, H. (2006). Exchange Rate Pass-Through in the Euro Area. *IMF Staff Papers,* vol.53, n°1.

[10] Fornero, J., Garretsen, H., Moons, C., & Van Aarle, B. (2007). Monetary Policy in the New-Keynesian Model: An Application to the Euro Area. Research Paper 2007-014, Faculty of Applied Economics, University of Antwerp, June.

[11] Franta, M., Saxa, B., & Smidkova, K. (2007). Inflation Persistence in the New Member States: Is it Different than in the Euro Area Members?. 10/2007, *Working Paper series,* Czech National Bank, December.

[12] Gagnon, J., & Ihrig, J. (2001). Monetary Policy and Exchange Rate Pass-Through. *FRB International Finance Discussion Paper*, n°**704**, July.

[13] Garretsen, H., Moons, C., & Van Aarle, B. (2007). Accession to the Euro-Area: A Stylized Analysis using a NK Model. *Research Paper* 2007-015, University of Antwerp, Belgium, June.

[14] Jondeau, E., & Le Bihan, H. (2005). Testing for the New Keynesian Phillips Curve. Additional International Evidence. *Economic Modelling*, vol.22, pp. 521-550.

[15] Leith, C., & Malley, J. (2002). Estimated General Equilibrium Models for the Evaluation of Monetary Policy in the US and Europe. *CESifo Working Paper,* n°**699** (6), April.

[16] Muscatelli, V.A., Tirelli, P., & Trecroci, C. (2003). Fiscal and Monetary Policy Interactions: Empirical Evidence and Optimal Policy using a Structural New Keynesian Model. *CESifo Working Paper*, n°**1060**, October.

[17] Rumler, F. (2005). Estimates of the Open Economy New-Keynesian Phillips Curve for the Euro Area Countries. *Working Paper* n°**102**, Oesterreichische Nationalbank.

[18] Sahuc, J. (2002). A 'Hybrid' Monetary Policy Model: Evidence from the Euro Area. *Applied Economics*, vol.9, pp. 949-955.

[19] Smets, F. (2003). Maintaining Price Stability: How long is the Medium Term?. *Journal of Monetary Economics*, Vol.50, n°6, September, pp. 1293-1309.

[20] Smets, F., & Wouters, R. (2002). An Estimated Dynamic Stochastic General Equilibrium Model of the Euro Area. *European Central Bank Working Paper*, n°171.

In: Inflation: Causes and Effects...
Editor: Leon V. Schwartz, pp. 165-178 ISBN 978-1-60741-823-8

Chapter 9

ESTIMATION OF ELECTRIC DEMAND IN JAPAN: A BAYESIAN SPATIAL AUTOREGRESSIVE AR(p) APPROACH

***Yoshihiro Ohtsuka*[1]* *and Kazuhiko Kakamu*[2]†**
[1]Tachibana. Securities Co., Ltd
[2]Faculty of Law and Economics, Chiba University,
1-33, Yayoi-cho, Inage-ku, Chiba, 263-8522, Japan

Abstract

In this chapter, we extend a spatial autoregressive AR (SAR-AR) model, which is proposed by Elhorst (2001), to SAR-AR(p) model and construct the efficient strategy of Markov chain Monte Carlo (MCMC) methods to estimate the parameters of the model. Our approach is illustrated with both simulated and real data sets. By the simulated data set, we present that Griddy-Gibbs sampler is more efficient than Metropolis-Hastings (M-H) algorithm in sampling the spatial correlation parameter. In the example by real data set, we examine electric demand in Japan. From the empirical results, SAR-AR(1) model is selected and we find that electric demand in Japan has a strong time correlation with the first order lagged dependent variable. Through the model comparison, we find that the spatial interaction plays an important role in Japan.

Key Words: Markov chain Monte Carlo (MCMC); Griddy Gibbs sampler; Spatial autoregressive AR (p) model.

1. Introduction

This chapter estimates regional electric demand in Japan and the spatial interaction among the regions from a Bayesian point of view. Electricity has been a main resource of the social and economic activities. In addition, the electric consumption is treated as

*E-mail address: y.ohtsuka@1ban.co.jp
†E-mail address: kakamu@le.chiba-u.ac.jp. Tel: +81-43-290-2406. Fax: +81-43-290-2406. (Corresponding author.)

demand in this chapter, because electric power cannot be economically stored and because the published data is the traded volume. On the other hands, a shortage of electric power supply causes severe loss. Therefore, the power industry need to estimate the demand accurately to balance demand and supply.

It is well known that the electric demand data has some features in Japan. First, there is a regional heterogeneity, that is, the volumes of electric demand are different in each region. Therefore, the intensity of time series correlations may be different among the regions. Second, the behavior of electric demand in a year has a seasonality as a common trend among regions. There is a sharp rise in demand for electric power in summer and winter. Furthermore, although it can not be observed from the data, there may be spatial interaction in the electric demand. The electric companies are connected by the overhead transmission lines and the undersea cables. They help each other if the company faces to the situation that the electricity is in short supply. It should be mentioned that the volume of the delivered electric power among the companies is an unobservable component, because it is not announced. Thus, we think it is important to consider spatial interaction in the model.

Many literatures have been taken for analysis of electric demand (*e.g.* Harvey and Koopman, 1993, Ramanathan *et al.*, 1997, Pappas *et al.*, 2008, and so on). However, these studies only focused on the aggregated demand, in spite of the fact that the data is observed over time and across a number of different regions. Therefore, in this chapter, we apply the idea of spatial econometrics to introduce the model with regional dependencies.

The spatial model has been widely used in geographical statistics, regional science, and other fields. Although the analysis using spatial model is popular in several research areas, spatial models have rarely examined in econometrics (*e.g.* Anselin, 1988, Elhorst, 2003 and Kakamu and Wago, 2008 examined from the view point of econometrics.). However, all the models mentioned above consider only spatial correlation. In other words, space-time correlations are not considered simultaneously. As is stated by Elhorst (2001), such a panel spatial models are special cases of space-time models, that is, the model supposes that serial correlation is zero.

In this chapter, we extended a spatial autoregressive AR (SAR-AR) model proposed by Elhorst (2001) to SAR-AR(p) model. Moreover, we construct the efficient strategy of Markov chain Monte Carlo (MCMC) methods to estimate the parameters of the model by Gibbs sampling approach (see *e.g.* Chib, 1993). In sampling the spatial correlation parameter, random walk Metropolis-Hastings (M-H) algorithm is widely used (see *e.g.* Kakamu and Wago, 2008). As an alternative approach, we proposed the Griddy-Gibbs sampler introduced by Ritter and Tanner (1992) for the acceleration. Through estimating the simulated data, we concluded that the Griddy-Gibbs sampler is more efficient than the M-H algorithm in terms of the inefficiency factors.

In the empirical analysis, we use the monthly electric demand data, which consists of Hokkaido, Tohoku, Tokyo, Chubu, Hokuriku, Kansai, Chugoku, Shikoku and Kyushu electric companies from January 1992 to July 2008. First of all, we transform the data to be a logarithm form. The demand data in Japan has seasonality. Therefore, we take 12 month difference to remove the seasonality. Then, we apply our SAR-AR(p) model to the transformed data. From the empirical results, SAR-AR(1) model is selected and we find that electric demand in Japan has a strong time correlation with the first order lagged dependent variable. Moreover, we find that the spatial correlation is close to 0.4. Finally, we compare the model with an univariate AR model, which is estimated with the aggregated data, from the view points of the DIC and the marginal likelihood. As the results, SAR-AR model is selected. Therefore, we find that the spatial interaction plays an important role in Japan.

This chapter is organized as follows. In the next section, we present the features of electric demand data in Japan. Section 3 introduces the Bayesian SAR-AR(p) model to analyse electric demand in Japan. Section 4 derives the full conditional distributions for our model and presents the efficiency of our sampling methods by simulated data. Section 5 presents the empirical results based on electric demand in Japan. Section 6 summarizes the results with concluding remarks.

2. Electric Demand in Japan

First we would like to explain the data set used in this chapter. The monthly electricity demand data are obtained from the Electricity Enterprises manual in Japan. Figure 1 plots the volumes of electricity delivery in nine regions in Japan from January 1993 to July 2008. [1]

In this chapter, the volume means the demand, because electric power cannot be stored economically. However, the electricity produced in one region is not necessarily used entirely in the same region, because the electric companies help each other if they face shortage of electricity supply. Moreover, there is no announcement of the delivery of electricity power from one company to another. Therefore, we consider the delivery as an unobserved component. We can see in the figure that volumes of electricity demand differ in each region. For example, the demand is highest in Tokyo and lowest in Hokkaido. On the other hand, we can confirm that seasonality as a trend is common to all regions. For example, there is a sharp rise in the demand in summer and winter. Therefore, we transform the data into logarithm form and take 12 month difference to remove the seasonality. Figure 2 plots the transformed data. Then, we apply our SAR-AR(p) model to the transformed data.

3. SAR-AR(p) Model

Let y_{it} and $\mathbf{x}_{it}$ for $i = 1, \ldots, n$, $t = 1, \ldots, T$ denote dependent and independent variables, where $\mathbf{x}_{it}$ is a $1 \times k$ vector on ith unit and tth period, respectively and first raw of $\mathbf{x}_{it}$ is set to be 1. Moreover, let $\mathbf{W} = \{w_{ij}\}$ and w_{ij} denote the spatial weight on the jth unit with respect to the ith unit. [2] Then, the SAR model conditioned on parameter $\boldsymbol{\beta}$ and ρ is written as equation (1),

$$y_{it} = \rho \sum_{j=1}^{n} w_{ij} y_{jt} + \mathbf{x}_{it} \boldsymbol{\beta}_i + u_{it}, \; |\rho| < 1. \tag{1}$$

[1] In Japan, electric power is supplied by ten companies: Hokkaido, Tohoku, Tokyo, Chubu, Hokuriku, Kansai, Chugoku, Shikoku, Kyushu and Okinawa. However, the Okinawa electric company supplies only to the Okinawa prefecture and is not connected to other companies. In addition, the proportional ratio of the volume of electricity demand is relatively small compared to the other nine companies. Therefore, we removed the Okinawa electric company from the analysis.

[2] The weight is row-standardized; that is, $\sum_{j=1}^{N} w_{ij} = 1$.

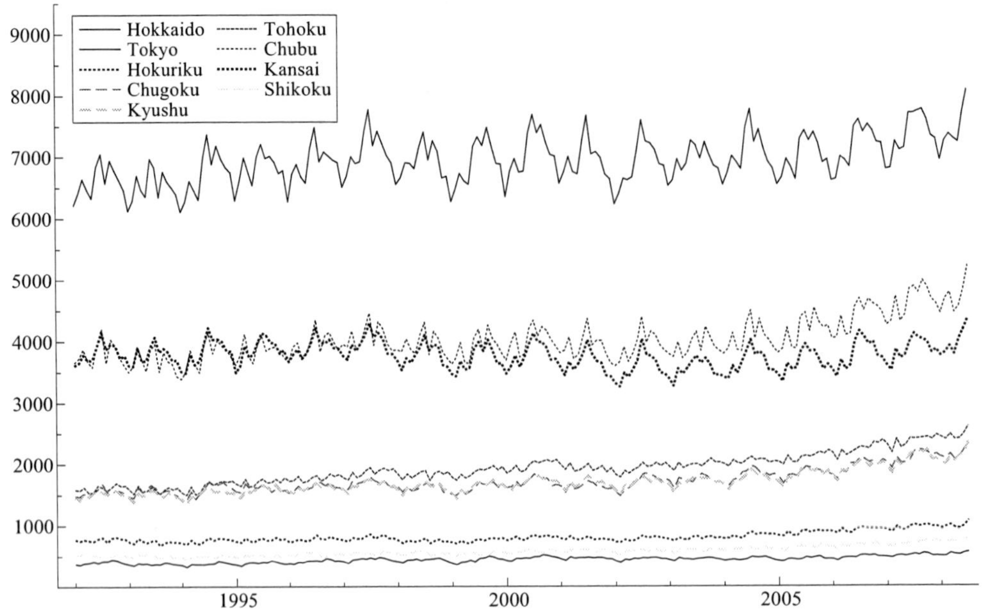

Figure 1. The volume of the electric demand ($1000 \times MWh$) of nine regions in Japan (1/1992-7/2008).

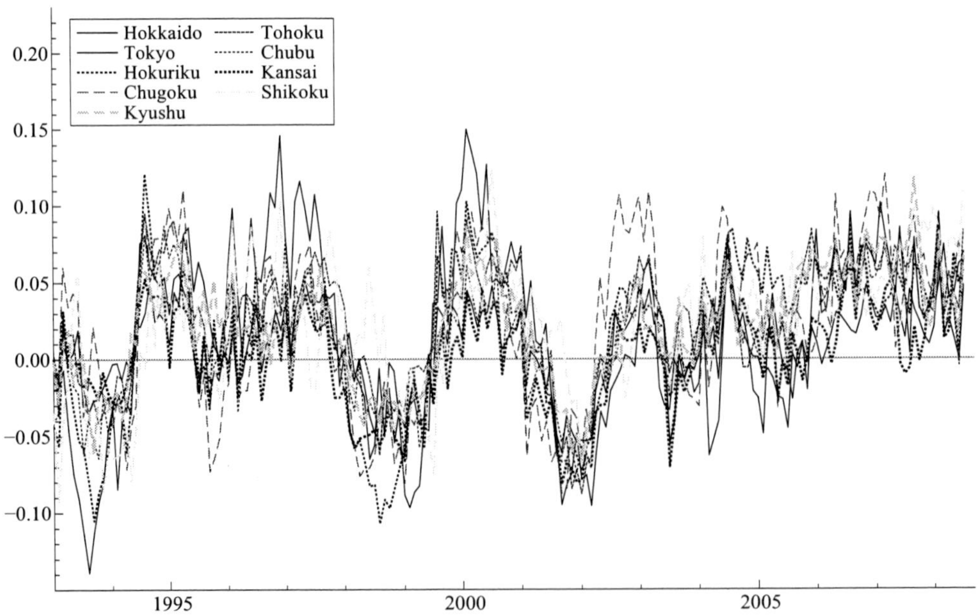

Figure 2. The transformed data of the electric demand in Japan (1/1993-7/2008).

where $\boldsymbol{\beta}_i = (\beta_{i1}, \ldots, \beta_{ik})'$.

Suppose that u_{it} follows an AR (p) process

$$u_{it} = \sum_{j=1}^{p} \phi_{ij} u_{i,t-j} + \epsilon_{it}, \quad \epsilon_{it} \sim \mathcal{N}(0, \sigma_i^2), \tag{2}$$

which is expressed in terms of a polynomial in the lag operator L as

$$\phi_i(L) u_{it} = \epsilon_{it}, \tag{3}$$

where $\phi_i(L) = 1 - \phi_{i1} L - \cdots - \phi_{ip} L^p$.

Then, we introduce the likelihood function of the model (1) and (2) as follows:

$$L(\mathbf{y}|\boldsymbol{\beta}, \boldsymbol{\Sigma}, \boldsymbol{\Phi}_p, \rho, \mathbf{x}, \mathbf{W}) = \prod_{t=p+1}^{T} f(\mathbf{y}_t|\boldsymbol{\beta}, \boldsymbol{\Sigma}, \boldsymbol{\Phi}_p, \rho, \mathbf{x}, \mathbf{W}), \tag{4}$$

where $\mathbf{y} = (\mathbf{y}_{p+1}, \ldots, \mathbf{y}_T)'$, $\boldsymbol{\beta} = (\boldsymbol{\beta}_1, \ldots, \boldsymbol{\beta}_n)'$, $\boldsymbol{\Sigma} = diag(\sigma_1^2, \cdots, \sigma_n^2)$, $\boldsymbol{\Phi}_p = (\boldsymbol{\phi}_{1p}, \cdots, \boldsymbol{\phi}_{np})$, $\boldsymbol{\phi}_{ip} = (\phi_{i1}, \cdots, \phi_{ip})'$, and

$$f(\mathbf{y}_t|\rho, \boldsymbol{\beta}, \boldsymbol{\Phi}_p, \boldsymbol{\Sigma}, \mathbf{x}_t, \mathbf{W}) = (2\pi)^{-\frac{n}{2}} |\boldsymbol{\Sigma}|^{-\frac{1}{2}} |\mathbf{I}_n - \rho \mathbf{W}| \exp\left(-\frac{\mathbf{e}_t' \boldsymbol{\Sigma}^{-1} \mathbf{e}_t}{2}\right), \tag{5}$$

where $\mathbf{I}_n$ is an $n \times n$ unit matrix and

$$\mathbf{e}_t = \mathbf{y}_t - \rho \mathbf{W} \mathbf{y}_t - \mathbf{x}_t \boldsymbol{\beta} - \sum_{j=1}^{p} \boldsymbol{\phi}_j \mathbf{u}_{t-j},$$

with $\mathbf{x}_t = (\mathbf{x}_{1t}', \ldots, \mathbf{x}_{nt}')'$, $\mathbf{u}_t = (u_{1t}, \ldots, u_{nt})'$, and $\boldsymbol{\phi}_j = diag(\phi_{1j}, \ldots, \phi_{nj})$.

4. Posterior Analysis

4.1. Joint Posterior Distribution

Since we adopt a Bayesian approach, we complete the model by specifying the prior distribution over the parameters. Therefore, we apply the following prior distribution:

$$\pi(\boldsymbol{\beta}, \boldsymbol{\Sigma}, \boldsymbol{\Phi}_p, \rho) = \left\{ \prod_{i=1}^{n} \pi(\boldsymbol{\beta}_i) \pi(\sigma_i^2) \pi(\boldsymbol{\phi}_{ip}) \right\} \pi(\rho),$$

Given a prior density $\pi(\boldsymbol{\beta}, \boldsymbol{\Sigma}, \boldsymbol{\Phi}_p, \rho)$ and the likelihood function given in (4), the joint posterior distribution can be expressed as

$$\pi(\boldsymbol{\beta}, \boldsymbol{\Sigma}, \boldsymbol{\Phi}_p, \rho|\mathbf{y}, \mathbf{x}, \mathbf{W}) \propto \pi(\boldsymbol{\beta}, \boldsymbol{\Sigma}, \boldsymbol{\Phi}_p, \rho) L(\mathbf{y}|\boldsymbol{\beta}, \boldsymbol{\Sigma}, \boldsymbol{\Phi}_p, \rho, \mathbf{x}, \mathbf{W}). \tag{6}$$

Finally, we assume the following prior distributions:

$$\boldsymbol{\beta}_i \sim \mathcal{N}(\beta_0, \Sigma_{\beta 0}), \; \sigma_i^2 \sim \mathcal{IG}\left(\frac{\nu_0}{2}, \frac{\lambda_0}{2}\right), \; \boldsymbol{\phi}_{ip} \sim \mathcal{N}(\phi_0, \Sigma_{\phi 0}), \; \rho \sim \mathcal{U}(-1, 1),$$

where $\mathcal{IG}(a, b)$ denotes an inverse gamma distribution with scale and shape parameters a and b.

4.2. Posterior Simulation

Since the joint posterior distribution is given by (6) is much simplified, we can now use MCMC methods. The Markov chain sampling schemes can be constructed from the full conditional distributions of $\boldsymbol{\beta}_i$, σ_i^2, ϕ_i for $i = 1, \dots, n$ and ρ. In the sampling schemes of the parameters except ρ, we adopt Chib's (1993) algorithm.

4.2.1. Sampling ρ

From (6), the full conditional distribution of ρ is written as

$$p(\rho|\boldsymbol{\beta}, \boldsymbol{\Phi}, \boldsymbol{\Sigma}, \mathbf{y}, \mathbf{x}, \mathbf{W}) \propto \prod_{t=p+1}^{T} |\mathbf{I}_n - \rho\mathbf{W}| \exp\left(-\frac{\mathbf{e}_t'\Sigma^{-1}\mathbf{e}_t}{2}\right).$$

This distribution cannot be sampled by the standard methods. Although Metropolis-Hasting algorithm is widely used for sampling ρ, we propose the Griddy-Gibbs sampler method for sampling the parameter.

Griddy-Gibbs sampler: Griddy-Gibbs sampler is proposed by Ritter and Tanner (1992). This sampling algorithm approximates a cumulative distribution function of the full conditional distribution by each kernel function over a grid of points and using a numerical integration methods, and is sampling method from the full conditional distribution by using the inverse transform method. Let the grid as follows

$$-1 = a_1 < a_2 < \cdots < a_m < a_{m+1} = 1,$$

and $\rho^i (i \in \{1, \dots, m\})$, which is centered in the interval $[a_i, a_{i+1}]$. Then, the full conditional distribution in the interval $[a_i, a_{i+1}]$ is approximated as follows

$$\omega_i = \frac{p(\rho^i|\boldsymbol{\beta}, \boldsymbol{\Phi}, \boldsymbol{\Sigma}, \mathbf{y}, \mathbf{x}, \mathbf{W})}{\sum_{h=1}^{m} p(\rho^h|\boldsymbol{\beta}, \boldsymbol{\Phi}, \boldsymbol{\Sigma}, \mathbf{y}, \mathbf{x}, \mathbf{W})}.$$

Thus, we select the grid a_i^* with probabilities,

$$\pi(\rho^i) = \frac{\omega_i}{\sum_{j=1}^{m} \omega_j}.$$

Finally, we sample ρ from the uniform (a_i^*, a_{i+1}^*).

Random walk M-H algorithm: We present M-H algorithm for ρ. The proposal distribution of ρ is

$$\rho^{new} \sim \mathcal{N}(\rho^{old}, s_i^2),$$

where s_i is turning parameter. In the numerical example below, we select the parameter such that the acceptance rate becomes between 0.4 and 0.6 (see Holloway *et al*, 2002). Next, we evaluate the acceptance probability

$$\alpha(\rho^{old}, \rho^{new}) = \min\left(\frac{p(\rho^{new}|\boldsymbol{\beta}, \boldsymbol{\Phi}, \boldsymbol{\Sigma}, \mathbf{y}, \mathbf{x}, \mathbf{W})}{p(\rho^{old}|\boldsymbol{\beta}, \boldsymbol{\Phi}, \boldsymbol{\Sigma}, \mathbf{y}, \mathbf{x}, \mathbf{W})}, 1\right),$$

and finally set $\rho = \rho^{new}$ with probability $\alpha(\rho^{old}, \rho^{new})$, otherwise $\rho = \rho^{old}$. It should be mentioned that the proposal value of ρ is not truncated to the interval $(-1, 1)$ since the constraint is part of the target density. Thus, if the proposed value of ρ is not within the interval, the conditional posterior is zero, and the proposal value is rejected with probability one (see Chib and Greenberg, 1994).

4.2.2. Sampling $\boldsymbol{\beta}_i$ and σ_i^2 for $i = 1, \ldots, n$

We transform the equation (1) following Chib (1993). Let $\bar{y}_{it} = \phi_i(L)(y_{it} - \rho \sum_{j=1}^{n} w_{ij} y_{jt})$ and $\bar{\mathbf{x}}_{it} = \phi_i(L)\mathbf{x}_{it}$ for $t = p+1, \ldots, T$. Then (1) is rewritten as,

$$\bar{\mathbf{y}}_i = \bar{\mathbf{x}}_i \boldsymbol{\beta}_i + \boldsymbol{\epsilon}_i, \ \boldsymbol{\epsilon}_i \sim \mathcal{N}(\mathbf{0}, \sigma_i^2 \mathbf{I}_{T-p}),$$

where $\bar{\mathbf{y}}_i = (\bar{y}_{i,p+1}, \ldots, \bar{y}_{iT})'$, $\bar{\mathbf{x}}_i = (\bar{\mathbf{x}}'_{i,p+1}, \ldots, \bar{\mathbf{x}}'_{iT})'$, and $\boldsymbol{\epsilon}_i = (\epsilon_{i,p+1}, \ldots, \epsilon_{iT})'$. The full conditional distributions for $\boldsymbol{\beta}_i$ and σ_i^2 can be obtained as

$$\begin{aligned} \boldsymbol{\beta}_i | \boldsymbol{\beta}_{-i}, \boldsymbol{\Sigma}, \boldsymbol{\Phi}, \rho, \mathbf{y}, \mathbf{x}, \mathbf{W} &\sim \mathcal{N}(\tilde{\mu}_i, \tilde{\Sigma}_i), \\ \sigma_i^2 | \boldsymbol{\beta}, \boldsymbol{\Sigma}_{-i}, \boldsymbol{\Phi}, \rho, \mathbf{y}, \mathbf{x}, \mathbf{W} &\sim \mathcal{IG}\left(\frac{\tilde{\nu}}{2}, \frac{\tilde{\lambda}}{2}\right), \end{aligned}$$

where $\boldsymbol{\beta}_{-i}$ and $\boldsymbol{\Sigma}_{-i}$ denote the parameters of $\boldsymbol{\beta}$ and $\boldsymbol{\Sigma}$ except $\boldsymbol{\beta}_i$ and σ_i^2, respectively, $\tilde{\mu}_i = \tilde{\Sigma}^{-1}(\Sigma_{\beta 0}^{-1}\beta_0 + \sigma_i^{-2}\bar{\mathbf{x}}_i'\bar{\mathbf{y}}_i)$, $\tilde{\Sigma} = (\Sigma_{\beta 0}^{-1} + \sigma_i^{-2}\bar{\mathbf{x}}_i'\bar{\mathbf{x}}_i)$, $\tilde{\nu} = T - p + \nu_0$, $\tilde{\lambda} = \bar{\mathbf{e}}_i'\bar{\mathbf{e}}_i + \lambda_0$, and $\bar{\mathbf{e}}_i = \bar{\mathbf{y}}_i - \bar{\mathbf{x}}_i\boldsymbol{\beta}_i$ like the Gibbs sampling in Gelfand and Smith (1990).

4.2.3. Sampling $\boldsymbol{\phi}_i$ for $i = 1, \ldots, n$

Let $\boldsymbol{\beta}$, $\boldsymbol{\Sigma}$ and ρ given, the equation (2) is rewritten as follows;

$$\hat{\mathbf{u}}_i = \hat{\mathbf{x}}_i'\boldsymbol{\phi}_i + \boldsymbol{\epsilon}_i, \ \hat{\mathbf{x}}_i = (\hat{\mathbf{x}}_{i,p+1}, \ldots, \hat{\mathbf{x}}_{iT})',$$

where $\hat{\mathbf{u}}_i = (u_{i,p+1}, \ldots, u_{iT})'$, $\hat{\mathbf{x}}_{it} = (u_{i,t-1}, \ldots, u_{i,t-p})'$, and $\boldsymbol{\epsilon}_i = (\epsilon_{i,p+1}, \ldots, \epsilon_{iT})'$. Then, the full conditional distribution of $\boldsymbol{\phi}_i$ can be obtained as

$$\boldsymbol{\phi}_i | \boldsymbol{\beta}, \boldsymbol{\Sigma}, \boldsymbol{\Phi}_{-i}, \rho, \mathbf{y}, \mathbf{x}, \mathbf{W} \sim \mathcal{N}(\tilde{\mu}_\phi, \tilde{\Sigma}_\phi)\mathbf{I}_{\phi \in S_\phi},$$

where $\boldsymbol{\Phi}_{-i}$ denotes the parameters of $\boldsymbol{\Phi}$ except $\boldsymbol{\phi}_i$, $\tilde{\Sigma}_\phi = (\Sigma_{\phi 0}^{-1} + \sigma_i^{-2}\hat{\mathbf{x}}_i'\hat{\mathbf{x}}_i)^{-1}$, and $\tilde{\mu}_\phi = \tilde{\Sigma}_\phi(\Sigma_{\phi 0}^{-1}\phi_0 + \sigma_i^{-2}\hat{\mathbf{x}}_i'\hat{\mathbf{u}}_i)$. We will draw from the untruncated multivariate normal posterior, and reject the draw if the roots of $\phi_i(L)$ lie inside the unit circle. S_ϕ implies a stationary error process; $\mathbf{I}_{S_\phi}$ denotes the indicator function of the set S_ϕ. The indicator function can be dropped if this restriction is not being imposed.

4.3. The Acceleration of Sampling ρ Parameter

This subsection illustrates our approach for the SAR-AR(p) model with simulated data in order to speed up the convergence of ρ parameter. The elements of the lower triangular matrix of $\mathbf{W}$ are generated from $\mathcal{BE}(0.6)$, where $\mathcal{BE}(a)$ is the Bernoulli distribution with probability of success a, and we set $w_{ij} = w_{ji}$. The example is described as follows:

$$\begin{aligned} y_{it} &= \beta_i + u_{it}, \\ u_{it} &= \phi_{i1}u_{i,t-1} + \phi_{i2}u_{i,t-2} + \epsilon_{it},\ \epsilon_{it} \sim \mathcal{N}(0, \sigma_i^2). \end{aligned}$$

The parameter values are set to be $\beta_i = 0.3$, $(\phi_{i1}, \phi_{i2}) = (0.8, 0.1)$, $\sigma_i^2 = 0.5$ for $i = 1, \ldots, n$, $t = 1, \ldots, T$ and $\rho = 0.8$. We set $T = 300$, $n = 4$ and $m = 100$, which is the number of grid points. For the hyperparameters, we set $\beta_0 = 0$, $\Sigma_{\beta_0} = 100$, $\nu_0 = 2$, $\lambda_0 = 0.01$, $\phi_0 = 0$, $\Sigma_{\phi_0} = 100 \times \mathbf{I}_p$. We perform the MCMC procedure by generating 8,000 draws in a single sample path, and discard the first 3,000 draws as the initial burn-in. All the results in this chapter are calculated using Ox version 5.1(see Doornik, 2006).

Table 1. Estimated result of the simulated data

Unit	Parameter	True value	Mean	Stdev	2.5%	Median	97.5%	CD	Inef
1	μ	0.3	−0.2190	0.8711	−1.1514	−0.2278	0.7500	0.61	1.00
	ϕ_1	0.8	0.7748	0.0579	0.6595	0.7749	0.8838	0.37	0.85
	ϕ_2	0.1	0.1155	0.0578	0.0021	0.1154	0.2312	0.07	0.96
	σ^2	0.5	0.5460	0.0462	0.4611	0.5433	0.6408	0.33	1.06
2	μ	0.3	0.0451	0.6336	−0.8815	0.0342	0.9933	0.69	0.81
	ϕ_1	0.8	0.8523	0.0588	0.7358	0.8520	0.9675	0.57	0.98
	ϕ_2	0.1	0.0477	0.0585	−0.0676	0.0477	0.1639	0.24	0.84
	σ^2	0.5	0.4444	0.0383	0.3753	0.4422	0.5267	0.02	2.38
3	μ	0.3	−0.2005	0.4748	−0.9610	−0.1938	0.5495	0.96	1.00
	ϕ_1	0.8	0.7869	0.0580	0.6718	0.7867	0.9008	0.96	1.07
	ϕ_2	0.1	0.0914	0.0578	−0.0183	0.0911	0.2058	0.47	0.98
	σ^2	0.5	0.4597	0.0385	0.3910	0.4568	0.5426	0.47	0.58
4	μ	0.3	0.4648	0.4259	−0.3225	0.4700	1.2294	0.02	0.46
	ϕ_1	0.8	0.8042	0.0589	0.6902	0.8041	0.9213	0.37	0.70
	ϕ_2	0.1	0.0712	0.0591	-0.0488	0.0719	0.1855	0.87	0.48
	σ^2	0.5	0.5400	0.0465	0.4555	0.5375	0.6382	0.62	0.83
	ρ	0.8	0.8083	0.0080	0.7858	0.8092	0.8194	0.32	2.26

Note: CD, Inef mean p-values of the convergence diagnostic(CD) test in Geweke (1992), inefficiency factor, respectively.

Table 1 present the results for the SAR-AR(2) by Griddy-Gibbs sampler, where Mean, Stdev, CD represent the posterior mean, the standard deviation, and Geweke's convergence diagnostics (Geweke, 1992), respectively. CD represents the p-value based on the test statistic on the difference between two sample means (i.e., dividing all the generated random draws into three parts, we compute two sample means from the first 10% and last 50% of the random draws), where the test statistic is asymptotically distributed as a standard normal random variable. We believe that the random draws generated by MCMC do not converge to the random draws generated from the target distribution when CD is less than 0.01(see Geweke ,1992, for a detailed discussion of CD). The inefficiency factor is defined as $1 + \sum_{s=1}^{\infty} \rho_s$ where ρ_s is the sample autocorrelation at lag s calculated from the sampled values and is used to measure how well the chain mixes. It is the ratio of the numerical variance of the sample posterior mean to the variance of the sample mean from the hypothetical uncorrelated draws. As the results, from statistics of CD, p-values of all parameters are greater than 0.01. It shows the convergence of all parameters of the example, and all the posterior means are included in the 95% credible intervals from the table.

Table 2. Comparison of the efficiency from the methods

Method	Mean	Stdev	Inef
Griddy-Gibbs	0.8083	0.0080	2.26
M-H	0.8095	0.0084	4.43

Note: Inef means inefficiency factor.

Table 2 summarizes a comparison of results from the Griddy-Gibbs sampler and M-H algorithm. The inefficiency factor from the Griddy-Gibbs sampler and M-H algorithm are 2.26 and 4.43, respectively. Then we can find that the Griddy-Gibbs sampler is more efficient than the M-H algorithm in terms of the inefficiency factors. Furthermore, Figures 3 and 4 show the sample paths and sample autocorrelation functions. The top of these figures is the results from Griddy-Gibbs sampler, and the bottom is the results from M-H algorithm. The sample path of Griddy-Gibbs sampler seem to mix well and autocorrelations die out very quickly from the figures. Therefore, these results lead to the conclusion that Griddy-Gibbs sampler is more efficient than M-H algorithm for sampling ρ parameter, and our approach for the SAR-AR(p) model has a practical use.

5. Empirical Results

5.1. The Weight Matrix

As the spatial weight matrix $\mathbf{W}$, we use the contiguity dummy variables (see Anselin, 1989). In this weight matrix, we consider the connection between the companies. All except one (Okinawa) of the electricity companies are situated on the four major islands: Hokkaido, Honshu, Shikoku and Kyushu. However, these four islands are connected by overhead transmission lines and undersea cables, although they are separate geographical entities. For example, the Hokkaido electricity company is connected to the Tohoku electricity company. Thus, we consider this dependence as first order contiguity between the neighborhoods, as illustrated in Table 3. In addition, a spatial weight matrix is used in row-standardized form.

5.2. Empirical Results

First, we need to choose the orders of AR, because we do not know these orders in advance. Thus, we use the DIC and the marginal likelihood to choose the orders. DIC is given by

$$\text{DIC} = \bar{D} + p_D = \hat{D} + 2p_D, \tag{7}$$

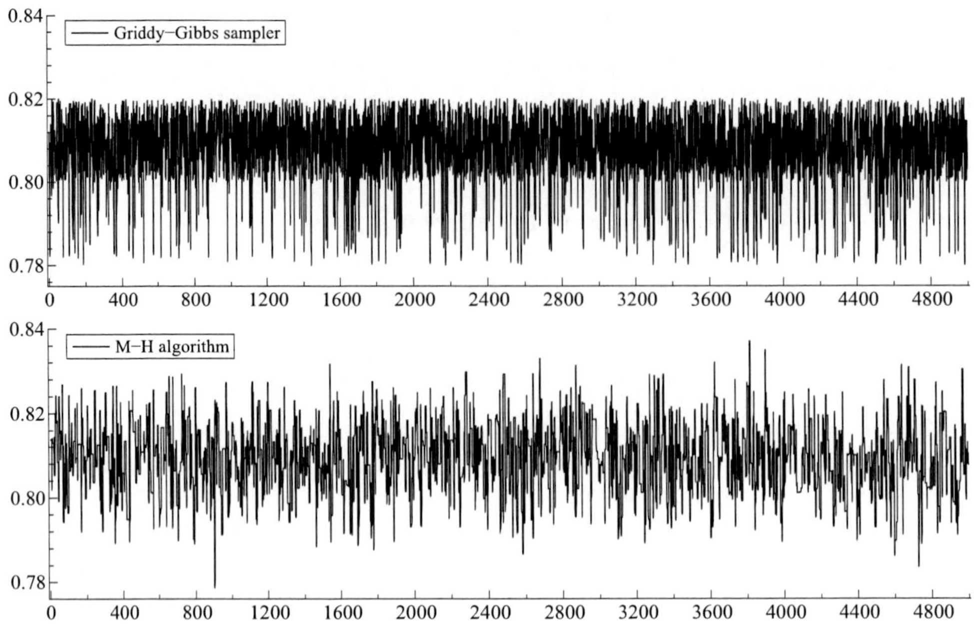

Figure 3. Sample path from Griddy-Gibbs sampler and M-H algorithm.

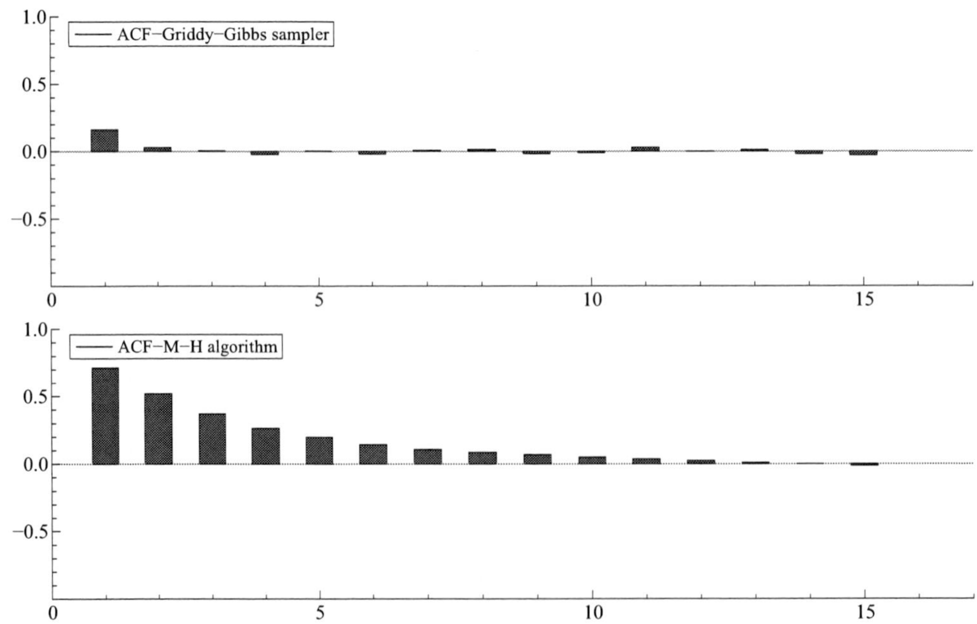

Figure 4. Sample autocorrelations from Griddy-Gibbs sampler and M-H algorithm.

where $\bar{D} = -2\mathrm{E}\{\ln[L(\mathbf{y}|\rho, \boldsymbol{\beta}, \boldsymbol{\Sigma}, \boldsymbol{\Phi}_p, \mathbf{x}, \mathbf{W})]\}$, $\hat{D} = -2\ln[L(\mathbf{y}|\rho^*, \boldsymbol{\beta}^*, \boldsymbol{\Sigma}^*, \boldsymbol{\Phi}_p^*, \mathbf{x}, \mathbf{W}))]$ and p_D, which given by $p_D = \bar{D} - \hat{D}$, is the effective number of parameters. We select

Table 3. First Order Contiguity, Japan Neighborhoods

Neighborhood	Contiguous to:			
Hokkaido:	Tohoku			
Tohoku:	Hokkaido	Tokyo		
Tokyo:	Tohoku	Chubu		
Chubu:	Tokyo	Hokuriku	Kansai	
Hokuriku:	Chubu	Kansai		
Kansai:	Chubu	Hokuriku	Chugoku	Shikoku
Chugoku:	Kansai	Shikoku	Kyushu	
Shikoku:	Kansai	Chugoku		
Kyushu:	Chugoku			

Table 4. The order selection of SAR-AR(p) model

Order	1	2	3	4
DIC	−11745.0	−11719.5	−11715.6	−11656.4
ML	5880.8	5870.8	5855.0	5823.4

Note: ML means Log marginal likelihood.

the order with the smallest value of DIC. We calculate the marginal likelihood using the harmonic mean proposed by Newton and Raftery (1994). Thus, we select the order with a higher marginal likelihood.

We run the MCMC algorithm for 3,000 iterations following a burn-in phase of 1,500 iterations. For the hyperparameters, we use the same values as in the case of the simulated data set. Table 4 reports the DIC values and the log marginal likelihood of SAR-AR(p) model for $p = 1, \ldots, 4$. From the table, we can find that SAR-AR(1) model shows the smallest value of DIC and the highest value of the log marginal likelihood.

Table 5 shows the empirical results of SAR-AR(1) model. From the statistics of CD, p-values of all parameters are greater than 0.01. Thus, it shows the convergence of all parameters. We will examine the results of each parameter. First of all, we will see the result of β_i for $i = 1, \ldots, 9$. We can confirm the individual trends in Tohoku and Kyushu from the table because parameters of these regions do not include zero in the 95% credible intervals. If we focus on AR parameters, we see that the parameters do not include zero in the 95% credible intervals in all regions. The largest value is shown in Hokuriku and the smallest one is shown in Tokyo. AR parameters in the regions, excluding Tokyo and Kansai, are approximately 0.8. These regions depend on a strong time correlation, although the effect is different in each region.

Finally, the spatial correlation ρ is greater than 0.4, and ρ does not include zero in the 95% credible interval. In addition, in order to compare our model with the univariate AR(1) model, we calculate the DIC and marginal likelihood values of the univariate AR model, which is widely used in estimating electric demand. Then the DIC value is -260.8, which is much larger than our SAR-AR(1) model. The marginal likelihood value is 527.2 and is

Table 5. Empirical result of SAR-AR(1)

Region	Parameter	Mean	Stdev	95%	Median	95%	CD	Inef
Hokkaido	β	0.00236	0.01122	−0.01943	0.00212	0.02440	0.05	0.75
	ϕ	0.78976	0.04694	0.69147	0.79083	0.87738	0.75	1.11
	σ^2	0.00096	0.00010	0.00079	0.00095	0.00117	0.80	0.87
Tohoku	β	0.02051	0.00764	0.00739	0.02034	0.03437	0.37	0.69
	ϕ	0.76711	0.05561	0.66356	0.76753	0.87799	0.63	1.71
	σ^2	0.00037	0.00004	0.00030	0.00036	0.00044	0.70	1.19
Tokyo	β	−0.00132	0.00295	−0.00705	−0.00125	0.00474	0.64	1.00
	ϕ	0.62986	0.06465	0.50277	0.63216	0.74957	0.79	1.06
	σ^2	0.00023	0.00002	0.00019	0.00022	0.00028	0.37	1.15
Chubu	β	0.00966	0.00536	−0.00111	0.00978	0.01971	0.10	0.73
	ϕ	0.72166	0.05519	0.61300	0.72079	0.82737	0.95	0.97
	σ^2	0.00039	0.00004	0.00032	0.00038	0.00047	0.67	1.48
Hokuriku	β	0.01266	0.01133	−0.00911	0.01266	0.03514	0.39	1.05
	ϕ	0.84122	0.04463	0.75143	0.84107	0.93031	0.18	1.20
	σ^2	0.00046	0.00005	0.00037	0.00045	0.00055	0.03	0.93
Kansai	β	−0.00567	0.00401	−0.01370	−0.00564	0.00205	0.01	0.87
	ϕ	0.66402	0.06035	0.54831	0.66562	0.77956	0.65	1.07
	σ^2	0.00031	0.00003	0.00026	0.00031	0.00039	0.77	0.58
Chugoku	β	0.01393	0.01214	−0.01163	0.01361	0.03781	0.45	1.42
	ϕ	0.81938	0.04609	0.72929	0.81843	0.91085	0.11	1.38
	σ^2	0.00068	0.00007	0.00056	0.00068	0.00082	0.50	0.82
Shikoku	β	0.01519	0.00784	−0.00038	0.01513	0.03045	0.51	0.88
	ϕ	0.71878	0.05241	0.62020	0.71910	0.82109	0.78	0.90
	σ^2	0.00084	0.00009	0.00069	0.00084	0.00103	0.97	1.55
Kyushu	β	0.01210	0.00489	0.00249	0.01193	0.02225	0.07	1.01
	ϕ	0.70676	0.05625	0.59695	0.70546	0.81315	0.26	0.70
	σ^2	0.00039	0.00004	0.00032	0.00038	0.00047	0.58	1.11
	ρ	0.42243	0.01511	0.39068	0.42359	0.45240	0.79	1.26

Note: CD and Inef mean p-values of the convergence diagnostic(CD) test in Geweke (1992), inefficiency factor, respectively.

Table 6. The result of model comparison

	DIC	ML
SAR-AR(1)	−11745.0	5880.8
AR(1)	−260.8	527.2

Note: ML means Log marginal likelihood.

also much smaller than our SAR-AR(1) model. Thus, we can conclude that our space-time model improves estimating performance of electricity demand in Japan. Therefore, we can confirm that spatial interaction plays an important role in Japan

6. Conclusion

This chapter has extended to the SAR-AR(p) model for electricity demand in Japan coupled with estimation using Griddy-Gibbs sampler in the Bayesian approach. The advantage of our SAR-AR(p) model is that it can be used to capture spatial heterogeneity and spatial correlation simultaneously. The estimation result using simulated data showed that the SAR-AR(p) model with Griddy-Gibbs sampler is of practical use. From the empirical results for electricity demand in Japan, we found that coefficients of autoregressive parameter differ in each region; that is, there is spatial heterogeneity. From AR parameters, electricity demand in Japan has a strong time correlation with a one previous value. Furthermore, we can also confirm that a strong spatial correlation because parameter ρ is greater than 0.4, and does not include zero in the 95% credible interval. Moreover, we compared SAR-AR(p) model with the univariate AR(p) model from the view points of the DIC and the marginal likelihood. Space-time model plays an important role in estimating electricity demand in Japan because our SAR-AR model is selected from the comparison.

Finally, we state some remaining issues. In this chapter, we construct AR process for capturing the time-series structure. However, it may follow more complicated structure like ARMA process. Moreover, we assume that each region has a different order of AR. Thus, we need to examine a type of modeling that has different orders in each region. These topics will be discussed in our future researches (*e.g.* Ohtsuka*et al.*, 2008).

References

Anselin, L. (1988) *Spatial Econometrics: Methods and Models*, Dordrecht: Kluwer.

Chib, S. (1993) "Bayes regression with autoregressive errors," *Journal of Econometrics*, **58**, 275–294.

Chib, S. and Greenberg, E. (1994) "Bayes inference in regression models with ARMA(p, q) errors," *Journal of Econometrics*, **64**, 183–206.

Doornik, J.A. (2006) *Ox: Object Oriented Matrix Programming Language*, Timberlake Consultants Press, London.

Elhorst, J.P. (2001) "Dynamic models in space and time," *Geographical Analysis*, **33**, 119–140.

Elhorst, J.P. (2003) "Specification and estimation of spatial panel data models," *International Regional Science Review*, **26**, 244–268.

Gelfand, A.E. and Smith, A.F.M. (1990) "Sampling-based approaches to calculating marginal densities," *Journal of the American Statistical Association*, **85**, 398–409.

Geweke, J. (1992) "Evaluating the accuracy of sampling-based approaches to the calculation of posterior moments," in *Bayesian Statistics 4* (Bernardo, J. M., Berger, J. O., Dawid, A. P. and Smith, A. F. M. eds), Oxford University Press, Oxford, 169–193.

Harvey, A. and Koopman, S. (1993) "Forecasting hourly electricity demand using time-varying splines," *Journal of the American Statistical Association*, **88**, 1228–1253.

Holloway, G., Shankar, B. and Rahman, S. (2002) "Bayesian spatial probit estimation: A primer and an application to HYV rice adoption," *Agricultural Economics*, **27**, 383–402.

Kakamu, K. and Wago, H. (2008) "Small sample properties of panel spatial autoregressive models: Comparison of the Bayesian and maximum likelihood methods," *Spatial Economic Analysis*, **3**, 305–319.

Newton, M. A. and Raftery, A. E. (1994) "Approximate Bayesian inference with the weighted likelihood bootstrap," *Journal of the Royal Statistical Society, Series B*, **56**, 3–26.

Ohtsuka. Y., Oga. T., and Kakamu. K. (2008) "Forecasting electric demand in Japan: A Bayesian spatial autoregressive ARMA approach," Working paper series, 08E045, Faculty of Law and Economics, University of Chiba.

Pappas, S. S., Ekonomou, L., Karamousantas, D. C., Chatzarakis, G. E., Katsikas, S. K. and Liatsis, P. (2008) "Electricity demand loads modeling using autoregressive moving average models," *Energy*, **33**, 1353–1360.

Ramanathan, R., Engle, R., Granger, C., Vahid-Araghi, F. and Brace, C. (1997) "Short-run forecasts of electricity loads and peaks," *International Journal of Forecasting*, **13**, 161–174.

Ritter, C. and Tanner, M. (1992) "Facilitating the Gibbs sampler: The Gibbs stopper and the Griddy-Gibbs sampler," *Journal of the American Statistical Association*, **87**, 861–868.

In: Inflation: Causes and Effects...
Editor: Leon V. Schwartz, pp. 179-185
ISBN 978-1-60741-823-8

Chapter 10

OUTPUT CONTRACTS FOR CENTRAL BANKS IN A MONETARY UNION: A WAY OUT OF THE DEFLATION BIAS

Juan Cristóbal Campoy and Juan Carlos Negrete
Fundamentos del Anlisis Econmico, Facultad de Economa y Empresa,
Universidad de Murcia, Murcia, Spain

Abstract

This paper presents a new advantage of output contracts vs. inflation contracts not yet considered in previous literature [Beestma and Jensen (1999) and Røisland (2001)]. The analysis develops in the common agency framework used by Dixit and Jensen (2003), which models the political pressures that national governments (principals) in a monetary union exert on the common central bank (agent) through inflation contracts. In this context, we show that the deflation bias obtained in this last article can be avoided if one government designs an output-related contract and its counterpart does the same or, instead, offers an inflation contract.

Keywords: Central Banks, monetary union, commnon agency.

JEL: E52, E58

1. Introduction

The relationship in which several principals simultaneously try to influence the actions of an agent has been the cornerstone of the common agency theory pioneered by Bernheim and Winston (1986) and later applied to political economy issues by Grossman and Helpman (1994, 2001) and Dixit, Grossman and Helpman (1997). Recently, Dixit and Jensen (2003) have extended the common agency theory to cover situations that arises in many macroeconomic policy contexts where the expectations over the agent's action affect the principals's payoffs. They applied their theory to the institutional design of the common central bank (agent) in a monetary union with multiple principals (i. e., member governments) and a rational private sector. In this context, the contract metaphor proposed by

Walsh (1995)[1] is used to model the political pressures that national governments exert on the common central bank[2]. In this common agency setting, Dixit and Jensen (2003) have concluded that, when principals non-cooperatively design inflation contracts which represent a cost to the principals, monetary policy has a deflation bias.

The aim of this paper is to propose a performance contract which, in the above context of a monetary union with common agency, avoids systematic deviations of inflation from the socially optimal level. We prove that such undesirable deviations will not take place if one government designs a contract which links performance to output and its counterpart does the same or, instead, offers an inflation contract.

The assumption that incentive schemes generate costs to the governments is crucial to understand these different outcomes. As will be explained in more detail below, in this setting, only when both contracts are linked to inflation, each principal will embark on a futile attempt to pass its share of the total incentive costs (paid to the agent) on to its counterpart. By contrast, no deflation (or inflation) bias can arise when at least one government offers an output contract. The reason is that average output cannot be influenced by the principals' behavior, since it equals the (exogenously given) natural level. In this sense, our paper shows a new advantage of output-related contracts (vs. inflation contracts), not considered by previous literature which has shown that this type of central bank contract is an appropriate state-independent delegation when the output is persistent [Beestma and Jensen (1999) and Røisland (2001)].

The rest of the article is organized as follows. Section 2 presents the model. Section 3 is devoted to the results. Section 4 concludes.

2. The Model

Our framework is based on the standard stochastic model widely used in the literature on credibility in monetary policy (see, for instance, Walsh [2003, chapter 8]). However, as in Dixit and Jensen (2003), we extend this setup to consider common agency in a monetary union. The world is made up of two countries $(i = 1, 2)$. The working of the economy is summarized by the following expressions:

$$y_i = \overline{y} + \alpha(\pi - \pi^e) - \varepsilon, \tag{1}$$

$$U_i^G = -\left[\beta\pi^2 + (y_i - y^*)^2\right] - \phi(A_i - b_i x_i), \tag{2}$$

$$U^{CB} = -\left[\sum_{i=1}^{2}(\beta\pi^2 + (y_i - y^*)^2\right] + \xi\left[\sum_{i=1}^{2}(A_i + b_i x_i)\right], \tag{3}$$

where $\alpha, \beta, \phi, \xi > 0$; and $y^* > \overline{y}$. Equation (1) shows that the economy possesses a Lucas supply function, so that the difference between output (y) and the natural level $(\overline{y})$ depends on the deviations of inflation (π) from its expected value (π^e) and on a supply shock (ε)

[1] Walsh (1995) modelled the process of delegation to independent monetary authorities as a contract within a principal-agent framework. Bernanke (2004) has stated that, over the past 25 years, this paper has been one of the most influential ones in monetary policy.

[2] A similar common-agency setput arises in a single country where the national central bank is the agent. In this sense, Havrilesky (1993, p. 118), has pointed out that "interest groups place strong pressures on monetary policymaking, either directly or indirectly through politicians".

with zero mean and finite variance (σ_ε^2). The private sector is rational, that is, $\pi^e = E\{\pi\}$, where $E\{.\}$ is the expectations operator.

We study a common agency with two principals (the governments) and one agent (the central bank). Expressions (2) and (3) are closely related. They represent the utility functions of, respectively, government i and the common central bank.[3] Their first terms (in brackets) express the corresponding player's concern over deviations of inflation and output from optimal levels, normalized to zero and y^*, respectively. In the case of the central bank, this concern arises since each government appoints one National representative to run the common monetary institution. The rest of both these equations shows that each national government tries to influence the conduct of the common monetary policy by offering the central bank a performance contract. For principal i, the incentive scheme takes the form $A_i - b_i x_i$; where x_i may be inflation, π [as in Dixit and Jensen (2003)] or the deviation of country i's output from the natural level[4], $(y_i - \overline{y})$.

Each government designs a performance contract, taking its counterpart's choice as given. Then, once expectations on (common) inflation are formed, the realization of the shock is observed by the central bank which, in turn, chooses the inflation rate. Parameters ϕ and ξ need not coincide since they represent, respectively, the weight that governments and monetary authorities put on the incentive scheme relative to the social loss arising from deviations of inflation and output from optimum levels.

Finally, two points are worth emphasizing. First, as Walsh (1995) and Bernanke (2004) have stated, performance contracts are best treated as a metaphor. That is, incentives need not be interpreted strictly as pecuniary since central bankers take into account many others aspects of their job, including their professional reputations or the prestige of the institutions in which they serve. Second, as it is standard in the literature on central bank contracts, we assume that the principals are constrained to design incentive schemes which are not contingent on the realizations of the random shocks. The reason is that it is prohibitively costly to specify all possible contingencies in advance, let alone to enforce such a hypothetical kind of arrangement [see, for instance, Hart (1995)]. In our paper, incentives are not linked to the realizations of the shock but to either inflation or the deviation of country i's output from the natural level.

3. The Results

We explore the strategic interactions between the governments, the private sector and the central bank. We solve the game by backward induction. In the last stage, the central bank faces the following problem (plugging (1) into (3)):

$$\underset{\{\pi\}}{Max} \quad -\left[\sum_{i=1}^{2}(\beta\pi^2 + (\overline{y} + \alpha(\pi - \pi^e) - \varepsilon - y^*)^2\right] + \xi\left[\sum_{i=1}^{2}(A_i - b_i x_i)\right].$$

[3]These quadratic functions are standard in the literature on credibility in monetary policy. On the other hand, Woodford (2002) has shown that this type of objective functions build on microeconomic foundations, since they can be derived from a representative agent in a general equilibrium model.

[4]Results do not change if we do not consider the deviations of output from the natural level but from any other reference value (e.g., the socially optimal level of output).

The solution yields the optimal response of the monetary authorities:

$$\pi = \frac{\alpha(y^* - \overline{y} + \varepsilon) + \alpha^2 \pi^e}{\beta + \alpha^2} - \frac{\xi\left(b_1 x_1' + b_2 x_2'\right)}{4\left(\beta + \alpha^2\right)}, \tag{4}$$

where $x_i' = \frac{dx_i}{d\pi}$. Therefore, taking expectations in (4) and solving for π^e one finds[5]:

$$\pi^e = \frac{\alpha\left(y^* - \overline{y}\right)}{\beta} - \frac{\xi\left(b_1 E\{x_1'\} + b_2 E\{x_2'\}\right)}{4\beta}. \tag{5}$$

Plugging this value for the expected inflation into equation (4) and solving for π, we obtain:

$$\pi = \frac{\alpha\left(y^* - \overline{y}\right)}{\beta} + \frac{\alpha}{\alpha^2 + \beta}\varepsilon - \frac{\xi\left(b_1 E\{x_1'\} + b_2 E\{x_2'\}\right)}{4\beta}. \tag{6}$$

Now, each government chooses its performance contract taking into account its counterpart's choice and the participation constraint of the agent. Formally, government i solves the following problem:

$$\begin{array}{ll} \underset{\{A_i, b_i\}}{Max} & E\{U_i^G(A_i, b_1, b_2, x_1', x_2', E\{x_1'\}, E\{x_2'\}, \varepsilon,)\} \\ s.t. & E\{U^{CB}(A_1, A_2, b_1, b_2, x_1', x_2', E\{x_1'\}, E\{x_2'\}, \varepsilon,)\} \geq u_0, \end{array}$$

where u_0, is some outside opportunity utility and the values of $E\{U_i^G(A_i, b_1, b_2, x_1', x_2', E\{x_1'\}, E\{x_2'\}, \varepsilon,)\}$ and $E\{U^{CB}(A_1, A_2, b_1, b_2, x_1', x_2', E\{x_1'\}, E\{x_2'\}, \varepsilon,)\}$ are obtained via the following sequence of computations: (i) substituting (1) into (2) and (3); (ii) plugging the values of π^e and π (appearing in equations (5) and (6)) into the resulting three expressions for U_i^G and U^{CB}; and, finally, (iii) taking expectations.

Notice that the participation constraint must hold with equality since, otherwise, principal i would not be maximizing its expected utility. Namely, it could be better-off by lowering A_i (in such a "small" amount that the central bank still found it optimal to accept the contract). Therefore, from the usual first-order conditions of the Lagrangian function we obtain that principal i's indifference curve must be tangent to the agent's, i.e., government i's marginal rate of substitution between A_i and b_i equals the central bank's:

$$\left.\frac{\partial A_i}{\partial b_i}\right|_{E\{U_i^G\} = \overline{E\{U_i^G\}}} = \left.\frac{\partial A_i}{\partial b_i}\right|_{E\{U^{CB}\} = \overline{E\{U^{CB}\}}}, \qquad i = 1, 2. \tag{7}$$

In the case considered by Dixit and Jensen (2003), where $x_i = \pi$, setting $x_1' = x_2' = 1$ in (7) one finds that:

$$\frac{\alpha\left(y^* - \overline{y}\right)(\xi + 2\phi)}{2\phi\beta} - \frac{\xi\left(\xi + 4\phi\right) b_i}{8\phi\beta} - \frac{\xi\left(\xi + 2\phi\right) b_j}{8\phi\beta} = -\frac{\xi\left(b_i + b_j\right)}{4\beta} \qquad i, j = 1, 2; \quad i \neq j. \tag{8}$$

[5]Notice that, since we know that x_i is π or $y_i - \overline{y}$, then x_i' is, respectively, 1 or α. Therefore, π^e is not included in the right-hand side of (5).

Solving simultaneously the two equations implied by (8) one finds the Nash equilibrium in incentive schedules[6]:

$$b_i^{DJ} = \frac{2\alpha\left(y^* - \overline{y}\right)\left(2\phi + \xi\right)}{\xi\left(\phi + \xi\right)}. \tag{9}$$

As a result, substituting the value of b_i (appearing in (9)) into (5) and bearing in mind that $x_1^{'} = x_2^{'} = 1$, we obtain that average inflation is negative, i.e.:

$$E(\pi^{DJ}) = -\frac{\alpha\phi\left(y^* - \overline{y}\right)}{\left(\phi + \xi\right)\beta} < 0.$$

Namely, as highlighted by Dixit and Jensen (2003), if governments in the monetary union non-cooperatively offer the central bank inflation contracts, a deflation bias will be present. However, we consider a way out of the problem:

Proposition: *In a monetary union, no deflation nor inflation bias arises if the incentives of the central bank are linked to: (a) output in one government's contract and to inflation in its counterpart's; or (b) to output in both contracts .*

Proof:

(a) In this case $x_1 = y_1 - \overline{y}$ and $x_2 = \pi$. Therefore, setting $x_1^{'} = \alpha$ (because of (1)) and $x_2^{'} = 1$ in (7) we have that:

$$\frac{2\alpha\left(\alpha^2\xi - 2\phi\beta\right)\left(y^* - \overline{y}\right)}{2\phi\beta} - \frac{\alpha\xi^2 b_1}{8\phi\beta} - \frac{\alpha^2\xi^2 b_2}{8\phi\beta} = \frac{\alpha^2\xi b_2}{4\beta} - \frac{2\alpha\left(\alpha^2 + \beta\right)\left(y^* - \overline{y}\right)}{\beta},$$

$$\frac{2\alpha^2\left(\xi + 2\phi\right)\left(y^* - \overline{y}\right)}{2\phi\beta} - \frac{\xi\left(\xi + 4\phi\right)b_1}{8\phi\beta} - \frac{\alpha\xi\left(\xi + 2\phi\right)b_2}{8\phi\beta} = -\frac{\xi b_1}{4\beta}.$$

Therefore, solving for b_1 and b_2 yields:

$$b_1^{y\pi} = \frac{4\left(y^* - \overline{y}\right)}{\xi}, \tag{10}$$

$$b_2^{y\pi} = 0. \tag{11}$$

Now, plugging this values of b_1 and b_2 (appearing in (10) and (11)) into (5) and setting $x_1^{'} = \alpha$ and $x_2^{'} = 1$ we have that average inflation is equal to zero, i.e.:

$$E\left(\pi^{y\pi}\right) = 0. \tag{12}$$

(b) In this scenario, $x_i = y_i - \overline{y}$. Therefore, by a similar process as the one described in above: i) setting $x_1^{'} = x_2^{'} = \alpha$ (from (1)) in (5); ii) solving for b_1 and b_2; iii) plugging them into (4) and bearing in mind, again, that $x_1^{'} = x_2^{'} = \alpha$, we obtain that no deflation nor inflation bias arises, i.e. $E(\pi^{yy}) = 0$. ∎

We now explain the intuition why the deflation bias arises when both principals offer inflation contracts but this bias is eliminated when any or both of these two incentive schemes

[6]Note that since A_i does not appear in (8), it has a rather residual role, namely, to guarantee that the participation constraint holds with equality. It is straightforward to check that it is also the case in all the contracts considered below.

is replaced by an output contract. To begin with, consider the case where both contracts link incentives to inflation. In this setting, why the non-cooperative behavior of the governments brings the economy into deflation, even though both of them dislike it? In other words, why each principal has incentives to deviate from the scenario where the inflation bias is null and move into an equilibrium in which a deflation bias is present? The answer to this question lies with the governments' intent to save on incentive costs. Therefore, if, say, government 1 increased its penalization on inflation by a "small" amount, deflation would arise and, as a result, it would: (a) increase its expected stabilization loss of both inflation and output (first term in (2)); and (b) increase its expected incentive transfer (second term in (2)) by an amount $\Delta T_1 > 0$. However, the central bank: (i) would increased its expected stabilization loss (first term in (3)); but it will also increase not only the incentive reward received from government 1 (by the amount $\Delta T_1 > 0$), but also the one provided by the other principal (by $\Delta T_2 > 0$). Therefore, ignoring (a) and (i), since in terms of the envelope theorem they are only second order effects (because we depart from an optimal stabilization of output and inflation), the total increase in the incentive rewards received by the central bank would exceed the increase in the incentive cost borne by government 1 $(\Delta T_1 + \Delta T_2 > \Delta T_1)$. Since that would relax the central bank's participation constraint, government 1 could take advantage and decrease the fixed part of its contract, A_1, by an amount greater than ΔT_1 (approximately, $\Delta T_1 + \Delta T_2$) so that the participation constraint held, again, with equality. To sum up, by increasing "a little" the penalization on inflation and readjusting the fixed part of its contract, the government could save on incentive costs. Applying an analogous reasoning, government 2 would also find it advantageous to deviate in the same direction from this ideal scenario with no deflation nor inflation bias.

It is worth noting that, the assumption that incentive schedules are costly to the principals is crucial for allowing for the possibility of a deflation bias arising when both contracts link incentives to inflation. The reason is that, when inflation contracts represent costs to both governments, each of them will try to save on them. How? As just discussed above, by manipulating its own incentive scheme with the aim of shifting its share of the total incentive transfer (received by the central bank so that its participation constraint is satisfied) to its counterpart.

Notice that such competition between principals cannot take place when one of them, say government 1, offer an output contract (irrespective of whether the other principal designs an inflation or an output contract). The reason is that, in this scenario, government 2, by altering its penalization on inflation or output (and taking as given government 1's contract), can no longer affect government 1's incentive costs. Why? Because, government 1's incentive costs are now related to output whose expected value is invariant (and equal to the natural level). Hence, in this setting, principals will not be induced to attempt to pass its share of the total incentive costs (paid to the agent) on to its counterpart, avoiding the deflation bias present when both central bank's incentives are related to inflation.

4. Conclusions

Dixit and Jensen (2003) have extended the contracting approach to central banking to the case of a monetary union where there are multiple principals (the member governments). Their model takes account of the fact that even the European Central Bank's constitution cannot, in practice, fully isolate monetary authorities from political pressures. In their setting, incentive schemes offered by member governments to the common central bank model such pressures. In this context, they have concluded that when principals non-cooperatively design inflation contracts monetary policy in the union has a deflation bias. However, our paper has shown that this result depends crucially on the variable to which incentives are linked (i.e., inflation versus output). We have shown that such bias is eliminated if at least one government offer the common central bank an output-related contract. Therefore, the presence of this type of contract prevents the 'politicisation' of the monetary policy from causing a deflation bias.

References

Beestma, R. and H. Jensen (1999), "Optimal Inflation Targets, 'Conservative' Central Banks, and Linear Inflation Contracts: Comment", *American Economic Review*, **89**, 342-347.

Bernanke, B. (2004), "What have we learned since October 1979?", Conference on Reflections on Monetary Policy 25 years after October 1979, Federal Reserve Bank of St. Louis, St. Louis, Missouri,
http://www.federalreserve.gov/boarddocs/speeches/2004/20041008/default.htm

Dixit, A. and H. Jensen (2003), "Common agency with rational expectations: theory and application to a monetary union", *The Economic Journal*, **113**, 539-549.

Hart, O. (1995), *Firms, contracts and financial structure* , Clarendon Press.

Havrilesky, T. (1993), "The political economy of monetary policy", *European Journal of Political Economy*, **10**, 111-134.

Røisland, Ø. (2001), "Institutional arrangements for monetary policy when output is persistent", *Journal of Money, Credit and Banking*, **33**(4), 994-1014.

Walsh, C. (1995), "Optimal contracts for central bankers", *American Economic Review*, **85**, 150-167.

Walsh, C. (2003), *Monetary theory and policy*, Cambridge, MA, MIT Press.

Woodford, M., (2002), "Inflation stabilization and welfare", *The B.E. Journal of Macroeconomics*, vol. 2, issu. 1, article 1.

INDEX

A

B

C

D

I

J

K

L

Y